STORM CLOUD

STORM CLOUD

MELBOURNE STORM'S
DEMISE AND RESURRECTION

PAUL KENNEDY

hardie grant books
MELBOURNE • LONDON

Published in 2013 by Hardie Grant Books

Hardie Grant Books (Australia)
Ground Floor, Building 1
658 Church Street
Richmond, Victoria 3121
www.hardiegrant.com.au

Hardie Grant Books (UK)
Dudley House, North Suite
34–35 Southampton Street
London WC2E 7HF
www.hardiegrant.co.uk

A Cataloguing-in-Publication entry is available from the catalogue of the National Library of Australia at www.nla.gov.au
Stormcloud
ISBN 9781742705989

Cover design Bluecork Design
Typeset in Sabon 10.5/14 pt by Kirby Jones
Printed and bound in Australia by Griffin Press

CONTENTS

FOREWORD

It was on the cusp of the 2012–13 summer that the new NRL chief executive officer first shook hands with the world of rugby league. He arrived full of enthusiasm from his years in the swank corridors of the Lloyds Banking Group, if understandably wet behind the ears when it came to the workings of an arcane sport.

Meet David Smith, the 44-year-old Welshman who declared boldly on that first day of public exposure that he had secured the 'best job in Australia'.

In the traditional open-neck-shirt style of the game, the new man was swiftly rebranded as 'Dave' Smith in sections of the swollen league media. The scribes and commentators wished him well.

But it was an Indian summer that proved to be remarkably brief. At the large media conference that introduced him, Smith fumbled some questions that were Dorothy Dixers to everyone else in the room – unable to name the current Australian captain (Cameron Smith) or identify key players (among them several household names) in a photo of the Indigenous All Stars team.

Akin to the four leading Australian cricketers who would be sent home from their tour of India a few months later, it seemed that Smith (or those cosseting him) had not done the required homework – in his case, laying down a platform firm enough to get him through this first 'meet the press'.

Things would only get tougher for the new man.

By the subsequent day of Smith's full-time arrival at League HQ in Moore Park, Sydney, in February 2013, the game was in a muck lather – which was not by any means unknown territory for the most volatile sport in the country. Emerging news of the implosion and subsequent suspension by his club of the dazzlingly talented Ben Barba (Canterbury Bulldogs) had rocked the league on the eve of the season kick-off. Barba had been stencilled in as the face of the game for the season's big opening – and, amidst great fanfare, would officially launch season 2013 on behalf of his fellow players. But the news broke belatedly that his personal life had gone badly awry, the Bulldogs had suspended him indefinitely, and he would be a non-starter at the launch and on the early-season playing fields. So it was (and not for the first time) that almost an entire promotional program package had to be placed in the shredder, and a hurried new approach sticky-taped together.

For Smith, hoping for blue skies and wide horizons for the game he would lead, it was the most bruising of kick-offs.

Just ahead, though, lay even grimmer news – something akin to a shoulder charge – that flattened the game *in toto,* and sent shockwaves across the whole spectrum of Australian sport. A 12-month investigation by the Australian Crime Commission (ACC) into the integrity of sport across the land had identified widespread use of prohibited performance-enhancing substances (including some that had not been approved for human use) along with strong links to organised crime identities and groups. The ACC report declared further that the relationship between professional sporting bodies and organised crime may have resulted in match fixing and fraudulent manipulation of betting markets.

On the question of the use of illicit drugs, fingers were pointed directly at the two major football codes: AFL and NRL. Former Australian Sports Anti-Doping Authority (ASADA) boss Richard Ings made the histrionic declaration: 'This is not a black day in Australian sport, this is the *blackest* day in Australian sport.'

In the aftermath of the first shock announcement in Canberra, there began a vastly publicised news/sport saga (in which weeks stretched into months) as the veracity of the claims that had been made were forensically tested. Rugby league found itself at the very heart of one of the biggest stories of its lifetime – and no single entity more so than the historically troubled Cronulla Sharks Rugby League Club. It was identified as a hotbed of suspicion for alleged illegal substance use amongst its ranks in season 2011, with the ripple effect spreading out to other clubs.

To David ('Dave') Smith it must have felt as if he had walked into the path of a tornado ...

Yet, in the robust territory inhabited by rugby league it has been ever thus. The resilient game's long haul (105 years) has been punctuated with regular episodes of skullduggery and high drama, controversy and monkey business. One former Australian Rugby League chairman, Ken Arthurson, had long ago talked of 'a game born in blood and conflict' but one that you could 'hit with an axe' with the certainty that it would rise to fight another day. Another ex-ARL boss, Kevin Humphreys, used to dread the arrival of 'ides of March' – which coincided exactly each year with the beginning of the new premiership season. Humphreys would ponder wryly the likelihood of some unforeseen controversy exploding on or off the field, and overtaking all else. He was rarely wrong ...

This book, the product of a relentless search for truth by author Paul Kennedy, records a particularly explosive episode in an old story. The tale this time is of a brilliantly performing outfit, the Melbourne Storm, that came to operate in a culture of deceit.

Taking its place in a hot field down the years, the Storm story stands as one of the game's biggest ever, hitting with sledgehammer effect in 2010. It concerned, after all, the club rated the best, the most professional and the most successful of the modern era. The peeling away of the layers of the story provided glimpses into the depths of deception and cheating that were shocking to the ordinary league punter although a study of history would show that dubious methods employed in the search for success on the playing fields, allied with generally shady dealings, have too often been a fact of life in rugby league.

The brief chronology recorded here goes some way towards placing the Storm saga in context – with this modern–day scandal taking its 'worthy' place in a history of dramatic events which, in turn, have played their part in making the game the rugged, raffish and disputatious floor show it remains to this day. They cover territory both on and off the playing field. And even if some of them can bring a wince to even the most loyal of rugby league faces ... these episodes from seasons past (and present!) are still woven into the fabric of what is arguably the toughest game in the world.

These are just a few of them:

1907–08 The game of rugby league is born out of internecine warfare featuring a breakaway from the pompous rugby (union) establishment via secret meetings under gaslight with deals struck aimed at luring disenchanted rugby players across. The capture by the 'new game' of rugby league of Dally Messenger 'The Master' on a nod of approval given by Dally's mother was the golden, clinching moment.

1909 The game dumps from office its three founding fathers: James Giltinan, Henry Hoyle and the great cricketer, Victor Trumper. There are initial accusations of 'secret funds' and 'ballot rigging' levelled. Mainly the sackings seem to have been to do with perceptions of secrecy in the league's financial dealings. The three men, rightly, are thoroughly restored in the story today – accepted as the trio that had the *most* to do with league's beginning.

Rugby league effectively wins the 'war' against rugby union by secretly signing more than half the Wallaby (rugby union) team, which had toured Great Britain in 1908–09. The coup is financed by colourful Sydney business identity James Joynton Smith.

1943 On raceless Saturdays during the War, betting on rugby league games is rife. One Saturday morning Souths star Jack 'Duck' Walsh answers his front door to be offered a bribe to throw a match against Easts that day. He says 'no thanks'. Souths lose anyway.

1944 Newtown club is accused (probably wrongly, and they brusquely denied it) of 'tanking' in a premiership final against Balmain, to ensure a windfall from a subsequent grand final gate. Favourite Newtown leads 11–nil in the match, but loses 19–16 ... and then loses the grand final too, 12–8, the following week!

1946 The NSW Rugby League sack the man who had been its Secretary since 1914, Horrie Miller. It is reported that at issue is 'missing money'.

1952 & 1963 Two referees, George Bishop (Souths v Wests, '52) and Darcy Lawler (St George v Wests, '63) are accused, albeit years later, of having cheated in Grand Finals – with both backing the respective winning team. The admired Jack Rayner, captain–coach of the beaten Souths team in '52, never speaks to Bishop again even though the pair live in the same suburb and often pass on the street.

1983 Kevin Humphreys, seventh president (and executive director) of the NSW Rugby League, resigns in the wake of Chris Masters's sensational *Four Corners* program ('The Big League'), centred on the circumstances of Humphreys having misappropriated $52,519 from Balmain League Club. The startling disclosures eventually lead to a royal commission and to NSW Premier Neville Wran standing aside from office for a time.

1990 Rugby league confronts its first major 'drug scandal' – although rumours of drug taking have been around the game for years. The news breaks that ten South Sydney players have tested positive to 'social drugs'.

1991 Rugby league's finest team of the era – Canberra – wears the tag 'cheats' after the revelation that the Raiders had substantially breached the salary cap in seasons 1990–91.

1995 Super League: the Rupert Murdoch/News Limited raid on rugby league arrives and progressively becomes the biggest, most decisive blow-up in the game's history, a 'war' that tears the game in half and destroys lifetime friendships. Even on its fragile settlement it leaves aftershocks that have resonated to the present day.

2002 Amidst a welter of revelations uncovered about secret payments, the crack Canterbury Bulldogs team is revealed as having blatantly cheated on the league's salary cap in 2001 and 2002, with plans to exceed it again (by $459,000) in 2003. The club is fined $500,000 and stripped of 37 premiership points, sending it crashing from first to last ...

And so it has continued year by year. The dramas, large and small ... the likes of the Storm, subject of this book, nailed in 2010 for their rorting; and of Canterbury forward Ryan Tandy becoming the first sportsman convicted of match-fixing in Australia following a police investigation into a $30,000 betting plunge on the Queensland Cowboys (against the Bulldogs) in a match played that same year ...

Paul Kennedy set out on a challenge as rigorous as playing 80 minutes of an NRL game when he began the quest of telling the true and inside story of the Storm's dodges and deceptions and the wider machinations surrounding the News Limited–owned club. There were hurdles at every turn – men who 'knew stuff' ... but wouldn't talk, or men who couldn't talk (on the record at least) because of rumoured arrangements made.

In the long and honourable tradition of investigative journalism, Kennedy dug deeper and deeper, sometimes picking up just one fragment or two of value in some of the scores of lengthy interviews he conducted. Quickly it became clear that there were those who did not want the book to be written.

For the author in his pursuit, it was a tangled web from the kick-off: the challenge was trying to sort out the exact role of the club and its officers, the players involved, the player managers, the NRL and News Limited ... amid the murky dealings that took place throughout the Storm's covert operation. The challenge beyond was to shine a light on the denouement, the uncovering of what had really taken place in defiance of NRL laws, and the identification of the breakthroughs that led eventually to the heavyweight penalties imposed.

Kennedy's quest from the beginning was honourable in the ancient tradition of the media defiantly doing its job in exposing infamy as thoroughly as it can. At the full-time hooter there existed a book that reads, in its piecing together of the story, like a racy thriller.

An aphorism written on the wall of the Green Bay Packers (NFL) team in 1962, and reflecting the hard-nosed view of famous coach Vince Lombardi, defines as well as anything the difficulties of Kennedy's chase for truth:

What you see here
What you say here
What you hear here
Let it stay here
When you leave here

Fifty years later the philosophy imprinted on that wall far away lives on here as strongly as ever – transported seamlessly and long ago to the world of Australian rugby league.

It is precisely why Paul Kennedy, far from Lombardi's time and territory, found the going so hard as he chipped away at what sometimes seemed an impenetrable wall ... before breaking through ... gathering the disparate elements of the story and writing this book.

In the time that has followed the Melbourne Storm experiencing their 'great fall', there have been other dramas, other shattering disclosures in rugby league. And so it is today that a new man at the helm, David Smith, is left cramming information as best he can about the reality of the game's historic compulsion to thrill and shock in equal measures, as it travels along the teeming, seething highways and byways of the seasons.

— Ian Heads

Ian Heads OAM has observed the passing parade of rugby league in Australia for almost 60 years, as fan, journalist, author and historian. In that time he has written words beyond counting on the game and its people, including more than 30 books.

AUTHOR'S NOTE

On 22 April 2010, the world's best rugby league team – Melbourne Storm – was given the harshest penalties in sports history for systematically breaching the NRL salary cap. Complicating the execution of the sanctions was the conflicted role played by Storm's owner, News Limited (Ltd), which half-owned the league and its pay television broadcaster. The company paid the bills, sat on the boards and then headline-raged with embarrassment at the behaviour of its employees.

The scandal caused anger, confusion and suspicion. A grim newspaper spat was waged between News Ltd and Fairfax. Sydney scorned Melbourne. The former News Ltd–appointed Storm CEO Brian Waldron fell publicly mute. Intense Storm coach Craig Bellamy stared back at the national media's glare and said, 'We will stand up for ourselves and we will fight our way back from here. That fight starts today. And tomorrow it starts on the field.'

Australia's phenomenal sports world was in shock. Hours after the penalties were announced on television, one of the game's ex-champions – Wally 'The King' Lewis – sat at his news desk and told viewers, 'If the message isn't loud and clear by now, people running the rugby league certainly need their heads read. As a former player it really does disgust me. And I feel very sorry for the boys [players] but not so their bosses or, in particular, the player managers.'

But finding fault in this caper is more difficult than The King made out.

Days after 22/4 (as Storm insiders call it), News Ltd CEO John Hartigan privately confronted the Storm footballers over their part in the affair and was met by a 'veneer of anger'. Three years on, Hartigan recalls his response: 'Hang on a minute, turn around and look at your own behaviour. That boat in the garage ... the fact that you were getting all this extra money, which wasn't catered for in the contract that was lodged with the NRL ... that was just the fairy godmother plonking it in your bank account ...'

The media boss is talking about some of the biggest names in sport, including Australian captain Cameron Smith, whose secret deal – or 'side letter' – was signed by the same hand that has lifted many trophies.

Then again, News Ltd ran the team. What were its failings? And who would investigate its role?

My aim in writing this book was to document the rise, fall and rise of a uniquely modern sports franchise – established in a city not fond of its trade, and bankrolled by Rupert Murdoch for broader commercial gains – that became a centre for excellence, greed, betrayal and resilience.

The majority of people named in these pages were happy to talk, anonymously or otherwise.

The book is not about blame or praise. It tells of deal-making and luck; and money, of course. In the reading, it must be remembered that few officials and players know everything about their scandals but fewer are the ignorant. As foundation Storm coach Chris Anderson says, 'There are no secrets in rugby league, mate.' The truth is in the context. So we must start at the beginning, before Melbourne Storm was a twinkle in Murdoch's eye.

PART ONE

CHAPTER 1

ORIGINS

On the evening of 8 June 1994, the Melbourne Cricket Ground was brimful of people in warm coats squinting through the smoke from fireworks. They had come to watch the foreign sport of rugby league in its most brutal and wholehearted expression.

'This is just unbelievable,' raved television commentator Ray Warren to his whopping national audience. 'An Australian record rugby league crowd has gathered in this great sporting stadium.'

Warren was stunned by how many Victorians, raised on the teat of a different winter football code, had bothered to turn up.

'Gets the heart pumping doesn't it Ray,' agreed ex-player Peter Sterling. 'We heard over the last seven days how many pre-sold tickets there were, figures of 65,000 or 70,000. In my mind I thought well I'll believe that when I see it. Here's the evidence tonight.' Sterling's scepticism was understandable. Rugby league had never been part of Victorian life.

Southern hearts and habits have been with Australian Rules football since the 1850s. Three-time Prime Minister Alfred Deakin acclaimed in 1908, while toasting a national carnival: 'I have yet to find a game that carries as much pleasure, as much harmless excitement, and as much stimulus as the Australian game of football. The game is Australian in its origin, Australian in its principle, and, I venture to say, Australian in its development.'

The noted orator knew the people. He understood their faith in 'muscular Christianity'. And he was a Melbournian. Victoria would be forever devoted to the game played on ovals by athletes free to roam.

*

Rugby league was born in the bleak north of England in the early 1890s. Australians adopted it in 1908. But it was never appreciated south of the Murray River.

In 1914 a rugby league match was played at the MCG between NSW and England. It was hoped the fixture would showcase the new game. Instead, it became an exhibition of violence. It has since been described as the dirtiest representative game ever played. In 1978 a 'Festival of Football' was staged at Fitzroy's Junction Oval. This saw Sydney clubs Wests and Manly clash brutally and famously in a contest triggered by a class war.

Only in the 1990s did rugby league dare to take its finest players to Melbourne to promote itself properly. It came with a boast: State of Origin.

Ray Warren went on, 'They're here in their thousands. Jammed into the Melbourne Cricket Ground. Just listen to them. I think the only thing that has come anywhere near this in my career as a commentator would be Wembley. The 1992 World Cup final. That was around 75,000. You can almost feel the crowd pulsating with the expectation that something special is about to happen.'

It was the second of a three-game series.

New South Wales Rugby League general manager John Quayle was strolling down near the fence, looking up at the faces of locals. He liked them. Sure, they were speaking a funny footy dialect, calling his game 'rugby' and talking about 'jumpers', not jerseys, maybe expecting a few 'touchdowns'. But that was okay. They were friendly, interested and most of them had paid to get in.

There was a modest cheer, followed by polite applause.

Quayle turned to watch 24-year-old New South Wales captain Laurie Daley lead his team onto the ground made world famous by test cricket and the 1956 Olympics.

It was Daley's eighth time as captain. He looked to be steeling himself. NSW had lost Game One after leading 12–4 with five minutes to go at the Sydney Football Stadium.

Queensland 16–12. Series: QLD – 1 NSW – 0.

Treading the MCG turf beside Daley was strength and power in the frames of Glenn Lazarus and Paul Harragon, to be employed as rams all night by hooker Benny Elias. Coach Phil Gould wanted to keep the attack narrow. Helping this ploy would be the world's best player, Brad Clyde, back in the Blues' team for the first time since 1992. His Canberra teammate Brett Mullins was on debut.

Warren breathed, 'I wonder what's going through *his* mind.'

Nearby walked sharp-jawed Andrew Ettingshausen, the most capped Blues player. Locals liked him immediately for his athleticism. Perhaps they imagined him playing for Essendon or Geelong or Collingwood.

Queensland walked out of the change room, beneath a flimsy XXXX (a beer company) banner held by rugged-up cheerleaders. In doing so, captain Meninga equalled Wally Lewis's record appearance tally (31 games). This was his farewell series. But the crowd was upstaging Big Mal.

Quayle watched the Maroons enter the arena then he resumed taking in the crowd; he reckoned there must be 90,000 fans present. If he wasn't smiling, he was laughing.

For two years Quayle had been trying to rent the MCG for 'Origin'. He wanted to advance the business of rugby league by making it a national game. Since taking the wheel at the NSWRL in 1983, he had expanded his competition by welcoming the Brisbane Broncos, Gold Coast-Tweed Giants (later Seagulls) and the Newcastle Knights. But Quayle wanted to spread his game in non-traditional rugby league territories, just as the AFL was doing with Australian Rules.

On his first visit to the ground, the NSWRL boss had spoken to the Melbourne Cricket Club secretary Dr John Lill and sensed some reluctance. So he went to the premier of Victoria, Jeff Kennett.

Kennett was elected in October 1992. He liked to brag about his 'big events'. He had wrangled the Formula One Grand Prix from Adelaide in 1993 and was on the lookout for other ways to advertise his patch at the expense of bordering states.

Origin is something quite different to rich and flashy motor racing. Quayle was nervous about meeting Kennett. His confidence was further damaged when he was late for his appointment. This was unfortunate. Kennett, as a personal rule, makes character judgements on three initial observations: fingernails (better if they're not chewed), shoes (well maintained, hopefully) and punctuality ...

Quayle blamed the pilot strike for delaying his plane. 'I apologise Mr Premier, but your airport held us up.'

'You blokes from up there [Sydney] would say that,' Kennett said.

The premier picked up the phone and dialled Melbourne Airport. He passed on Quayle's charge to a dismayed official, who assured the politician flights had been delayed by an operational fault in *Sydney*. Kennett relayed this information to Quayle, hung up the phone and nodded.

Quayle shrugged and got on with his pitch.

State of Origin was not entirely new to Melbourne. In 1990, Game Two was staged inside the running track at Olympic Park, on a mild night in front of almost 30,000 people. The fireworks over the city and Debbie Byrne's full-band national anthem preceded a minute's silence for well-known former Australian Rules administrator, Jack Hamilton, who was killed in a car crash that day.

Queensland's Gary Belcher kicked off. The dashing Ettingshausen, with black stripes under his eyes to dull the light towers' glare, caught the ball and ran it back – so beginning one of the toughest and most thrilling Origin stanzas. The players found the surface too slippery but the sell-out crowd could not have hoped for harder hits if they were ringside looking up at Mike Tyson and Buster Douglas in Tokyo.

The match finished with controversy, Langer penalised for pinching the ball after prop Lazarus had been tackled. Rod Wishart turned the mistake into a two-point lead for NSW. Minutes later, with Queensland desperate to conjure a long-range try, Blues' back Brad Mackay intercepted an errant pass and scored a try to end the Maroons' night and series. NSW 12–6.

Elias, captain of the first Blues Origin trophy win since 1986, was hoisted onto shoulders. Tina Turner's cult song 'Simply the Best' blared from speakers while players thanked the crowd. 'We Are the Champions' (by Queen) had the satisfied fans humming their way to exits. In his second Origin appearance, Ricky Stuart was man of the match. Australian Rugby League Chairman Ken Arthurson presented him an envelope and seemed thoroughly satisfied. Arthurson said, 'The thing that I'm most pleased about tonight is the magnificent response from the public of Melbourne.'

Two test matches were subsequently played in the southern capital. New Zealand upset Australia on 3 July 1991 at Olympic Park. It was the first time a rugby league test match had been staged in Australia outside New South Wales and Queensland. The following year Australia lost to Great Britain at Princes Park, an AFL stadium (future administrative home of Melbourne Storm). Again the crowd was tightly packed, noisy and impressed. But these games were all in secondary venues – off-Broadway. Quayle wanted the big stage for his show of muscle, which had grown into one of the great spectacles of Australian sport from its inception in 1980. It was, and remains today, the highest standard of rugby league in the world.

Kennett was sold.

'What do you mean you can't go to the cricket ground?' the premier asked.

'Well the cricket ground don't want us to play there,' Quayle repeated. 'I believe I could attract 50,000 people and I think a lot of people would travel down here.'

Quayle showed Kennett the television ratings from previous series. It was the number-one TV sports show in the nation, even though it wasn't shown live in Melbourne.

Kennett picked up the phone again. This time he dialled the MCG, looking to speak to Dr Lill. 'I'm sending John Quayle over there,' the premier stated. 'I think this is a great tourist event for Melbourne.'

Quayle said goodbye to Kennett and drove from the government's offices at Spring Street to the stadium, less than a kilometre away. This time, Dr Lill was accommodating. 'How many [spectators] do you think you can get?'

'Look, I've gotta get fifty thousand or it's going to be a failure,' Quayle explained. 'That's my aim.'

Dr Lill, a respected, longstanding MCC chief, recalls experiencing some trepidation over how it would work. He says he wasn't against rugby league. The obstacles were scheduling and price.

'Well this ground costs a lot of money you know,' he told Quayle.

'Well, how much will it cost me?' Quayle posed. Dr Lill ummed and aahhed and proposed a per-head fee. Quayle said, 'Look, what about if I give you $50,000.'

Dr Lill said he needed time to think about it. He rang Quayle the next day and they made an agreement for $80,000. Sweetening the deal, Quayle said all MCC members could have a free ticket, although Dr Lill insisted it was unlikely the members would come.

When the code's chief took the agreement back to the Australian Rugby League board he saw the directors purse their lips and frown.

Ken Arthurson said, 'Oh, mate, this is our best product ...'

'Trust me Ken,' said Quayle. Arthurson, perhaps remembering the successful 1990 excursion at Olympic Park, agreed to give it a go.

So began the campaign to win over the public. Sydney and Brisbane football lovers were unhappy. 'Awwww, not again. What right have you got? Who do you think you are? This is *our* game!' Ticket sales were slow, early. Meninga and Daley went to Melbourne for promotions. Quayle arranged through his AFL counterpart and friend Ross Oakley to use broad-minded Australian Rules coaches Tommy Hafey and Ron Barassi as cross-code spruikers.

As the match loomed, Quayle was called to appear before the ARL once again.

'You did tell us 50,000, we're told there's only been 40,000 seats sold.'

'Yeah, but we're a month out,' Quayle explained. He could sense some of his colleagues wanted to abandon the fixture and bring it back to Sydney. But as soon as the final whistle was blown on Game One, Origin II started to sell.

The smoke did not clear before the lovely Kate Ceberano sang *Advance Australia Fair* to a packed coliseum.

Quayle made his way from the sidelines of the field to a grandstand corporate function of 250 people. James Packer, son of media mogul Kerry, sidled up and nudged: 'Well Quayley you've done it. This'll be massive on television.'

It was a dull game, worse luck.

NSW coach Phil Gould was delighted with the win and the final scene was of him cuddling his charges. 'I'm quite sure we'll see rugby league in Melbourne again. It's nice to be the first and just an absolutely sensational night to be here on the ground in front of that crowd and come up with a win.'

A flag in the crowd read: *MCG: The new home of rugby league.*

The Queensland team had not enjoyed its trip to Melbourne any more than it had four years ago. One of its players was particularly downcast. On the bench sat Chris Johns, who would become the Melbourne Storm's first chief executive. Lazarus would be Johns's highest profile recruit (by then an injured warhorse).

Next day, the *Herald Sun* – Melbourne's big-selling News Ltd tabloid – ran the parochially defensive headline: *Great show but AFL still rules.* The newspaper's owner had not yet made an investment in rugby league.

Jeff Kennett (an Australian Rules tragic and future president of Hawthorn Football Club) wasn't threatened by the successful turnout for Origin. To a radio audience he said, 'I think it's [a rugby league presence in Melbourne] good for the game. I think it's obviously financially very beneficial and I think it's good for the character of this sporting city.' He privately said to Quayle, 'Son, what's next year?'

Quayle's achievement in briefly winning over Melbourne was a highlight in his life serving sport. He scooped state and national tourism awards for Best Promotion of a Sporting Event 1994. MCC secretary Dr Lill later said to him: 'You're welcome back at this ground anytime Mr Quayle.'

State of Origin did return to the MCG in 1995. Queensland won Game Two in front of a crowd of 52,000 people. In 1997 it was tried again but Quayle had left the sport by then and Super League players were prevented from competing. Only 25,000 people turned up to watch. Perhaps it was the strongest indication to league administrators that Melbournians were not as enthused about rugby league as they were about 'big events'.

In ARL discussions about expansion, Quayle always knew setting up a professional team – a franchise – in Melbourne would be difficult. He had spent years compiling evidence that weighed against it.

Back in 1990, the NSWRL had sent to the city of Aussie Rules three of its junior development coaches – Martin Meredith, Ted Johnson and Frank Ponissi – to spend six months in rotated stints preaching the game's worth. At the time, the Victorian Rugby League was based in a little office at Glenferrie Road, Hawthorn. There were two people in there: a full-time manager and a part-time receptionist. The NSWRL development coaches had twin aims. They desired to build up the existing junior league; and make people aware of the game by talking about it.

Twenty-three years later, Frank Ponissi recalls a harsh reality. 'We went around to schools. To be honest with you, it was so foreign. There was no pay TV. There was no free-to-air [coverage]. We're only talking 1990 but it was foreign. People would ask us, which rugby is that? Is that the Wallabies? I can tell ya, rugby league back in 1990 in Melbourne was as alien, as foreign as you could possibly imagine.'

'We never had a junior base [in Victoria],' John Quayle says today. 'That's why we chose to go to New Zealand and Perth [in 1995]. But our plan was a reduction of teams in Sydney and then Melbourne the next step.'

The conception and survival of any Melbourne-based professional rugby league club would need an owner with arm-deep pockets and a broader commercial interest.

Rugby league fell into turmoil during the 1995–97 seasons. It was subjected to an ARL–Super League power struggle, a dispute waged for players' services in a grab for control of the code in Australia and its broadcasting benefits. It was Rupert Murdoch's News Ltd (Super League) versus Kerry Packer and Optus Vision (ARL). In 1997, after two years of bitter feuding in courts and boardrooms, rival tournaments were held. The sport was damaged and relationships strained. Fans were disenchanted.

Roy Masters wrote about the conflict in his book *Inside Out: Rugby League under scrutiny*. He stated the calamity was 'as painfully simple as two children seeing who can hold his breath the longest'.

In May 1997, Murdoch's son Lachlan made the decision to further expand Super League by basing a team in Melbourne. That there was not an obvious rugby league market in Victoria did not deter the rich and powerful young man. It was part of an overall business strategy to attract national advertisers to his competition. It was conceived only after News Ltd sought the approval of Premier Kennett, who recalls the proposal:

> I remember it very clearly. Ken Cowley, who was the head of News Ltd in Australia at the time, working under Rupert, came into see me. I was sitting in my office at Parliament House and he said, 'I want to bring a rugby league team to Melbourne'. I said, 'We support that, we're a city of many cultures, many codes, many sports but don't give me a second-rate team. If you're gunna bring a team down here give me one that is competitive.'

A team was being hastily prepared for the following Super League season. But then rugby league's war reached a truce. The ARL and Super League came together. A new competition was formed. The National Rugby League would be half-owned by News Ltd and ARL. Murdoch had secured pay-TV rights through Fox Sports, and News Ltd placed representatives on the NRL board, which would decide the future of the sport in Australia. Some clubs were scrapped (South Queensland Crushers, Western Reds and Hunter Mariners) and their best players found new homes. News Ltd sent many of its still-contracted players to play in purple jerseys for its newest franchise, called Storm.

CHAPTER 2

'A STORM'S COMING'

Some silences before the contest can be more thrilling than winning. They fall at moments of wide possibilities – when no-one fears you, rates you ... even *thinks* about you; and you believe in yourself because your coach or wife told you to and they're honest and trustworthy, like your mother and father were when you were a boy, back when nothing in the world seemed impossible.

It was Saturday, 4 March 1998. The team bus headed south along the uneven New South Wales coast. Melbourne Storm's coach, Chris Anderson, listened to the groaning gears and whining brakes. He was looking out the window through the light rain, wondering how the boys were goin' mentally. Mate, they were quiet.

Storm players, led by first captain Glenn Lazarus, didn't know how to consider their circumstances. In a few hours they would play their first match in the new NRL. The teammates didn't know each other well. Although they had sweated together over summer, trial matches had offered no evidence of their worth. Results were so far inconsistent. Talent and some experience existed on that bus. But there were no promises. The footballers did not know whether they were any good collectively. It made them restless, introverted and determined.

Sydney sportswriters and commentators had forecast mediocrity. Other teams expected Storm to be 'competitive' at best. Anderson and his pioneers had used such predictions as fuel for harder training. They had talked about overcoming the difficulties of unfamiliar playing combinations, heavy interstate travel and hostile crowds. But now, in a clanking bus a long way from their new home ... who knew anything? If the people really wanted to watch them play, why did the NRL send them to debut in Wollongong?

Among the passengers were two newsmen: Michael Westlake and Chris Appleby.

Appleby was the team's first media manager. He had quit his job as a *Herald Sun* reporter to join the new football franchise. Appleby was a rare breed of Melbourne journalist: he liked rugby league, owing to the years he lived in Canberra on a basketball scholarship at the Australian Institute of Sport; and he was optimistic about Storm's first match, mainly because he had heard an omen on the Channel Ten weather report that evening: 'A storm's coming.' Also, he was still feeling a glow from the night before, having enjoyed a lusty dinner with the team management in Sydney. Present at the nosh-up were club managing director and part-owner John Ribot, chief executive Chris Johns and the coach.

Appleby recalls, 'We stayed at the Brighton Le Sands Hotel – because Anderson knew the owner of a seafood restaurant across the street [the owner was a supporter of Canterbury, Anderson's previous team]. We had a night-before meal.' It would turn into a ritual on away trips. 'Players'd be all downstairs slumming it and we'd be upstairs easting lobster. Great wine,' Appleby grins.

Reminded of his prematch lobsters, Anderson quips, 'Tell Chris Appleby he remembers too much.'

Of the bus trip, Appleby tells, 'NRL players are unusual. Church mice before games and mental after it. No-one knew what to expect, we'd done okay in the preseason. I remember Howsey (Rodney Howe) being zoned in the whole trip. A lot of guys had headphones on. Hardly a word was spoken. Even the jokesters of the team were silent. Locked in.'

Westlake was the new rugby league reporter for the *Herald Sun*. The scribe felt lucky – and a bit cheeky – to be on the bus. If he tried to get on a team bus now they'd laugh at him and shut the door in his face. Bloody journo. But this was a unique assignment. He was 21 years old, a cadet hired by the *Herald Sun* from the *Townsville Bulletin* to write about a sport few Victorian readers cared for. Access was important. It was Appleby's suggestion to have a beat reporter travel with the team.

'I said to the board we need to guarantee ourselves coverage, which means we've gotta take journos on the road,' Appleby explains.

'There'll be a commitment from the paper if one of their guys is at the venue ... Sydney Football Stadium or Newcastle. We just needed something.'

Westlake did not feel his role at the paper was notional. Most days he had to fight for column inches from Phil Gardner, the imposing sports editor. Gardner judged stories on merit, measured them against other sports. This day-to-day editorial approach existed despite the *Herald Sun*'s close relationship with Storm. Except on Fridays. Every week the newspaper, determined to give a full page and sometimes two to Storm – graphics, team lists, a column. You weren't going to miss that there was a game on if you were reading the *Herald Sun* on Friday.

Forget about it on television in Melbourne. It didn't rate a mention, just didn't register. The Australian Football League was king.

Westlake is now a senior journalist at Queensland's *Courier Mail*. He remembers, 'My brief from Gardner was pretty specific – main role was to cover Storm and he outlined that if I missed a story it was my arse.'

Herald Sun Editor-in-Chief Peter Blunden was a great help to the new club back then. He would become one of Storm's biggest supporters and remains so. Now a News Ltd managing director, Blunden says, 'I was fortunate 'cause I grew up in Sydney. I was a passionate Balmain supporter. Relatives played for the club etc. Had a great passion for it.'

The other major newspaper in Melbourne – *The Age* – was a Fairfax-owned broadsheet. It covered sport almost as comprehensively as its competition but had no obligations to Storm.

'*The Age* was a bit more of a battle, 'cause they weren't into it,' Appleby says. 'They only did the home games. [Reporters] pushed where they could but they're not the guys you need to impress, it's the sports editors who make decisions on copy space.'

In the earliest days, News Ltd gave Appleby a credit card for schmoozing journalists, producers and editors. His entertainment budget was $20,000. 'I reckon I used about $2000 to $2500 a year,' he says. 'It was unbelievable. Nobody wanted to have dinner with me. Nobody wanted to talk rugby league.'

Westlake was the exception.

Soon, the Storm reporter would have to find his own way to the stadiums. Westlake was an independent thinker and would inevitably have to write critically of the team, as required by his employer. He was a journalist, not a cheerleader. 'I was always very conscious of getting too close to the players because that's the way I hold myself,' he says. 'Avoid the situation of it becoming too personal.'

This was not a one team–one town love affair, like Queensland had with the *Courier Mail* and Brisbane Broncos. It was not worth the *Herald Sun's* time and effort to care so much about Storm, beyond its Friday preview. Primarily, it had newspaper copies to sell. AFL and crime headlines would do that. Rugby league? Not so much.

Westlake still remembers the silence on the bus. It was exciting, despite the grim weather. When they arrived, the players and media men stepped off and looked up at the Illawarra Steelers' home stadium, unimpressed.

'It was an archaic, shitty old place,' Appleby remembers, 'just like ours.'

Soon the players were dressed in uniform and listening to Chris Anderson, one of the finest coaches in the game, speaking in succinct sentences about the challenge they faced, the responsibility they carried in being the first to represent Melbourne. Anderson wore big prescription glasses and looked like a school principal. His hair was grey but his approach was black and white. An intuitive coach delivers his prematch edict for his simplest charge to comprehend. That way, all understand what is expected of them. As it turned out, Anderson's squad was intelligent, adaptable and sensitive.

Storm team V Illawarra, Win Stadium, Round One 1998

Robbie Ross
Craig Smith
Aaron Moule
Paul Bell
Marcus Bai
Scott Hill
Brett Kimmorley
Rodney Howe
Danny Williams
Robbie Kearns
Paul Marquet
Ben Roarty
Tawera Nikau

Reserves
Glenn Lazarus (C)
Richard Swain
Russell Bawden
John Carlew

Coach: Chris Anderson

Win Stadium was on the water's edge; the Tasman Sea made a wild backdrop to Storm's debut game. Retired footballer Steve 'Blocker' Roach was making special comments for the television coverage on Fox Sports. He observed, 'The most important thing for Melbourne

Storm tonight is to play with confidence but don't be too hasty with the ball early. Don't let that nervous energy build up. If they do that they'll be well in this match.'

Illawarra was only slightly more experienced than Storm in first-grade matches played (average 60 per player, compared to Melbourne's 49 – although if you took out Bell, Kearns and Marquet that number dropped to 29). Another commentator, Mario Fenech, tipped Illawarra to win.

Lazarus started on the bench. He was still recovering from an injury sustained playing for the Broncos the previous year. New Zealander Tawera Nikau – with his spiky-top, straight-back hairdo – led Storm onto the field. There was half-hearted booing from the crowd. Centre Paul McGregor led Illawarra out, Trent Barrett at his shoulder.

Young Storm halfback Brett Kimmorley caught the kick-off. He was an important player who almost didn't make it to Melbourne. When his previous team (Hunter Mariners) was axed, News Ltd determined to split up the halves. One would go to Melbourne, the other to Canterbury – another Super League team. When five-eighth Scott Hill decided to go with Storm, Kimmorley looked to be a Bulldog until he flew south and handed a signed, otherwise blank piece of paper to chief executive Chris Johns as his commitment to the new club. Simply, he wanted to stay with his Hunter mates. They were very close, as were their girlfriends and wives. Johns argued successfully with league management for the compact ball player to be a Melbourne boy.

Kimmorley passed the ball to the tanned and chiseled prop Howe, who ran into the breaking wave of tacklers. Three were required to wrestle him to the ground.

Fenech: 'Pretty good crowd down here. I'm not too good with maths but I'd assume there's about 10 or 12,000 people.'

Danny Williams – recruited from North Sydney – ran directly up field from dummy half, and made Storm go forward.

After a few minutes, a Trent Barrett cut-out pass caused Storm to make its first error in defence and Steeler Craig Wilson scored a try. Four minutes later hometown lock Brad Mackay stepped by Paul Marquet and passed to Illawarra halfback Will Robinson, who bent down and touched the ball upon the grass tips. The rain fell heavily. Storm was down by 12.

Twenty-six minutes were gone and Melbourne still hadn't scored. Anderson's stern countenance told his concern. Then Lazarus came onto the field. And everything changed.

Glenn Lazarus was the centrepiece of Storm recruiting. He had won premierships at two other clubs, Canberra and Brisbane. 'We were keen to get him to make a statement to other players,' foundation CEO Johns explains.

Like Hollywood films, impatient new sports teams need a proven lead actor.

Lazarus, the man that brilliant comedy duo H.G. Nelson and Roy Slaven nicknamed 'The Brick with Eyes' was starting to dry out and crack when Storm called. He was recovering from a broken leg and his devoted following was thinning. Five years earlier Lazarus was on the cover of *Inside Sport* magazine, in his prime. The Brick had not long been at Brisbane (after leaving Canberra when the Raiders ran out of money).

He told *Inside Sport*, 'The turmoil started at the Raiders in 1991 when they were having to cut back the salary cap and take 20 per cent [off player payments]. I don't know whether I was filthy on them for taking money off me or what it was, but I just wanted to come to Brisbane.'

Lazarus was a habitual winner.

In 1992, he helped Brisbane win the Winfield Cup, New South Wales the State of Origin and Australia the World Cup. He was the best forward in the game. Tellingly, he conceded to *Inside Sport* his body was suffering: 'I tell you, the day after the game I can be very sore, very sore indeed. Some days I can hardly move. But it's all forgotten after the first training session.' That was 1993, when he was 27. By 1998, he wasn't pushing back time and tacklers so easily. But his first run in a jersey that flashed lighting bolts inspired his new teammates.

Storm's Marcus Bai had returned a Barrett kick 60 metres to set up the visiting team's attack. Approaching Illawarra's line, Lazarus took the ball and did not deviate, piggy-backing a trio of defenders like small boys. He was suddenly a metre away from the line. A quick play-the-ball saw Scott Hill run onto a short pass. He stretched out while being tackled to record Melbourne Storm's first try. Craig Smith converted.

Nearing the end of the first half, the commentator Roach was falling in love with Rodney Howe, who had run with the ball 16 times in under 40 minutes.

'That is an amazing effort,' Roach explained. 'I was speaking to Anderson before the match and he said Rodney Howe was his fittest player.'

At half-time Storm trailed by six. Of new football clubs, Cronulla was the last team to win its first away match. That was in 1967. Storm looked every chance of matching that on this frigid night: it was wearing the Steelers down, just as Anderson had planned.

Anderson has won almost every piece of weighty silverware in rugby league. He played 232 first-grade games for Canterbury–Bankstown from 1971–1984, eight tests for Australia and State of Origin. His career in charge of teams began when he successfully captain–coached Halifax in England for four years. In 1989 he returned to serve the Bulldogs as Under 21s coach, then took over the first-grade post. He later led his team to Grand Final victory in 1995, defeating Manly. In 1999, Anderson would start coaching Australia.

Ribot and Johns had chased Anderson to lead Storm. It wasn't a difficult courtship. The coach wanted to come. He'd secretly harboured a desire to ply his craft beside the Yarra River.

'As a coach you never get the opportunity to join a club and pick your own team,' Anderson says. 'I had a style of football I wanted to play and this was an opportunity to start from scratch and pick the players I wanted in that side.'

Johns remembers wanting Anderson more every day.

> We had to put a team together who knew how to win and had a winning culture about it so the first meeting with Chris Anderson really stuck out in my mind. He was the man for the job. I could see the passion ... he wasn't coming for the big pay cheque or because he was disheartened by another club, he was genuinely excited about the opportunity to be the person who built the culture of the club and build it from the ground up. The main thing was we had to get winners involved, right?

Players had to be fetched from around the nation, but before Anderson wrote down names he penned his priority positions.

'I thought out a style of football I wanted to play,' he explains.

> Worked out a salary cap [more accurately it was a budget, as there was no true salary cap in 1998] on that basis before I put any names to it. I spent a lot of money – two-thirds of my money on front rowers and halfbacks because they were the most important things to the style I wanted to play. I apportioned a good amount

of the salary cap on that, and the rest of it we filled in with athletes.

Anderson recruited Lazarus, Kearns, Nikau and Howe – all internationals – to lead his pack. He stresses it was important for him to know where the money was going.

'It's an important part of having a happy team,' he says. 'If you go outside of that you're giving the team reasons not to be happy.' The coach believes players know what teammates earn.

'There's no secrets in rugby league,' he says. 'Everyone knows what everyone's on. But if it's within your structure it's an easy thing to explain. To keep harmony within the group you need to have structure before you put names on positions.'

Nobody knows players' value better than the coach, and often the position is worth more than the footballer. For instance, a club is not wise to spend $400,000 on a winger. Though he might give the crowd goosebumps, a winger doesn't make anyone else in the team a better player. Front rowers and ball players do that.

Not much has changed since Anderson coached Storm, except the hooker and fullback have become more important. The role of the five-eighth has diminished slightly. Coaches don't play halfback, five-eighth, centre, centre anymore. They have halfbacks either side of the ruck. Five-eighths have become more running players.

So any team with an accomplished hooker, fullback and halfback will be very dangerous.

In England, Anderson learned his trusted approach: flat attack, building a base for the forwards so the backs can score the tries; mix in some 'ad lib' football and play the ball quickly, if possible, but keep everything structured.

'We used to wear 'em down,' Anderson says. 'You could wear the opponent down 'cause you didn't have the interchange that you've got now so the game opened up a bit in the last ten minutes of each half.'

Anderson came to Storm after Super League, a stressful time for him, indeed. The coach and his Bulldogs went with the News Ltd breakaway competition but four players famously crossed back to the enemy – ARL – after arguing then–Super League boss Ribot signed them unfairly. Anderson considered the four men disloyal and shunned them. One of those footballers, Jarrod McCracken, wrote a revealing book on the distasteful events – *A Family Betrayal: One man's Super*

League war (with Daniel Lane). McCracken had few kind words for Ribot and Anderson.

On Super League rushing to contract the players, McCracken wrote,

> We were all taken aback when Ribot produced contracts and said if we didn't sign the dotted line there and then we'd be left out in the cold once the competition was up and running. It was the closest thing possible to having a gun placed at our heads and while I believed Ribot's actions were unethical, my fear of being left ... was very strong ... I didn't want to end up an unemployed footballer.
>
> I was later to learn that feeling of apprehension was just as powerful among the other blokes. Like me, they wanted to go home and discuss the implications involved in becoming a part of Super League with our advisers, solicitors, agents and families. However, Ribot was adamant that because of the top secret nature of the competition, it was a case of having to sign immediately; the pressure was mounting.

McCracken recalled Anderson's reaction to the four players subsequently baulking at Super League: 'Anderson didn't take the news well at all. He stood up, knocked his chair to the ground and snarled at all four of us, "I can't believe you blokes! You can all go and get fucked!" It was a far cry from the calm, cool and collected man we were all used to dealing with.'

In the second 40 minutes at Win Stadium, Rodney Howe kept banging away like a playful rhino. Illawarra lacked urgency in attack and struggled to get the ball out of its own half. Stormed pressed, lucked a penalty. Smith – recruited from Canterbury reserve grade – knocked it through with his left boot. 8–12.

Three minutes remained. Storm was ten out. Desperate tackles were completed before Kearns, from dummy half, went to Hill, who cocked his body and shot straight through a maybe-gap to score a try. A conversion would win the match.

Anderson knew he needed a reliable kicker. That's why he selected Smith. Playing his third first-grade game, he sealed it with a sweetly timed left-foot strike.

Roach: 'They've just overpowered this Steelers' forward pack.'

The crowd went quiet. Storm was unloved and jubilant. The commentator called it a famous victory.

Rodney Howe, looking fresh, spoke to Mario Fenech post-match. 'Were just glad to win. Very happy boys. It's a great start. Melbourne are not here to muck around. We're gunna be here for a long time to stay. We read the papers all week and that spurs everyone on.'

Beer was brought to the victors in the change room. It was a gesture of appreciation from the coach.

'Psychologically, having a few beers after the game was a great thing,' Anderson looks back.

> We worked really hard all week to put a performance on and we needed a letdown. We get carried away with the physical side of the game [these days] and not enough with the mental side of the game. After the game you need a letdown so our letdown was two or three beers. [It was me] saying listen we prepared as well as we could, regardless of the result we've given it our best shot. For me that was telling the players I believed in them and that they all go out and give it their best shot.

The days of a beer straight after the game are long gone, replaced by sports science–inspired remedies for recovery, often at the expense of enjoyment.

Innovative world champion rugby coach Rod Macqueen penned in his stellar book – *One Step Ahead* – a subchapter called 'Smelling the roses'. He revealed that in 1997 his Brumbies had secured a home semifinal against the Wellington Hurricanes. As each player turned up to training that week, Macqueen gave him a rose.

'It's a time I will always remember,' Macqueen wrote. 'How important it was to sit back and reflect, to savour the achievement. Even though we had not finished the season we had attained an important goal. It was important to appreciate the special moments in the journey.'

Anderson agrees: 'Conditioners [fitness staff] have taken over a bit and they rule the world now. The physical recovery is important but they've lost track of the mental recovery.'

Media manager Appleby remembers the buzz of Storm's first big night.

> The change room was just a party. Relief. Excitement. We were on to something here. We've just beaten Illawarra. They're alright.

They're not a bad team. At their venue. No-one gave us a chance to win. We were tipped to finish last in the whole comp. We were on the bus by 10.30pm. Straight back to Brighton Le Sands. I remember there was singing. Everybody got on the microphone at the front of the bus. Tell a story or a joke. The adrenaline and excitement was like nothing I've witnessed since. We were away.

CHAPTER 3

OLD STEEL TURNSTILES / GRAND SUCCESS

Storm made its home at Olympic Park, or 'The Graveyard', as it became known. It stood downhill from the MCG, on the banks of the Yarra River, and was the dilapidated mecca of athletics in Australia. Tennis was played just across the street at Rod Laver Arena and basketball was the sporting attraction next door at The Glasshouse. A greyhound racetrack and betting ring existed on its other flank. In this company, Storm stood out like a sixth finger.

The team's first home game was on 3 April 1998. Within an hour of the match, there were several organisational headaches for Ribot and his front office. One concerned the broadcast media boxes.

'It's a disgrace,' said radio commentator Ray Hadley, protesting his poor view of the field.

Hadley was down from Sydney to describe the action. Storm had won its first three matches on the road and was becoming a story beyond the pages of the *Herald Sun*. Hadley wanted to move closer to the halfway line.

'It's just not good enough,' he yelled.

Today Hadley is an influential Sydney talkback jock with some national recognition. In the late 1990s, he was best described in Mike Colman's excellent book *Super League: The Inside Story.*

> Hadley, a former cab driver and auctioneer who had called country race meetings for no pay to break into the game, had clawed his

way to the top of the unforgiving and highly competitive world of radio sports journalism by having a go. He was loud, pugnacious and dogmatic. Once he took a position, he dug in his heels and by, a combination of verbosity and volume, ground down opposition callers. If that didn't work he flicked the switch on them. On day two of the Super League–ARL war, Hadley showed which side he had chosen and went on the attack, as he did from that day on.

Hadley was anti–Super League, which made him anti–John Ribot. A famous episode of Channel Nine's *The Footy Show* pitted Ray Hadley and NSW State of Origin coach Phil Gould (who helped sign players for the ARL during the Super League dispute) against John Ribot and Chris Johns, Super League's players' representative.

Before the program began, Ribot turned to Johns and said, 'This is lions and Christians stuff here. We're about to get fed to the lions.'

On air, Ribot began. 'The [Super League] vision is about taking the game to the rest of the world. It's about giving the patrons and fans a better deal than what they've had in the past ...'

'What a load of crap,' Hadley interrupted. 'It's about pay television, John. It's about lining people's pockets with money and for you to sit here and say differently is just an absolute farce.'

On it went for a long time. At the end of the can't-look-away debate, Ribot was peeved.

Now Hadley was sitting somewhere near the tryline at Olympic Park. It was a bit like turning up to a wedding and being seated near the toilet when you thought you should've been on the bridal party table.

Appleby was handing out 'game notes'. He recalls,

> Ribot had made a point of making sure Ray Hadley's mob were far [away], at the end, almost on the 10-metre line. Not a great spot. So I go to take the notes in and he blew up at me. Could not believe it. 'Our ratings compared to that mob up there ...' It was all by design. He'd been shitcanning us. As if we're gunna roll out the red carpet to you.

There was a more serious problem outside the stadium, a public relations calamity no less.

True to tradition, a large Melbourne crowd had turned out for this unprecedented event. But thousands of people could not get in to watch the game. They were just standing around outside The Glasshouse. Five million dollars had been spent upgrading Olympic Park but the old steel turnstiles were still in place and they were preventing patrons entering in a hurry. Ticketholders were left bunched and furious. One woman rose above the bay of denied spectators by climbing a lamppost. She had the bewildered look of a parent who had lost a child.

A news reporter recorded patrons' complaints.

'We're absolutely amazed at the debacle that has occurred,' said a young woman.

'If I'm willing to put my cash up front in order to obtain a ticket, I expect to walk through that door,' fumed a middle-aged man.

Ribot went to fix it.

The match was about to start. Retired champion, now commentator, Wally Lewis said he was looking forward to Melbourne's pack testing the more fancied North Sydney Bears.

> Everyone thought that they [Storm] were gunna have a couple of good players, maybe stick their nose up every now and then in the competition, but Glenn Lazarus really has led from the front and I'm sure that's the bit that has gained them respect from other teams. I'd like to see Melbourne win. I think it'd be great for spreading rugby league, especially down here in Victoria.

Storm's new sponsor, Honda, had a car parked on a stage near one of the corner posts. Ribot had approached businesspeople all over Melbourne seeking corporate support. At Honda he found Tony Devers, who would become one of the club's most loyal backers. Devers had just crossed from Volvo to Honda as director of sales and marketing. Honda was only selling 10,000 cars in those days. Research suggested the cars were seen as feminine.

'Aligning ourselves with a more masculine team sport was part of our strategy,' Devers remembers. 'I made a decision straight away that we would join them. John [Ribot] didn't know much about Melbourne. His strategy was good. He wanted to get connected with the movers and shakers of Melbourne business.'

The sponsor made the most of the partnership, hosting regular barbeques for his staff with all the players present. 'I lived on a couple of acres, and they'd play tennis and swim and eat ... I'd never seen people eat so much.'

Ribot had held off signing a jersey sponsor. No company would meet his $1 million price.

The recruitment company Adecco, an international business merged from the Swiss Adia and French Ecco, was a signage sponsor from day one. Adecco's Australian CEO, Archie Fraser, liked rugby league and understood its appeal in NSW and Queensland.

'Anybody we took [to the matches] there just loved it, the closeness of the contact and the ferocity of the contact,' Fraser says.

> That was a different experience for a Melbourne supporter to see Rodney Howe running headlong at somebody and the wind being expelled from him on a cold night at Olympic Park and you're only a few metres away. So we had no trouble with it being a different form of corporate entertainment.

Fraser liked Storm so much that when he left Adecco he joined the club as head of commercial operations in 1999, before moving into a new international business. Ribot impressed him. 'As a person in sports branding, a marketer, a "I get it" type of person, he is as good as I've come across in any walk of sport.'

Several years later Archie Fraser would return to sports administration as chief executive of AFL club St Kilda, replacing a likeable but flawed man called Brian Waldron.

Storm players were once again very quiet in the change room. Anderson bounced a ball. Nikau sat mute on a seat. Ben Roarty drove his shoulder into a brick wall with disturbing force. Matt Geyer, brought in as replacement for injured Robbie Ross, did some push-ups. The other player included in the starting side was 22-year-old hooker Richard Swain (for Danny Williams). No-one could know the two newcomers – Geyer and Swain – would be club champions. They were just nervous rookies.

Storm team V North Sydney, Olympic Park, Round Four 1998

Matt Geyer	Ben Roarty
Craig Smith	Robbie Kearns
Paul Bell	Tawera Nikau
John Carlaw	Reserves
Marcus Bai	Paul Marquet
Scott Hill	Russell Bawden
Brett Kimmorley	Wayne Evans

Glenn Lazarus	Ben Anderson
Richard Swain	
Rodney Howe	Coach: Chris Anderson

A boy band called C.D.B. sang the national anthem. Fireworks went off and the game began with many fans still stuck on the street. Lewis hailed, 'Melbourne people are the true sports fans of Australia.'

North Sydney, through its Billy Moore–led forwards and halves Jason Taylor and Ben Ikin, immediately pressured Storm. But Melbourne was its equal in all skills. Work-hungry Howe led the hit-up count again (he was also leading the league). Kimmorley kicked smartly. Then came the tries. Paul Marquet left his teammates with a fond memory by becoming the first man in a purple lighting 'V' to score a four-pointer at Olympic Park, carrying Taylor on his back. Ten minutes later Scott Hill charged past defenders. And then Marcus Bai snatched the ball after a Hill bomb.

Bai had arrived at Storm to give his career one last shot. The PNG speed merchant had played absolutely no rugby league as a junior but represented his home country at the 1995 World Cup. He had stints at Hull, in England, and Gold Coast Chargers before being recruited by Ribot and Johns. 'I went through two clubs and thought that [Storm] was my third club and if I didn't succeed I'd be going back home – back to PNG,' Bai recalls. 'I have eight brothers and two sisters and my eight brothers got stuck into me. They said this is an opportunity and you've got two years at Melbourne so this is your last chance, you won't get a fourth chance so you better show us you can make it and go all the way.'

History says Bai did go all the way. On this afternoon, he flew like a dart into the corner. The Bears got one back through Michael Buettner but trailed by eight at the break.

Ribot eventually opened the gates (the crowd overflow sat on the athletics track). He shook his head all evening. 'That's something we've gotta apologise for, something we've gotta address,' he told a news crew. 'Some people have paid money, they've been inconvenienced but we'll certainly rectify that problem.'

That Ribot was genuinely contrite says a lot about his single-mindedness. He could have been forgiven for not being *too* distressed. People had actually turned up. The dark cloud brought its silver lining. But Ribot was aware he could not be satisfied with a grand entrance into a crowded Melbourne sporting market. Most of these people were browsers.

On this night a reporter asked a watcher, 'Can you tell the difference between a scrum half and a dummy half?'

'Absolutely not,' was the reply. 'That's why I'm gunna buy one of those books [team information booklet], without a book I'm gunna be in trouble.'

John Ribot (formerly John Ribot de Bresac) was a Queensland footballer in the 1970s. He had a stint at Newtown but it was at Western Suburbs that he thrived under coach Roy Masters.

Masters (*Inside Out*):

> Newtown's 1979 coach, Warren Ryan, had little regard for Ribot and the young forward was desperate to play first grade. He was immediately popular with the Magpies players because he was unassuming, unaffected and, despite what Ryan believed, unafraid.
>
> Some of his critics say I selected him on the wing at Western Suburbs in 1980 because he could not concentrate sufficiently to play the role of lock. This is unfair. He was a second-grade lock when I chose him on the first-grade flank, and he was a sensation within a few weeks.

Ribot fulfilled his playing potential. He played for Australia against France in 1981. He then signed with Manly, made his State of Origin debut and toured with the 1982 Kangaroos. Post-retirement, Ribot became Queensland Rugby League Development Manager, which led to him becoming the successful first chief executive of the Brisbane Broncos and an opponent to the game's traditionalist administrators. At the time, he said,

> my abiding philosophy was the one set down by the Broncos board – to pursue business principals while also really looking after the players so they'd never want to leave the joint. What the board wanted overall was quality, quality, quality, all the way along. The best staff, the best players, the best coach.

It became the Super League mantra. And it came with him to Melbourne.

The funding structure of Storm was unique. The company with the licence to run the club was called Valimanda. It was Ribot's family business. At the very start, Storm was Ribot's franchise. It was a present for his service during the 'war'. News Ltd gave it to him. He had planned to entice other shareholders but wanted assurances Storm would remain in the NRL. The league was proposing to cut its competition from 22 to 20 clubs at the end of 2000. There could be no promises.

'Things happened so quickly,' Ribot recalls. 'I went back to News [News Ltd boss Ken Cowley] and said "Hang on, all the rules are changing by the minute here. What are we gunna do? I'm getting caught in the politics. Who's gunna pick up this bill?" They came back and said, "Don't worry, there's a bigger picture on this."' News Ltd agreed to indefinitely pay all the bills.

Ribot did not want to own the club outright. He knew from the beginning it would struggle to be profitable. It was better for News Ltd to own a majority and provide ongoing funding.

News Ltd took 70 per cent of Storm and gave Ribot 30 per cent. He gifted 5 per cent of his cut to Chris Johns. Valimanda was responsible for all commercial deals, including sponsorship and merchandising. The company would become important much later in Storm's trials, during the 2010 salary cap scandal. But for many years it was not even a name that required explaining. It was just a holding company.

As Storm Managing Director, Ribot's first job was to create a name, jersey and symbol. A poll was held for readers of the *Herald Sun* to contribute ideas. Ribot, Johns and Appleby sat down and had a discussion. Lachlan Murdoch had weighed in; he wanted 'Melbourne Monarchs', but it was taken by a baseball team. A short list was made ... Stormers, Bay City Stormers, some animals. Appleby, influenced by his eye for American sports, liked punchy names like 'Heat' and 'Jazz'.

Storm it was.

It was powerful, strong and a statement about Melbourne's weather. Next? Logo. Johns suggested Thor the Thunder God. Appleby tossed up having a thunderbolt 'V' for Victoria. It was Ribot's call to have purple in the uniform, as Johns explains: 'Reebs had a lot of friends in the textile industry and he was really pushing for the blue and purple and yellow because they were really strong with women. The old adage: if you're not a good footballer, at least look like you're a good footballer, be well dressed.'

Ribot trumpeted in 1998, 'I feel great, this is gunna work. I don't think I'm being arrogant saying that but this is something I'm passionate about.'

Number-one recruit Lazarus said before the first match,

> Aw look, I think the Melbourne public are pretty ignorant of rugby league and of course the Melbourne Storm and that's no fault of theirs, they've been brought up on Aussie rules and that's fine. It's up to us to convince these staunch AFL supporters to come across and have a look and see what we've got to offer.

But the club's marketing strategy wasn't to crack Aussie rules nuts, rather to befriend yearning rugby league expats living in Victoria. Ribot, standing next to Lachlan Murdoch, hinted at his tactics in a speech at the team's ritzy launch.

'We're never gunna be a threat [to AFL] here,' he said. 'Even if we take 20,000 people to our games that won't even dint their crowds.'

A large part of the Storm budget was spent on scouring Melbourne suburbs looking for anyone who came from a rugby league stronghold – not just NSW and QLD but Canberra, Tonga, Samoa, New Zealand, South Africa and England.

Ribot and Johns trawled through census figures, rugby league ticketing data and consumer research lists. The Storm made a map in the office and coloured in targeted areas, charting the location of 'Rugby League expats'. They then went to individual houses to flog club memberships. Ninety per cent of the first members came from that approach. Player recruitment complemented promotional campaigns – Tawera Nikau billboards were erected near Kiwi populations. One billboard showing a large Lazarus head boomed: *Melbourne Takes Rugby League by Storm.* Homesick Canberrans or Queenslanders would have been giddy knowing 'The Brick' was now in their town.

Ribot pronounced, 'I think it's ripe for Melbourne to have another football code down here but if we weren't to do it right I think we could put rugby league under pressure about future ventures into Melbourne. But we haven't come here to fail.'

Everything had worked well so far, except the old steel turnstiles.

The next phase of marketing was under way. It was the most important part of setting up a successful, privately owned franchise in hostile – or worse, ambivalent – territory. Winning.

Eight minutes after half-time, Marcus Bai did something so extraordinary people would talk about it for years. It was a kick return that caused the sensation. Carrying the ball, Bai charged straight into big Bear Josh Stuart, dipping his body across and into the tackler's flat stance. Right shoulders collided. The North Sydney forward rocked back and then folded like an accordion. Bai leapt forward, through the impact zone and kept going a few more metres. Play was stopped while Stuart hobbled off muttering simple phrases. People are run over by cars, not wingers. Simply, it was an awesome display of strength. Storm could not lose now.

Two more tries were scored. It ended 24–16.

The lap of honour was a strange and wonderful sight. A standing ovation – the world's slowest Mexican wave – followed the players around the athletics track. The crowd was the largest the club ever saw at Olympic Park over 11 seasons. Wally Lewis called Storm's performance against the NRL heavyweight North Sydney, 'Some of the brightest attacking football that we've seen over the last 12 months.' He pointed out that Storm's premiership odds – 600–1 before the season – might be shortening.

The team was followed not only by female cheerleaders but young men doing backflips in the dark.

'And I just remember being so proud when we won that first because we had to go down there [Melbourne] and we knew no-one,' Chris Johns recalls.

> In Sydney and Brisbane they've heard of Ribot, they've heard of me, they knew rugby league but walking down to CUB [beer company], walking into the corner office looking for sponsorship, they knew nothing about us and they were all mesmerised by the AFL.
>
> We knew we had to win games for credibility so we could go in, create corporate support and our community support as well. If we were gunna have a bum football team it was gunna be hard to put bums on seats, it was gunna be hard for them to come in and support us. That was a massive relief to be able to win our first [home] game.

AC/DC's 'Thunderstruck' was played over the loudspeaker, more fireworks went off and the people vowed to barrack (or show support) for Storm from now on. The bandwagon was filling up fast. But make room for Jeff Kennett. Wearing a shirt, a tie and a smirk, hanging a jacket over his shoulder, he said, 'We keep adding pieces to the jigsaw, that's what makes us different. Others work off a template that is set, we keep adding to parameters of that template.'

After the players showered and dressed they joined their new followers for refreshments at the dog track next door. About 3000 people attended to worship at the temples of Nikau, Bai and co.

Appleby recalls, 'T [Tawera Nikau] was the messiah. Marcus [Bai] was everyone's cult hero.'

The players loved it. Dog track drinks became part of their routine. And there was never any trouble despite CUB recording that Storm's per-game consumption of beer and bourbon was way ahead of every AFL club in town.

Later that season, Melbourne Storm was on top of the NRL ladder when its all-muscle prop Rodney Howe tested positive to a drug test. On 25 June 1998, NRL chief executive Neil Whittaker announced Howe was the second Australian representative in a month guilty of taking a banned substance.

'There could be more,' Whittaker told the media. 'We would be naïve to think there could not be more.'

Head of the Australian Sports Commission's medical advisory panel Dr Ken Fitch accused the NRL of doing 'next to nothing in the war against drugs'. 'Rugby league seems to have paid lip service to steroid abuse. How many positives have there been that we haven't heard about?'

Howe said he took the drug stanozolol (used by Canadian sprinter Ben Johnson at the Seoul Olympics) to help him recover from a knee injury sustained in a test match in 1997. After a four-hour hearing, he was suspended for 22 weeks. The player was too distressed to comment after the sanction was announced. But Ribot said Storm would support its enforcer, formerly of Newcastle Knights and Western Reds, and better educate its players.

Howe found no such comfort from the opposition. Bronco Shane Webcke wrote in his autobiography (with Ian Heads):

> When Melbourne's Rodney Howe was caught out as a [performance enhancing] drug cheat in 1998 and suspended for 22 matches, I thought he was a pretty weak bastard. I was probably even dirtier on him because he played so well via the stuff he took.

Gordon Tallis (another Bronco) would later sledge Howe when he played the Storm in a match at Olympic Park – and in a subsequent interview did not back away from the things he said. 'If he's a big enough man to inject himself with steroids, he should be a big enough man to cop the flak out on the field,' said Tallis. 'Did he really think he wouldn't be sledged? Did he really believe that guys like me who work their arses off in the gym to reach their physical peak are going to welcome back to the game a bloke who has taken the easy way out?'

During the match Tallis called Howe 'The Chemist' and 'Stanozolol' and kept up the verbal pressure. Afterwards, Storm officials were up in arms about the 'treatment' afforded Howe. But Tallis's post-match comments reflected a wider anger in the team. 'He cheated on every guy who trains his guts out ... he cheated on the game of rugby league that I love,' he told *Rugby League Week*'s Tony Durkin.

Some mud stuck to Storm, no doubt. How much is hard to quantify.

Aussie rules former champion Wayne Carey, in his book *The Truth Hurts* (with Charles Happell), told about a confrontation with Howe at Crown Casino.

> I did an interview on Triple M in Melbourne and said that Melbourne Storm front rower Rodney Howe should be suspended for life. I happened to run into Howe one night ... and he came up and challenged me about what I'd said. I thought, here we go, there might be a bit of trouble here. But I didn't back down. I said, it's great to see you back playing, but I feel drug cheats shouldn't get a second chance, that's just my opinion. I think he'd thought I was going to back down. He walked away in the end, his aggro having died down, and we agreed to disagree. He actually seemed like a decent bloke.

Three days after the Howe news broke Storm fell from its one-week perch atop the competition table. After leading 21–18 near the end of the match against Auckland, Warrior Stacey Jones kicked a bomb for winger Tony Tatupu, who scored a try that the video ref took five minutes to award.

Typically honest, Anderson after the match conceded the Howe affair was troubling. 'It had made it difficult to concentrate on footy all week.'

Without Howe, Storm faded slightly to finish third in 1998, losing a semifinal to Brisbane, the eventual title winner. Next year, Storm again came third – behind Cronulla and Parramatta but ahead of Sydney City, Canterbury and St George Illawarra.

Melbourne hosted its first final in 1999 at Olympic Park but lost 10–34 to the Dragons. From the outside, the campaign looked ruined, but the coach was not without hope. He thought his boys had 'competed well'. Anderson's biggest worry was the condition of his son Ben, who had been playing five-eighth. There is still some debate over what led to the popular player's subsequent omission. Ribot says he urged Anderson to drop his underperforming boy but Anderson argues, 'It was my decision not to play him. He was carrying an injury. In the end you have to put the team in front, you don't want to take an injured bloke into a semi final. Ben had given everything [so] it was disappointing for him to miss it.'

The changes the coach made to his team worked well. Geyer was moved from wing to number six. That relieved him of kicking conversions and penalties, for which he was thankful. His accuracy had dipped 10 per cent in recent weeks, due to the yips. Left-foot kicker Craig Smith came back into the team on the wing.

The next week Storm and Canterbury played a thrilling match. The Bulldogs led 22–18 in the 69th minute. They had just made a 68-yard gain. Fifth tackle. Twenty out. Bulldog Ricky Stuart executed a grubber kick that didn't grub. Instead the ball bounced high on its end and introduced itself to Geyer (having a nice day?) who grabbed it and took off like he'd swiped a giant bank cheque.

Caller Ray Warren piloted him to the line: 'Matt Geyer comes up with the ball. He goes for full pace (... back arches past a tackler ...). HE'S AWAY. HE'S AWAY. CLEAR THE TARMAC. MATT GEYER IS GOING IN. HE'S GUNNA LAND IT. RIGHT SMACK BANG NEXT TO THE UPRIGHTS.'

Craig Smith conversion ... Storm won. 24–22.

The victory began a frantic week for media manager Chris Appleby as he tried to lobby Channel Nine Melbourne to broadcast the preliminary final between Storm and Parramatta live on Saturday night. For two years Appleby, Ribot and Johns had lobbied executives at Bendigo Street, Richmond, to show their club on the box at a decent time. They could not crack it on Sunday afternoons. Movies went there.

'Bambi was gunna rate better,' Appleby recalls. 'We belted our heads against that Channel Nine brick wall for years. Lots of cool lunches in their boardroom, nice wine ... just didn't happen.'

Finally, with the image of Geyer's try vivid and inspiring, they struck an agreement. It was on prime time. By game day Appleby started taking notice of omens again – this time upsets. Storm wasn't tipped to beat the Eels. In the AFL, Carlton beat Essendon in a final at the MCG by one point. Lazarus had become a Blues fan. He and Appleby watched the Sydney hotel lobby the afternoon before the preliminary. That's a massive upset. That'll do. Then another outsider looked like toppling the unbeatable: Jeff Kennett. The Victorian election had been held. By the time Storm started warming up it was very possible former teacher Steve Bracks would be the next premier of Victoria.

Appleby thought it was great. Not that he was an Australian Labor Party devotee, although he could've been. He just liked omens. Then someone got a message to him – Channel Nine was rescheduling, staying with the election coverage, dropping the footy. No Storm live.

Storm beat Parramatta in front of about 25,000 people. The win was driven by a maturing self-belief. Again, Anderson's men had come from behind. No victory feels better. For the second week in a row Storm had won by two points. How's that for an omen? Crowded on the sideline, watching the final seconds disappear, the substitutes and staff yelled. 'Shit, we're goin' ta the Grand Final.'

But to win the premiership Melbourne would have to beat the combined might and dazzle of St George Illawarra.

Storm team V St George Illawarra, Stadium Australia, Grand Final 1999

Robbie Ross
Craig Smith
Aaron Moule
Tony Martin
Marucs Bai
Matt Geyer
Brett Kimmorley
Glenn Lazarus
Richard Swain
Rodney Howe
Paul Marquet
Stephen Kearney
Tawera Nikau

Reserves
Matt Rua
Danny Williams
Russell Bawden
Ben Roarty

Coach: Chris Anderson

The sky was lumpy grey. The stadium held 107,000 people. A fighter jet swooped low. It was Melbourne's first Grand Final but it was The Brick's last. Lazarus would retire after 80 more minutes of short runs and violent collisions. The coach asked him to say a few words before the match. Blokes listened in awe to their leader's very personal goodbye to the game.

Grand Final anticipation can torture you. The fear seizes your insides and won't let go, makes you go to the toilet over and over. Your mind's eye flashes images of imminent failure, until you train it to see only success. Only experience can immunise against these symptoms but even that is not a cure-all. Batsman Michael Hussey said on walking away from his international cricket career, 'There's gunna be a lot of things I won't miss, like the real sick feeling in your stomach before you go out to bat in a Test match.'

What Hussey felt at the final stages of sporting life was a double dose of pre-performance nerves. In the veteran athlete fear of failure is made worse by fear of the end. Soon all the crowd noises and the sweet silences of change rooms will be taken away. The comfort of knowing teammates better than anyone else in the world – their quirks and jokes and fury and whisperings – will be gone. Sure, we can still be friends. But not like we were under the stadium, between those concrete walls, our private play area: our youth.

So it was for Lazarus, who began to stumble on his words and cry. He desperately wanted to pass on his experience. He continued bravely, 'Just remember, you may never play in another one of these ...' said Lazzo. 'Don't waste this opportunity.'

The captain's life contradicted his message. He was about to play in his sixth Grand Final. That aside, he was right. Sometimes you only get one shot. Don't come back later and say I wish I could have my time again.

The big man tried to finish his speech. But in the end he had to quit. A sudden sadness of living through one last preparation was too much. Wearily, Glenn Lazarus hung his head. The room of footballers was stunned. What just happened? Weeping caught on. Anderson's preparation was wrecked.

Ribot had chartered a plane for wives, girlfriends and sponsors. They sat in their grandstand seats and waited.

Anderson, wearing a shirt and tie, had a silent moment and thought about the Dragons, the team paying wages totaling $7.2 million, more than twice the salary cap (this was not against the rules of the time, as Super League contracts were still distorting the numbers and the Dragons were a merged team). His private fear was 'they were more experienced than us in big games'. But he felt his team had become more resilient since they last met the Dragons a few weeks ago.

He told Channel Nine's Peter Sterling ... 'I'll jus' think we'll guts it out. We'll run over the top of them.'

Appleby was outside, watching the reserve grade decider, taking in the enormous crowd. He says, 'I remember feeling really confident, we've got the game, we've got the players. I was quietly calm.'

Westlake, the young beat reporter, was covering the match for News Ltd. He sat in the press box and opened his laptop.

'It was a seven o'clock flight out of Melbourne and you knew it was going to be a massive day,' he recalls fondly. 'It was special to me to cover it. I started writing in the first half. Most stories were about how they were blowing the big occasion because they were playing crap.'

Lazarus led the team out.

Commentator Ray Warren: 'This is one of the true sporting stories of Australia. Two years in the top grade – they brought them together from all over. The Storm of Melbourne.'

By any measure the Storm players were too emotional from the captain's address to play anywhere near their best.

St George Illawarra – $1.45 favourite – with nine Steelers from that first match against Storm 18 months earlier, was virtually the same team that had beaten Melbourne at Olympic Park four weeks before. Players to watch were Anthony Mundine (three tries in the preliminary final), Nathan Blacklock on the wing and halfback Trent Barrett.

Hugh Jackman sang the national anthem with vim. He fluffed not a line but Storm fouled many.

Fifteen years later Brett Kimmorley confides he has never watched a replay of that train-wreck first half. 'It was one of the worst feelings you could ever imagine. I think with the emotion of what happened pregame to then running out and how the first half played out – at half-time [down 14–0] I was thinking the game was over and we played horrible ...'

In the first minute, Storm knocked on. Next minute, Swain, now starting hooker, was staggered in a tackle and had to leave the field. He would later return to lead the tackle count at half-time. In the fifth minute, Kimmorley kicked out on the full. Rodney Howe knocked on.

The Dragons approached Storm's line. A Mundine kick rolled under the posts. There were no Storm players back to help fullback Robbie Ross and it was a simple try to Craig Fitzgibbon.

Howe had the ball in centre field but didn't pass ... kicked it. Turnover. Players were slipping over.

Craig Smith returned a kick but dropped the ball. Danny Williams gave away a penalty for knocking the ball from a tackled player. 8–0.

Storm was flat. St George Illawarra kept going wide to avoid Melbourne's strength. Blood streamed from Craig Smith's face. Referee Bill Harrigan sent him off.

'Too much claret.'

Thirty minutes gone, Kimmorley chipped midfield. The ball bounced to Nathan Blacklock, who didn't hesitate or swerve. He ran fast and straight for 68 metres. Kimmorley and Ross could be seen banging into each other like two stooges, as if blown dizzy by Blacklock's jet engine. Lazarus, resting on the bench, shook his head dolefully.

Storm sensed it had lost the opportunity to take the title.

In the press box, Westlake had his lede. 'I wrote that they were overawed.'

At half-time Anderson, sleeves rolled up, did what Lazarus could not do. He spoke. The statistics – possession 42 per cent; missed tackles 13; completions 13 from 20; tackles 166 to 121 – meant Storm should've been completely out of the game. But it wasn't. 'Even though we were behind by 14 points we had a positive half-time talk that we were still in the game,' Anderson says. 'St George probably had a negative one because they bombed a try before half-time that probably would've killed us off.

'[I said] we've probably had the worst half of football in our year and we're still in the game.'

Appleby remembers Anderson's nerve as the pivotal tool.

'Ando just said we're not doin' it right. I really saw him give direction on strategy and structure. Let's just go and play some footy.'

Kimmorley would win the Clive Churchill medal for rallying his team in the second half. But it was Tawera Nikau and Stephen Kearney (recruited from Auckland at the end of 1998) who started the Storm motor with fierce tackling and bold runs.

'They put a bit of fear into the Dragons,' Kimmorley remembers. 'All the nerves disappeared too because we just started playing a bit of natural football again.'

Only Lazarus continued to struggle, making several mistakes.

The we-can-do-this moment came when Mundine should've scored in the fiftieth minute. Craig Smith disturbed the ball's carriage as Mundine reached for the line ... it would have been the winner, the nail: final bullet to the head. But it wasn't. It was Mundine being 'The Man', backing his ability (he could've passed to unmarked men outside). But it didn't come off this time. An omen? Maybe we can do this, do you think?

Kimmorley slid a kick behind the tryline. Repeat set. Geyer went to the blindside, issued a flat (looked forward) pass to Tony Martin. He stretched. Try.

Lazarus caused another turnover. Dragon halfback Barrett chipped to the line. Rod Wishart leapt. So did Bai. The ball landed with Paul McGregor, who scored. Wayne Bartram missed the conversion. Wishart returned the kick-off, spilt the ball. Kimmorley found Roarty. Try. 18–12.

The Brick banged one more time. Kearney ... Swain ... Marquet ... hands in the play-the-ball. Penalty. 18–14. Storm was within reach.

There were only a few minutes remaining when Kimmorley, just metres out, trying to create something, went to kick along the ground. He saw Dragon acting fullback Jamie Ainscough come in, anticipating, so he changed it and lofted the ball toward the sideline ... just deep enough for Craig Smith to run in and catch and get knocked out before he could land the ball.

What followed was underscored by tension. Bill Harrigan referred the decision to the video referee.

Ray Warren: 'I think Bill Harrigan is about to make one of the biggest calls ever in 100 years of rugby league.'

Storm players watched the replay. They knew it would be a penalty try. The uncertainty was where the kick should be taken. With Craig Smith unconscious, Geyer had to take the conversion to break the tie. He had not practised goal-kicking for weeks. His hands were shaking when someone handed him the ball. Lazarus, fed up with trying to influence the result, went and told his young teammate, 'Over to you, you're on ya own.'

Geyer lied and said there were 'no worries'.

Harrigan pointed under the posts. Still Geyer wasn't confident. He had missed one of these kicks a month ago. He took deep breaths and forgot his stepping routine. As he lined up, Sterling said to more than a million viewers, 'We are about to have the most unbelievable end to a season that you could ever imagine.'

Warren, not finished, called it 'the most historical Grand Final ever. A sporting miracle'.

Geyer hit the kick well and Storm won the premiership. Lazarus became the only player to win three titles with three teams. He finally quit the game. In a long and distinguished career, Kimmorley didn't play in another premiership. He says, 'It was the greatest thing I achieved as a player 'cause I chased one for the rest of my career and wasn't able to find another one.' The young halfback travelled home in the cockpit of the team plane, while the rest of the players sat in business class, eating meat pies and drinkin' beer.

Anderson recalls of 1999, 'The whole year was a highlight. Highlights are the interactions you have each week with the players. I enjoy that. If you're there just for winnin' Grand Finals you're gunna have a lot of lowlights.'

Westlake spent the second half of the Grand Final hitting the delete key. After the game he went downstairs to witness the celebrations and get his interviews, then went back upstairs and resumed filing his match review and breakout stories. He pushed the send button on his copy as a taxi delivered him to Sydney Airport.

> I think it was six or seven pages of copy that I filled up essentially by myself. I was mentally exhausted on that plane and just snoozed. I got back to Melbourne and the *Herald Sun* sports department was having a celebration following the coverage of the AFL Grand Final. I came straight from the airport around midnight.

He walked straight into the pub with his bags and laptop.

'They all stood up and gave me a massive round of applause and a great big cheer – as a journalist I guess it's as close as you come to winning a Grand Final.'

Fourteen years later, he recognises, 'It was probably the greatest day of my career.'

A group of 400 supporters watched the Grand Final together in a marquee back in Melbourne. New number-one fan Dally Messenger III – grandson and namesake of the sport's first hero – said no-one saw Geyer convert the penalty try. 'I looked around the tent and everyone was looking the other way – they couldn't look at the screen. They all turned around when they heard the cheer.'

Ribot and Johns had done it. It had all worked. What now? Financially there were immediate concerns. News Ltd did not want to own Storm for a very long time. Lazarus was leaving. Nikau was also likely to depart. One hope was that recruiting would not be difficult. Delirious in victory, The Brick told Anderson the game's best players would beat a path to the premiership club.

As it turned out, Storm didn't need to entice the game's best. While the winning footballers went out and got premiership tattoos on their bum cheeks, Ribot's scouts in Queensland were hard at work recruiting three short-limbed boys called Cam, Cooper and Billy, who would redefine the sport.

CHAPTER 4

DISCOVERING THE BIG THREE

Architects of the best 12-month scouting streak in rugby league history say it was mostly luck that saw future internationals Cameron Smith, Billy Slater and Cooper Cronk land at Storm. But there was more to it.

When Ribot was gifted Storm he shrewdly purchased a team in the Queensland state league that became the country's finest football nursery. Norths Devils (Northern Suburbs Rugby League Football Club) has a proud history of winning premierships. It was particularly successful in the 1960s under legendary coach Bob Bax, who would later mentor Wayne Bennett. By the 1990s, like many teams in the Queensland Rugby League, Norths was dirt poor. It would've folded if not for the Storm partnership.

Ribot thought Norths 'smelled right'. 'Their history was really important for us,' he says. 'And we could live off that and that could flow on into what Melbourne Storm was all about. It could accommodate players not selected for first grade and develop teenagers through a Colts team.'

Ribot's ex-teammate Mark 'Muppet' Murray was made boss of Norths. Murray then employed a Colts coach to help with scouting: Anthony 'Hook' Griffin.

'It was something that had never happened in the game and I guess I was a bit concerned how it was all going to work across two cities, but it was something that I enjoyed the challenge of,' Murray recalls.

'It probably shaped a lot of things, particularly the way the game is in Queensland now with the feeder systems to NRL clubs.'

Murray, a former Australian and Queensland representative, was Norths' last premiership captain (1980). He retired at 27 after an accident in a bar. He was mucking around with mates, fell over and was speared by glass. Normally you'd expect 100 stitches from such an incident but he had two. A splinter of glass went through the eye. It was a freakish injury.

A physical education teacher, Murray eventually went into coaching and football administration at Redcliffe. The Queensland competition was strong back then but the Brisbane Broncos started up in 1988 and necessarily drained the local teams of their best youngsters. Under Murray, Redcliffe was one of the better performed teams and the Muppet was poached by the great Jack Gibson to coach Eastern Suburbs in the NSWRL. Murray stayed in that role for three and a half seasons, until he was sacked and replaced by Arthur Beetson.

'I came back to Redcliffe then in an admin role, but I was keen to get back into coaching,' he says. Then the call came from Johns and Ribot in late 1997.

Storm's understudy, Norths, won the Queensland title in 1998. Geyer played in that team. Murray was then selected to coach Queensland in State of Origin for the next two seasons. But it was his unseen work in player development and talent spotting that most benefitted his employer.

Melbourne had its New South Wales recruitment managed by Theo Burgess, whose nickname, 'Tok' (Tree of Knowledge), hinted at his quality. It was Anthony Griffin's job to trawl the junior carnivals in Queensland. He was not like the old scouts you read about in classic books like *Prophet of the Sandlot* (by Mark Winegardner) – hunched over, low hat, cigar, narrow eyes and a gut feel – lookin' for a kid with the 'right stuff'. No, Griffin wasn't like that at all.

Cameron Smith

You can spot recruiters if you look for them – identify them not by what they wear or smoke but how they move and where they position themselves on the sidelines; at youth tournaments they announce themselves by their solitude. They watch, really watch, holding a list of player names in one hand, maybe a pencil in the other. They all know each other and might mouth g'day sometimes or nod, but it is a competitive business and not just a game. It is where success is won or missed forever. Three-time world heavyweight champ Muhammad Ali once said, 'The fight is won or lost far away from witnesses. Behind the lines, in the gym, and out there on the road, long before I dance under those lights.'

In the NRL, 'out there on the road' is where recruiters source silverware. Thanks to a High Court ruling involving Terry Hill back in the early 1990s, there is no draft. So scouts (and agents) wander up and down the sidelines of fields far flung to catch a prospect, get the signature first; don't wait or you'll miss out.

Griffin stood on the sidelines in Rockhampton watching the Queensland Under–17 carnival. It felt good to be there. Griffin had previously been a player/coach in 'Rocky'. He knew people in town. But truth be known, Griffin didn't actually *love* this part of the job. He preferred coaching and had ambitions to be an NRL boss one day. This was a way to get there.

He was dedicated.

Two years before, Griffin set up a Brisbane carers' house for Storm players recruited from country Queensland. Storm paid the rent. Griffin was charged with finding a host or nanny for the players but decided to do it himself, with his wife, Helen.

At this particular carnival he was watching teams from all over the state, representing regions including Brisbane, Wide Bay, Gold Coast and North Queensland. He was not alone. The other hawks were around. After Super League, NRL clubs were more organised than they had been. Most clubs had recruiters travel everywhere. Griffin was always aware of the Broncos' staff.

> We were the first NRL club to base ourselves in Brisbane so it was a massive challenge to try and get kids off the Broncos because in those days, you know, they were winning and Wayne [Bennett] was the coach and if a young kid got a call from Wayne, it was pretty hard to knock back for a Queenslander not to go to the Broncos.

While he checked out all the players, Griffin was particularly interested in a boy he had seen play for Logan Brothers a few weeks earlier. His name was Cameron Smith.

At representative level, junior football quickens and hardens. Some club players can't cope. They appear rushed or timid. Nerves can play a part early in matches so learned scouts pay little attention to a fumble or misstep until about ten minutes in. That's when the rhythm of the contest evens out. That's when you can see the best more clearly.

Smith has never been hurried, in football or life. And if the pace of the game went up, he looked even more comfortable, making decisions for the team, problem-solving under the threat of violent collisions as easily as selecting socks from a drawer.

'I'm not saying I'm any genius and found him and no-one else found him,' stresses Griffin. 'He's just someone that always had a little bit extra time about what he did, you know, similar to what he does now. Recruitment's a bit of a lucky dip sometimes; guys that tell you they know what they're doing and get it right all the time are lying.'

Griffin's modesty is admirable but paying attention to Smith's poise should not be overlooked. Scouts can make a rich living signing athletic kids and playing 'lucky dip'. Go for the boy with broad shoulders ... long legs ... vertical leap ... movie-star looks. That's *Moneyball* in reverse. But the recruiter who can identify and trust strengths like composure or durability provides his club with the truest value.

Griffin already had a record of appreciating unspectacular but critical traits.

Teenager Dallas Johnson was identified and signed by Griffin because the boy made his last tackle of the youth tournament with as much gusto as he had the first.

'I just thought I've gotta sign this kid out of effort alone, you know,' Griffin recalls. 'I thought he was a real tough kid.' Johnson, raised on his family's farm on Queensland's Atherton Tablelands, could easily have been a country footballer for the next two decades had Griffin not noted his work rate. The lad was otherwise unremarkable. (Johnson is still playing in the NRL.)

Not everyone saw value in Cameron Smith. He was not selected in the Queensland team after that carnival in Rockhampton. A boy from Wide Bay was chosen as hooker because he ran faster than Cam. That didn't deter Hook and Muppet, who moved to the second phase of their assessment of the earnest teen from Marsden High School.

Murray had a recruitment blueprint, which included judging character. This was always subjective.

He explains, 'He'd [Griffin] come back and draw up a list and I would go with him to meet the parents and sit down and talk for an hour with them. Usually at their homes so we got a feel for the nature of the kid and the upbringing.'

It is often the best and quickest way of measuring values.

'We had an unwritten philosophy on what we were looking for,' Murray continues.

> When you watch them play, footy talent is an easy thing to spot – if he can tackle, if he can run ... that's the easy part to assess and I think a lot of scouts jump all over that – they think geez I gotta get this kid, I gotta get that kid – and that was a tendency because of what he can do on the field but I think it takes a complete package to play at that level [NRL] so if you haven't got the right make-up and right temperament and the right character – commitment, dedication and all those sorts of things, a bit of intelligence.

Smith's father, Wayne, had played for Easts Tigers in Brisbane against Murray, who recalls the lounge room meeting as unremarkable. 'He's got an economy of words, Cam. But his old man, having been a footy player, did most of the talking.'

Smith sat and listened. The men discussed his future – ambitions and desires beyond football. Whether Smith was able to make it all the way to the NRL could not be determined. But his start to life had been a good one. He had humility and respect and a calm confidence that gave him a chance to reach his potential.

Griffin and Murray, on behalf of Storm, signed the future Australian captain for $5000.

'From the day he came over and started to play,' Murray says, 'I've never seen Cam play a bad game. I've seen him have good games and better games but he was just one of those kids from day one – he was composed, very consistent and he was a natural at it. I always felt he was going to go places.'

Cooper Cronk

Scouts can't be everywhere all the time. It's important to know blokes who can help you.

Storm had a pool of seven spotters spread across Queensland and northern New South Wales. These men were ex-footballers in positions to watch regular matches of junior football (teachers or coaches). Technically, Melbourne employed them. Each man was paid a bag of Storm merchandise and an annual trip to Victoria, to meet Ribot and socialise for a couple of nights. Of course, those meagre rewards were a bonus. The men acted as informers because it was thrilling to be, in a small way, attached to professional football. Also, it would feel exceptionally rewarding if one day a boy you discovered turned into one of the finest players in the country. Wouldn't that be nice?

Gavin Darwin was one of Storm's spotters. He was a teacher at St Laurence's College in Brisbane and one of its rugby coaches. Darwin had been a university rugby union representative and also a rugby league player for Brothers and Valleys in the Brisbane competition. He knew both codes well.

Darwin first noticed Cooper Cronk as a ten-year-old.

'He just came through the primary school as a young fellow from Acacia Ridge,' Darwin recalls. 'He was just a delightful multi-talented kid.'

Cronk was an outstanding baseball player. He could run and hit and throw. His balance and coordination stood out. Actually, he shone in most sports. Hurdling was something he did easily.

Darwin remembers Cronk breaking his arm in a rugby game against Gregory Terrace (St Joseph's College) in primary school. The teachers at St Laurence's knew with Cronk winged the hope of a premiership was lost for the season.

In 1998 Darwin began coaching the First XV at St Laurence's. Cronk was much younger than the senior players but the teacher wanted to select him. He successfully requested permission from the boy's father.

'I just remember being at training and he was a real intent listener,' Darwin explains. 'Some of the boys at that age they think they know it all and whatnot but Cronk would listen intently and go and try everything that you showed him.'

When Cronk became one of St Laurence's best players, Darwin rang Anthony Griffin with the tip-off. Griffin asked whether Cronk had ever played rugby league; Darwin said he had – for Souths Acacia Ridge.

The Storm scout agreed to watch Cronk play. But the day he turned up, Cronk caused no goosebumps of excitement. It was hard to know whether he was special, because he did not often touch the ball.

Nevertheless, Darwin kept Griffin informed from that day.

After Cronk was selected in the Queensland B team and then the Australia B side, Darwin called Hook and said, 'You've gotta get this kid. He may never be a world-beater but he'll be your best clubman week in, week out. He'll do whatever you tell him to do.'

No contracts were drawn up. In 2000, Cronk was selected in the Australian schoolboy team. Unknown to Griffin, the teen was a self-driven trainer. He was determined, above all else. Given time and opportunities, he would improve.

The 2000 St Laurence's yearbook read:

> His nonstop talk was crucial to keep our team's game on track and he always put his hand up when times became tough. Coops proved to be the team linchpin, able to turn the game around.

Griffin recalls the crucial decision to recruit Cronk. It was not born of inspiration but fear. 'I thought shit I better sign this guy on a little contract [about $3000] in case he does something.' It was as simple as that.

Importantly, Cronk and Smith became friends. They travelled to Norths Devils training sessions together. A bond and understanding was formed between the pair that would last many years and make the boys quite rich and very famous.

Murray says,

> Cooper [Cronk] was always a well-mannered and well-spoken kid. He wasn't as obvious as a standout talent at the time but he was a real solid kid and at the time he was worth a chance. He played centre, we tried him at five-eighth and fullback. He went to dummy half. Back row. He won a few man of the match awards playing in the back row in Norths' first-grade side. When he went to Melbourne – he was loved around the place – he trained hard but we didn't have a position for him. He went down there and impressed [future coach] Craig Bellamy.'

Now deputy head at Anglican Church Grammar School, Gavin Darwin looks back, 'There are certain kids that you remember and you teach a thousand of them over ... 20 years I've been teaching now ... but there are kids you bump into that you always remember and he was one of them.'

Billy Slater

The discovery of Slater, who was born on the very same day as Smith, cannot be told without the mention of thoroughbreds. It is well known he rode horses as a track work jockey in Sydney for leading trainer Gai Waterhouse before breaking into the ranks of elite football.

As his legend grows, Slater's story has potential for mythology, like Michael Jordan getting cut from his high-school basketball team (he did not) or Cassius Clay throwing away his Olympic gold medal (he lost it). For the record, it happened this way ...

The Slater family is from Innisfail.

Slater's father played rugby league all his life and also coached. His son was bred into the game and started playing when he was four. Eight years later the small and nimble child started riding horses. His father was a punter and had mates who trained nags. Slater rode country track work until he was 16. Then he moved to Sydney. From the Waterhouse racing operation Slater learned a robust work ethic. He rose at 3am and rode til nine. In the afternoons he'd sit in the saddles again. It was a seven-day-a-week job for six months.

On returning to Innisfail, Slater wanted to play football again. He was disappointed to find there were not enough players to form a Colts team.

Ribot picks up the story.

> His dad said, 'Look, I know a barman that works at Norths, why don't I give him a call and they might be able to give you a trial'.
>
> So he spoke to a barman and the barman went to Mark Murray and said, 'I've got a guy from Innisfail, they wanna come down, would you give him a trial?'

That was on Tuesday. The trial was on Saturday. Murray said, 'Yes – if he wants to come all that way he'll be able to try out.'

Slater and his cousin drove an old beat-up Mazda from Innisfail to Brisbane. Murray remembers their first trial.

> They weren't outstanding, they were solid and I said to Slater afterwards you're welcome to stay, we can't offer you accommodation but if you've got that set you're welcome to stay on and be part of our Colts squad. He was a good average Colts player from what I saw in that first game. He didn't score a heap of tries – we thought he was a half or five-eighth in those days – and that's what he'd been as a junior. To his credit he said thanks. His cousin went back after three weeks. By the end of that first year we put Billy on a Storm deal.

In the beginning, Slater made too many errors. It was obvious the teenager could run the football but defensively he needed a lot of work. By the end of 2001, Slater's deal was expiring. It was then he started to dramatically improve, breaking defensive lines and running faster. Then, in a Queensland Cup game against Toowoomba (the Brisbane Broncos feeder club) Slater excelled. Broncos coach Wayne Bennett called a meeting with the player. By now Storm wanted to re-sign him. Murray was nervous. 'Wayne could be very convincing with young people,' he says.

Broncos offered Slater $25,000. Storm had him on a two-year deal worth $5000.

It wasn't a difficult decision. Storm matched the Brisbane offer and Slater was happy to stay. He was a loyal person. Also, Ribot and Murray made sure the club paid attention to its recruits, bringing them to Melbourne to make them feel part of the NRL environment.

'One of the main things for this club from the start was this club was never gunna chase blokes with a chequebook,' says Anderson.

> We had to have the facility, we had to have the best team, we had to have the best coaching staff, we had to have the best culture ... so when we bring a player down for an interview to come with us, we've got that wow factor. It was so important that the number one focus [for the potential recruits] was that they wanted to play for us not for a pay cheque or a bigger salary, but because they could see they were gunna become better footballers.

Not long after the recruitment of Smith, Cronk and Slater the modest but wonderfully successful scouting team of Murray and Griffin was finished, moving on. It was a short, game-altering partnership.

In 2001, Griffin would be called to Melbourne to be Anderson's assistant at Storm. Mark Murray would join him in Victoria as head coach after Anderson departed in mid–2002.

Today, Murray is CEO of Norths Devils.

Griffin kept chasing his dream of coaching an NRL team. His hard work paid off and he now coaches Brisbane Broncos. He spends no time dining out on his outstanding stint as a talent scout.

'I wish I hadn't picked [Smith] up now,' he laughs, meaning the hooker would be more useful to him as a Bronco. 'No, I mean I'm not trying to downplay it but I mean I was just doing my time, doing my job at the time and I didn't know what I was doing back then, you know, or where it would all end up.'

Boys and young men selected to enter the ranks of professional football face many hardships, including crippling injuries, constant criticism from coaches, media and fans, and a high probability of personal failure and disappointment. A very small percentage plays more than a decade and finishes on the shoulders of teammates being applauded by strangers.

But a freshly scouted teen does not waste thoughts on the future's reality. He is too happy dreaming. His legs are strong and his mind is uncluttered so that when he runs as fast as possible it feels like he could fly.

A team photo adorns the Norths Devils website. All players have been cropped out but three. There they are: neat haircuts, fists on knees, smiling like it's Christmas. Cronk, on the left, and the diminutive Slater, in the middle, look younger than Smith, who already has a beard shadow. The picture was taken when few people knew their names. The trio was in light blue and as long as they stayed together – shoulder-to-shoulder – the rest of their lives would be golden.

CHAPTER 5

REMEMBERING MICK MOORE

A year after Melbourne won its first NRL premiership, Australia staged the Olympic Games. One of the most dramatic moments was the host nation beating USA in women's water polo. The Stingers had earlier lobbied the International Olympic Committee to have their competition included on the schedule. They bailed up international delegates at the airport wearing only swimwear to plead their case. That did the trick. They were in. Australia made the final. Scores were level with 1.3 seconds left in the match. Yvette Higgins was the calm 21-year-old who took the shot to win her team and nation gold.

After the game, one of the Stingers tackled her coach into the pool, watched by greats of Australian sport, including Dawn Fraser. The drenched coach was Istvan Gorgenyi.

Dr Gorgenyi represented Hungary in water polo at the Munich Olympics, winning a silver medal. The next year his team won a world championship. After retiring, Dr Gorgenyi coached extensively in Europe before he landed in Australia. In between, he earned a Doctorate in Law and Political Science and worked in Hungarian psychiatric clinics as a social worker and family therapist.

Dr Gorgenyi has since developed a fascinating way of looking at team sports – called the Hunting Territory. It deals with group dynamics and performance. It is useful to keep in mind while considering what happened to Melbourne Storm as it fell apart after the 1999 premiership.

Dr Gorgenyi believes that sports teams develop through the same five stages: 'Disintegration', 'Infighting', 'Formation', 'Settled Team' and 'Dynamic Balance'. Some teams never experience dynamic balance, which is the state of being in perfect formation, all players and coaches forgetting about personal differences and desires to work for a common goal.

For an example of a team in dynamic balance think West Indies cricket in the 1980s. Ex-captain Viv Richards described his team's harmony in the documentary *Fire in Babylon*. 'These were a special bunch who felt the same way – had the same special consciousness. It was a magnificent combination.'

Often, football clubs don't go through more than two or three stages of Dr Gorgenyi's cycle of team life. When the infighting stage becomes too arduous – or the media increases the pressure for change – officials sack the coach. Back to the bottom of the cycle they go. Detractors then announce such a team is crippled by a 'losing culture'.

Anderson's Melbourne Storm raced through the stages of development so quickly that it reached dynamic balance in the 1999 finals, just two years after formation. It was almost inevitable that the disintegration stage would happen sooner rather than later.

Even great teams fall apart in the end. Players get older. The salary cap squeezes. A coach leaves. Extroverts within the team eventually clash. The symptoms of the disintegration stage manifest differently depending on club management strength. In the English Premier League, it doesn't look like much for Manchester United; maybe the team dips for a season. But the EPL does not have a salary cap, so poor performances, like cracks in a wall, can be plastered over by big signings. Money can repair faults or hold a team together for longer.

But not for Storm Mark I. Despite ritualistic player promises to stick together and forge more success, the organisation in Melbourne was already fracturing. The coach's relationship with Ribot and Johns was fraying over the player roster. Contract talks happen constantly at NRL clubs. Someone is always 'coming off' (a term for approaching the end of a deal). In Melbourne, young players needed more pay. Older players were retiring or going overseas.

Enough talent remained to win some big games but not another premiership. No way. And then something happened that no-one expected. Nor will they ever forget it.

On 22 January 2000, Melbourne played the UK Super League champion St Helens in the World Club Challenge. Not many more than 13,000 people watched in cold silence as the visiting Storm won 44–6 against an inferior opponent. Scott Hill and Robbie Ross crossed for two tries each. Tawera Nikau was in England but did not play, as he was now a member of the Warrington Wolves. Glenn Lazarus was resting his bones in retirement. Robbie Kearns was the new captain. The off shore celebrations were worthy of world champions.

Fifteen days later the NRL season began. Anderson's team had to play in Auckland, New Zealand. The fired-up Warriors won 14–6. However, Storm's predicament was relatively positive. One of the world's finest sporting competitions, America's Cup, was also being contested in Auckland. The host city was packed with partygoers and it was a pleasant place to drink away a defeat.

The fun was around Prince's Wharf. Hotels were crammed with smiling people admiring the view of unattainable yachts and cruisers in Viaduct Harbour. Storm players started socialising at a bar. The team and officials later split up, as happens when the liquor takes ahold. Among them was beloved football manager Mick Moore.

Like many Storm people, Moore had come to Melbourne from the Broncos. He was previously a strength and fitness coach, working at a police gymnasium, then at Brisbane Souths Rugby League Club, then for Brisbane Broncos second grade. He applied for the same type of job at Storm but missed out. Ribot and Johns made him football manager instead. He moved south a month ahead of his wife Tracey, who was pregnant with their third child. Early in his tenure Moore was the person who met all newcomers at the airport and showed them to their accommodation in the strange city.

Marcus Bai recalls landing in Melbourne on 8 November 1997,

> I was picked up by Mick and his son. He made me feel at home straight away. I will never ever forget that day. It was the eighth, which was on a Sunday. He said to me 'Hi Marcus' and you know the voice, Robbie Kearns and all the boys would know the voice. During that time I didn't speak English well. I said, 'I'm good.' He said, 'Why aren't you speaking to me? Don't you like me?' I said, 'No, no, no, I do like you.' He started laughing and said, 'There's only one person who says they like me and that's my wife and not you.' And that's how I had the relationship with him. I knew this

guy is a good guy. The next day he rang me to make sure we were training and things like that. It was great.

By Round One, 2000, Moore was 35 years old and had three young children. He was extremely popular for his warmth and sense of humour. He loved a beer and a dare, due to his competitive streak.

Moore's work colleagues had never seen him upset or unhappy. It was this personality that allowed him to be a peace broker in times of dispute between the football department and front office. Geyer says, 'Moore was the one guy universally loved. With us he was a pretty straight shooter but was also your best mate.'

His job at the club was closer to a team manager than today's football managers. Simply, Moore organised the athletes to be ready to play. Usually Moore shacked up on away trips with media manager Chris Appleby. Just two weeks before the NZ game, they had shared a room in England.

Appleby now laughs at the memory of Moore's steam train–loud snoring. At bars and pubs Appleby used a proven routine to ensure maximum rest. He used to tap Moore on the shoulder and give him a nod that said, 'Gimme a half-hour, big fella.' That way, when Moore turned in, Appleby was sound asleep and less likely to be up all night. 'The boys loved him,' Appleby recalls. 'He was the kind of guy, if you ever had kids, you'd say I'll model my kids on you.'

That night, Appleby roomed alone. Moore had arranged to share an apartment with the physiotherapists to oversee player massages. As the media manager was leaving a busy bar he saw a distressed woman approach Rodney Howe. He didn't know what to make of it. Oh well. It's late. Off he went.

Bai was one of the last to speak to Moore. Earlier in the evening he was in his hotel room, feeling miserable for knocking out Warrior Ivan Cleary during the match. It was an accident. Cleary was tackling Bai. But the Storm winger felt guilty.

Here Bai tells the story.

I will never ever forget that day. He [Cleary] went to the hospital and I felt really bad about it. Moore was the person who went up to my room and he said to me, 'Marcus, you better get out of the room or I'm gunna break this door down.' I said, 'I don't want to go out.' He said, 'You listen, you get dressed, you're coming with me and we're gunna have some drinks together.' He put some good words into me and he was the person who took me out. We went and had a drink and then we moved to another nightclub and I said, 'We're moving' and he said, 'you boys go and I'll come.' That's the last time I spoke to him. My hair still stands when I talk about it.

At 6am the next day Appleby's phone rang. He answered it. Ribot's voice said, 'We've lost Mick.'

Confused and maybe still dreaming, Appleby hung up the phone. He rang Ribot back. 'What did you say?'

'We've lost him. He's been in an accident.'

The press reported later that day that the 'manager of rugby league's world club champions has died after a late-night prank outside a bar'.

Moore's body had been recovered from Waitemata Harbour. He had jumped off a nearby wharf after drinking. An Auckland police spokesman said, 'He basically ran out of the bar – a bit of high jinks, skylarking, whatever way you want to put it – and propelled himself off the wharf.'

It was thought Moore struck his head on a pontoon. He was either unconscious or dead when he hit the water. The Italian America's Cup team jumped into the water, trying to save him. But it was too dark, too cold. It was an unforgettable scene. Ribot still remembers standing over his mate's body in the cruel morning light.

He told the media that day, 'Michael was always someone who brought a laugh to the office. He was easily the most popular member of the club. He was just a magic bloke.'

Back in Melbourne, Tracey Moore was told by police her husband was not coming home alive. She had to explain it to her children, aged six, four and two.

It was Ribot's duty to inform the players; they gathered in the corporate meeting room of the motel, just sat and stared at nothing. Some people make the room lighter with their presence, warmer with their touch. And when they are gone life is diminished.

Storm was never the same.

After the plane trip and funeral came the crash. For several weeks the team grieved and lost football matches. Commentators criticised Anderson's men for having a 'lack of focus'. Then came the so-called Grand Final rematch. It was at the MCG. St George Illawarra boasted it was better than Storm, despite losing the last season decider. Storm players' emotions felt volcanic by then. Something extraordinary was about to happen.

In the first 90 seconds of the match Moore's mate Bai scored a try and jogged away, without any apparent feeling. In the fifteenth minute, with Storm in front 18–0, Robbie Ross returned a Trent Barrett kick from deep in his team's half. He charged it back and passed to Bai, who dummied and shovelled the ball to Tony Martin, down the sideline, back inside to Ross in support. The Dragons could not touch him. 22–0.

Ray Warren announced from the commentary box, 'It's embarrassing at the moment.'

Peter Sterling added, 'Chris Anderson, whatever he said to his team, has hit the right note.'

Storm went on to win the match 70–10. It experienced the free sensation of being in dynamic balance one final time – albeit a deeply sad and empty version of selflessness. When it was done and the stadium siren sounded, there were few smiles. The victors in purple were thinking of Mick.

Kimmorley says, 'He was an outstanding football manager and the bloke that held it all together. He was such a caring, loveable bloke ... it was certainly tough.'

Richard Swain (winner of the Mick Moore Club Person of the Year Award in 2000): 'He was a champion bloke of the club, had a great family, so it really rocked us. I remember being really flat for the next few months.'

Storm went on to finish sixth in 2000, finally ejected from the tournament by a qualifying final loss to Newcastle at Marathon Stadium.

'It wasn't a surprise that things fell apart the way that they did,' journalist Westlake observes. 'It was a great shame because there was still the makings of a terrific club there. Unfortunately the personalities and the circumstances didn't mix so well.'

Without Moore to keep everyone together and happy, the dynamic had changed completely.

CHAPTER 6

SALARY CAP

The shock value of sports scandals should be zero.

American father of sports writing, Grantland Rice, penned his life story (*The Tumult and the Shouting*) in 1954, the year of his death. He said in all his years he remembered only two scandals, one being the infamous World Series corruption of 1919 (involving the tarnished Black Sox). He pointed out politics is more heavily 'loaded with crooks and cheats'.

But, Rice wrote:

> Sport today is, however, much more commercial and much more stereotyped than in my heyday. I doubt if we will ever again have the devil-may-care attitude and spirit of the Golden Twenties, a period of boom, screwballs and screwball antics. The almighty dollar, or what's left of it, hangs high. The magnificent screwballs have been crowded to the wall. The fleet Washington outfielder who, when asked to race Mickey Mantle against time before a recent Yankee–Senators night game, replied, 'I'll do it ... for five hundred dollars' is testimony to the times.

Rice wrote that almost 60 years ago. Since then the likeable athletes, the nutty but adorable managers and the larrikin (more a compliment now than in Rice's Golden Twenties) administrators have thinned to invisibility. Scandals, like bushfires, are sparking and raging more intensely every year. The dollar, or what's left if it, hangs higher still.

Where there are rules in professional sports there will always be rule breakers. Some are motivated by the rewards of success. Others are inspired by the fear of what happens if they keep losing; for these people, only one question remains – what are the chances of getting busted?

Like many professional sporting competitions all around the world, the NRL has a salary cap, which serves two functions: to prevent richer clubs stockpiling all the best footballers and making the competition uneven; and to stop bidding wars sending poorer clubs broke.

One of the most common ways of cheating in the NRL is to secretly pay players higher wages than the salary cap allows. Such a tactic comes with the threat of being exposed by the league's salary cap auditor or investigative journalists. It is a risk-and-reward equation, similar to speeding in your car. How far you are willing to go over the limit depends on how prepared you are to pay the consequences, a fine or worse.

Some types of payments outside the cap are allowed. These are called legitimate third party agreements or TPAs. They exist so the best players can boost their earnings through some casual work or marketing – guest appearances on television programs or modelling for a clothing company, etc.

The NRL website states the following on TPAs:

> Income that a player earns from parties not related to his club is generally not included in the Salary Cap, however, the details of the agreement must be advised to the club by the player. The club must get approval for the agreement from the Salary Cap Auditor in order for the remuneration to be excluded.

If the league rejects a proposed TPA but the payment goes ahead anyway, the club is in breach of the salary cap.

The NRL disallows TPAs if it is thought the money coming from a company or benefactor is a sweetener for the players to sign a contract. The deals are to reward players for services to their employers, not induce them to serve.

For many years the NRL also banned club sponsors giving individual players extra cash or goods. This caused angst because car companies, for instance, are prolific sponsors of football teams. The sponsors *wanted* the players driving their cars. But a leased vehicle declared to the salary cap auditor would take up about $25,000 of the club's money under the cap. Five players equaled $125,000. It was not insignificant. In a tight cap, every bit of room was valuable. A common way around that was for the club to officially lease a car to a front office worker and then give the keys and the wheels to the athlete for a year. Therein lies a breach.

The salary cap was first introduced by the NSWRL in 1990. It struck problems immediately. In 1991 the powerful Canberra team went broke. League boss John Quayle, while looking into the club's finances, discovered the club had been spending way over the limit.

Quayle recalls, 'The Raiders were last year's premiers and announced they couldn't pay. And they were doing things behind the scene.'

It was soon revealed other clubs were also ignoring the new cap. So Quayle started a practice of personally signing every contract from every club. Once contracts totalled the salary cap limit ($1.6 million) teams weren't allowed to register anyone else.

'And then they were going out and paying extra monies,' Quayle recalls. 'But so many of them couldn't pay players legitimately let alone under the table.'

The NSWRL did not have the resources or the inclination to investigate payments outside the cap.

'We knew they were doing it,' Quayle says.

> It didn't matter if they were getting a car from a sponsor back in those days, two cars from a sponsor or certain things [from] a certain wealthy benefactor of a club. No different to what happens today and what happens in AFL and all sports around the world. I didn't care that if all of a sudden Mal Meninga was getting whatever – $100,000 – to play the game and was getting a paper deal and was signing with a radio company. I didn't care 'cause it wasn't coming out of the club's money.

Other NSWRL clubs complained about this attitude because it favoured rich clubs like Brisbane, which could draw from its vast supporter base for cash and services to recruit and keep stars. But at that time the NSWRL was not likely to apply the handbrake to Brisbane's success. The Broncos were 'growing the game', Quayle says.

Penniless Canberra was forced to shed athletes. Some wanted to leave. Money owed to individuals was not entirely paid. Quayle remembers a meeting with the footballers, who were arguing about their losses. One person stood out. It was Craig Bellamy. Quayle says,

> When we went down, a number of the players – and I'll only use the words very senior players – said this is the league's problem and the league are gunna have to pay us or we're not gunna play, we're not gunna do this and we're not gunna do that. Bellamy was one player who stood up as an individual and said, 'Look, as far as I'm concerned I don't think it's the responsibility of the league and if the proposal being put to me means I'm gunna get 55 per cent of my money, I'm gunna accept it'. And he walked out of the meeting.

Bellamy was independent enough to walk alone, no small feat in a change room of male egos and insecurities.

During the recession of the early 1990s, some clubs didn't even want to pay the limit of the salary cap. 'George Piggins, who was president of Souths at the time,' Quayle tells,

> he said we're broke and my board still wants to spend $1.3 million, and I want you to tell us we can only spend $800,000. And that's what we had the authority to do. It was the league that gave the clubs the grant and we would say you're not getting your grant until your debts are paid so you'll not be further into debt.

In 1994 the salary cap was raised to $1.8 million. But then players started to sign for Super League or commit to ARL during the mid-1990s dispute and wages went bananas.

Jarrod McCracken's book (*A Family Betrayal*) lists all the contracts, from the top earners to the bottom feeders, who were still smiling at opportunities to make healthy bonuses. Atop the list was Raider Bradley Clyde – $4.3 million over seven years.

In 1998, the new NRL announced a $3.25-million salary cap (for clubs' top 25 players) would be introduced in 1999. There would have to be an adjustment period because many inflated Super League and ARL contracts were yet to expire. It was unreasonable to expect all clubs to immediately fall under the cap. In the meantime, the league measured some players not on their real wages but on 'notional values' (a player's estimated value on an open market). This was seen as a way of balancing out the competition until everyone eventually fell under the cap with new deals in place. In 1999, a meeting of NRL chief executives, chairmen and NRL board directors decided to retain the $3.25-million figure for another two seasons.

Former player Ian Schubert was given the job as salary cap auditor. He remains in the job today. His role is to allow or disallow payments to players, using his discretion under the rules, and to investigate breaches.

All NRL player contracts are lodged with Schubert. At the start of every season the auditor receives a statutory declaration from each club, signed by CEOs and chairmen, stating player earnings in relation to the cap. Schubert follows up with teams through the year to make sure they are abiding by the laws of the game. He often relies on media reports to find potential cap breaches. Contract negotiations sometimes play out in the press or on television. It's all part of agents playing off clubs, and vice versa.

Schubert holds a mighty and polarising position in the NRL yet rarely speaks publicly about his job. To fans he is an invisible man. To most people within the game he is helpful and friendly, albeit hard to read. He has immense self-belief. That is something he carried into business from his playing days.

He was recruited as a teenager to Eastern Suburbs by legendary coach Jack Gibson. In 1975 – his first season – Shooey was a sensation as a long-striding fullback.

The book *Grand Finals of New South Wales Rugby League* (by Alan Whiticker) describes:

> During the year, Ian Schubert, an 18-year-old schoolboy from Wauchope in north-western NSW, emerged as the most promising rookie in Australian Rugby League. His role in the brilliant Easts backline ... took on new importance with a sickening injury to Russell Fairfax midway through the year. Schubert moved from the wing to fullback with amazing success.

Gibson's glittering side was without Fairfax for the Grand Final against St George. It didn't matter. Easts won it romping. The final try went to a kid named Ian. 'Schubert brushed aside Billy Smith's covering tackle as if he was non-existent to run in Easts' eighth try which took the final score to 38–0,' Whiticker wrote.

The performance won Schubert acclaim and a spot on the Australian World Cup touring squad.

His career hit a flat spot after its meteoric start and by the 1980s it seemed Schubert's best was a memory. He moved from Easts to Western Suburbs, back to Easts, over to Manly, and finally returned to Wests.

Unlike most athletes, he finished his career impressively, as a second rower who kicked goals. He was Wests' leading points scorer from 1986 to 1988 and was later named vice-captain in the Western Suburbs Team of the Eighties.

In business shoes, he has been similarly tenacious and resourceful. During his early post-playing days he sought education and training to prepare him for years in the NRL's front office. After a brief stint at Canterbury as a lower grade coach, Schubert worked in administration at Easts. He then took up a role at the NRL, eventually falling into the unique position of salary cap auditor.

It could be argued his execution of the league's rules has been exemplary. The NRL is an even competition. No team has won the Grand Final in consecutive years since the cap was introduced. This is due to a constant trading of players between clubs. If one team reaps too much success, the winning players' prices shoot up and up. The cap serves to ensure the talent must spill over, like water from a brimful bath. A simpler way to test Schubert and the league's salary cap worth is to calculate broadcasting rights. On this count – currently valued over $1 billion – Schubert receives an A+.

Although club officials pan Schubert endlessly for his rulings on payments, the criticism is rarely personal. The recruitment managers and chief executives are like coaches with referees: they are constantly trying to get the most out of the rules for their own benefit. Schubert cares about precedent. He can appear to be at odds with teams but generally plays an even hand well.

If a club wants a ruling on a proposed deal, Schubert is obliging. In fact, he encourages administrators to keep in touch.

Schubert uses his elephant-thick skin to ride out controversies. This extends to criticisms from within his organisation. Being a salary cap auditor is perhaps the most thankless task in professional sport. Even referees get to run around, have a bit of fun, soak up the crowds' electricity. Most days Schubert, because of his title, is about as adored as a parking inspector.

It is difficult to understand how one man has stayed in such a position for so many years. In short, his energy is regenerated by a delight in the game's success. He sees himself contributing to the quality of the brand. He sits in the grandstand on Grand Final day with his wife and imagines the better team winning. Giving everyone in the stadium hope that their team can triumph on an even playing field thrills him as much as seeing a winger creating havoc, just as he did as a teen almost 40 years ago. He must enjoy those quiet moments, for when he walks away after the celebrations are complete he knows the next salary cap drama is not too far away.

In August 2002, the NRL's best team, Sydney (formerly and subsequently called Canterbury) Bulldogs, was revealed to be cheating the salary cap.

Newly appointed league chief executive David Gallop said at the time it was a bitter day for the sport. The ex–Super League lawyer added, 'Indeed the game has had its heart broken in an unexpected way.'

The Bulldogs' bust was not made by Schubert; rather it was *Sydney Morning Herald* reporters Kate McClymont, Anne Davies and Roy Masters who attained and published documents to detail the overspend. Their lede was this:

> A *Herald* investigation has found the Bulldogs breached the NRL's salary cap by more than $1.5 million over the past two years.
>
> Clubs are limited to spending $3.25m a year on their top 25 players. However, this year the Bulldogs have exceeded the cap by more than $700,000, with at least eight players receiving additional payments.
>
> An internal document seen by the *Herald* shows, for example, that boom five-eighth Braith Anasta receives a base salary of $205,000 plus match payments. But the club has arranged for him to receive an additional $250,000.
>
> Darrell Trindall gets $60,000 on top of the $115,000 he is supposed to be receiving, while New Zealand international centre Nigel Vagana receives an additional $50,000 on top of his official $200,000.

McClymont and Davies won Australian journalism's highest prize – the Gold Walkley – for their reportage. It is worth noting reactions from the NRL and the Bulldogs' hierarchy in that first exclusive story.

Schubert said, 'A breach of that scale would be something which would have to go to the NRL executive board. The board have the right to do anything they like with regard to excessive breaches.'

Ultimately the league stripped the Bulldogs of 37 competition points and fined the club $500,000.

League executive chairman John Chalk was apparently blindsided. 'I thought everyone was behaving themselves and falling into line. I'd be extremely surprised if this happened.'

'I am not going to comment on a document that I haven't seen,' stated Canterbury Leagues Club President Gary McIntyre. 'I don't know what it could be, so look, I can't comment further.'

Bulldogs chief executive Bob Hagan cried innocent. 'This is news to me,' he said. 'We have had the usual audit from Shooey [Schubert] and had a couple of issues on minor matters such as payments to players for duties outside the club – servicing sponsorships – but they have been resolved.'

After later admitting guilt, McIntyre and Hagan lost their positions. Twelve years later, the duo says the club needed to overpay to survive, if not thrive, after Super League. Canterbury was still angry about losing players during the ARL–Super League struggle.

Hagan, whose preferred method of keeping players happy was to pay for holidays or arrange leased cars, recalls, 'Ambiguity was rife around third-party deals.' He says most clubs paid sweeteners outside the cap, including house deposits in wives' names and mortgage repayments. 'That would have been done for about five or ten players at each club I'd reckon.'

Hagan points out player managers were instigating deals. The agents worked in groups, which helped them know what all players were earning. They would play clubs off against one another ... This is what they're offering. What can you pay? This is what we're expecting. Basically, the managers were doing their jobs well by pushing the wages boundaries, testing the rules of the game. And the Bulldogs' administrators were not able to resist. Calling a bluff meant potentially losing a player and losing a player meant fewer wins. Fewer wins meant no silverware. So goes the conundrum. It was one in, all in, according to the family club. Rightly or wrongly, there was always a genuine belief that other clubs were overpaying their footballers.

There are facts to support this assumption. NRL records show eight clubs were sanctioned for salary cap breaches in 2000, three in 2001, six in 2002 and eight in 2003. No less than 29 breaches were recorded during this period. Fines were issued. The Bulldogs' breach was the only one that attracted a loss of competition points.

Hagan says he does not regret his part in the salary cap scandal because it threatened no lives, although it cost him personally. His ties to the club were damaged. He now lives on the Sunshine Coast and holds a directorship of the national board for Men of League, assisting ex-players with medical assistance and support.

> It was just something that was evolving, and the money that was coming into the game. If you were looking for the player and you had the money you'd give it to him. If you were a smart CEO you would be getting the best players and the blokes that weren't too bright – they were picking up the dregs. The cap was a bit of a joke for the clubs.

It may have been a joke before Gallop sent the Bulldogs crashing to the bottom of the ladder. Thereafter, it was serious.

The reaction by opposing teams to the Bulldogs' cheating was varied. Some opponents tut-tutted the offenders.

Replacement ladder leader, New Zealand, was apparently appalled. Warriors' chief executive Mick Watson stated: 'It was a severe penalty, but in essence it was a deceitful web of cheating.' (Ironically, New Zealand was the next club to be stripped of points for breaches in 2004/2005.)

Melbourne beat Penrith 42–10 the weekend the Bulldogs were caught out. Coach Mark Murray offered honesty in this analysis: 'I'm not surprised, it's been going on for years.'

Storm hooker Richard Swain, who had recently been sacked by the club (so it could fit under the salary cap) but allowed to play out the season said, 'I'm not going to comment on what's happening there but it would have been nice to get that sort of help to keep me here.'

Murray added, 'All I know is that our organisation is doing the right thing by the cap and it's disappointing to lose Richard.'

Storm was not doing the right thing by the cap. According to Ribot, bringing wages under control after Super League was like 'putting a square peg in a round hole'. Melbourne went over the salary cap regularly. In 2000 it was $121,641 beyond the limit due to a disallowed TPA. The club did not try to hide anything from Schubert. It simply disagreed with his ruling. A fine was paid for $24,300.

In 2001, a similar TPA ruling took Storm $177,404 over the cap. This time the fine was larger: $89,904. The following year Ribot was frustrated by another deal that was 'reclassified' by Schubert. Storm was $133,396 over the cap for the 2002 season and subsequently fined $66,698.

Ribot says money paid to players over the cap was never from News Ltd. 'I could never get involved in that sort of stuff,' he says. 'Because I was a shareholder that's a dangerous thing for me to do. I have a fiduciary responsibility as a shareholder to News. I couldn't do that without telling News. I'd end up in bloody jail. I'm playing under a different set of rules.'

The most he could do was arrange sponsors to pay players for a bit of work. He mounts a strong defence for arranging TPAs for players in those early years.

'Sponsor wants to give him [the player] money outside of what he's giving to the club for a totally different or independent reason,' he explains.

> I can't control that. It's no different to Brisbane ... Brisbane had Thoroughbreds [a group of businessmen supporting Broncos]. And I was part of Brisbane then and it was all above board where blokes, because of who they were and their profile, realised if they were smart ... people would start taking care of you outside of football. It's a bit like in rugby union for the first 50, 100 years, there's an amateur game but there's all these opportunities made available to players. If you're a good bloke things could happen for you.

Ribot was frustrated with the fines being issued by Schubert every year.

A solution he favoured was to receive salary cap concessions from the league. He thought he should be able to pay more money to his players because he was in Melbourne and it was harder for him to keep players from leaving. For years he pleaded for permission to at least pay recruits 'relocation money' outside the cap.

To assuage the anger and resentment from Sydney-based clubs, Ribot stressed at the time:

> We don't want to spend more money under the salary cap, but if we bring players down here, we'd just like a concession to house those players. It's that simple. People really get confused and say, 'We're going to go and buy players.' We're not going to do that.

> All we want is to stop losing the internationals we develop. As we bring them in, they're falling out the other end.

Richard Swain was used as an example.

At the beginning of the 2003 season, Ribot finally secured what seemed like a commitment from NRL boss David Gallop for his salary cap concessions. (Ribot and Gallop knew each other well. Gallop was hired by Ribot to be his lawyer during the Super League–ARL dispute.)

At the club's annual launch, Gallop said simply, 'I support them getting some assistance. I think at the moment that a salary cap concession is the obvious one. At the same time salary cap concessions are something you should not give away lightly.'

Previous league boss John Quayle says, 'If I was running the game in Melbourne, they would've got certain benefits as the AFL did and has done with all their new clubs.'

The AFL gave healthy concessions (up to a million dollars) to its Queensland and New South Wales–based teams to 'grow the game'. It should be remembered Victorian AFL clubs (part of the Victorian Football League before 1990) have not always supported different rules for expansion teams. Former VFL president Allen Aylett wrote in his autobiography *My Game* (with Greg Hobbs) about the relocation of South Melbourne Football Club to become the Sydney Swans in the early 1980s. Aylett wrote:

> In the VFL, Collingwood headed a minority of clubs which continually spurned the Swans; snide remarks that the Swans were receiving preferential treatment and healthy hand-outs ... were hurtful. It was disturbing that the essence of South being in Sydney was sometimes forgotten: the spirit of pioneering our game in Australia's biggest city and that South could this way be saved. Did Collingwood *want* South to die?

Former Storm coach Chris Anderson commented on the issue in March 2003.

> It's a tough one because they've had the opportunity down there and in a lot of ways they've buggered it. Now things aren't going good and they want dispensation and I can understand clubs being dirty, but the important thing rugby league has got to look at is we

> need a team to be viable down there. This is something the league has to do. This is a direction the league has to take. We need the game to be making a decision that's best for the game and not for each individual club who's going to be saying, 'We don't want it'.

Gallop said a decision on the issue would be made at the next chief executive board meeting, with concessions 'coming into effect immediately'. But the NRL boss was in a tough spot. He did not entirely operate the NRL. The Sydney-based clubs still largely controlled the ARL, half owner of the league.

At this time, News Ltd's company secretary and business development manager Peter Jourdain had been appointed to the Melbourne Storm board. His role was to oversee budgets, as he had done through the Super League era. Jourdain suspected Ribot had no chance of receiving concessions if it was left to the other clubs to decide.

'I was absolutely supportive [of concessions] because if you look at what the AFL did,' Jourdain says.

> But I also was in my own thinking realistic. Very difficult to get all the other clubs to agree to that. All the clubs recognised it [Melbourne] is a market that rugby league needs to be in and they're 100 per cent supportive of the Melbourne concept as long as they don't have to give them any concessions. It was never gunna get up.

Ribot turned up to the chief executives' board meeting with high hopes to finally ratify his concessions. He says the other clubs savaged him like wolves.

'I said this decision's been made, we don't want to be treated any differently,' Ribot recalls. 'They [other CEOs] said oh it's a joke, you get your players, you've won a premiership, you want more concessions.'

Perhaps it was part of the Super League hangover. The old scars, the old wounds.

The headlines in the sports pages the next day talked about Melbourne 'withdrawing' its bid for cap concessions. Ribot was quoted: 'In the best interest of the game, we're reviewing our position with regards to the proposed relocation concessions because there is a misconception amongst the clubs that this is about the salary cap.' But Ribot felt double-crossed by the league.

A decade on, Gallop says there was never a promise for Storm salary cap concessions. It was only ever a proposal.

Storm kept overspending.

NRL records show Ribot went over the salary cap by $261,912 in 2003. He did not hide it. The league gave him a fine discount of 50 per cent. $130,956.

Gallop explains, 'We had a general principle that where we knew about the breach, we would fine at a lesser amount than if we discovered something that hadn't been disclosed to us.'

In 2003 Ribot completed an 80-page plan for the next ten years of Storm in Melbourne. The NRL projects manager, Shane Mattiske, helped with the mission statement, which included topics like junior development, marketing and scheduling. The document was revealed in the press to bat away speculation Storm would be uprooted because of poor financial and on-field performances. 'Hopefully it will put those rumours to bed because there's a lot of things that have happened that have never been warranted,' Ribot told journalists. 'We're not going to go away.'

He was right. Storm would endure. But Ribot's time in charge was running out.

CHAPTER 7

NEWS LTD'S PLAN

Less than three years after News Ltd decided to plant rugby league in Melbourne's fertile sporting field, Storm's finances became an annoyance for the owner.

Ribot had tried everything he could to limit financial losses but the club could not raise its revenue anywhere near expenditure. Crowds were low. Without the sensation of reasonably aiming for a premiership, the reality of simply existing in an AFL town was more burdensome. Swiftly, attention turned to the bottom line. Melbourne had by now established a pattern of haemorrhaging millions of dollars a season.

News Ltd was peeved but not enough to bail out. The media company's interest in Storm has always been part of a much bigger picture. Year-to-year shortfalls stole the headlines. But the franchise served its master in other ways. When the NRL was established, following Super League, the game's new co-owners ARL and News Ltd had struck a deal to evenly split $16 million in revenue every season.

News Ltd used $8 million to fund its three teams: North Queensland, Brisbane and Melbourne. The Broncos have always been profitable. The Cowboys just about broke even. Storm was the only team losing cash. But it wasn't $8 million a season, so News Ltd, from all its rugby league interests, was actually still in front.

'I had sweat beads coming down every year with bloody budgets,' Ribot recalls. 'But in the back of my mind I knew, hey look, they [News Ltd] won't acknowledge this but I know it's good for business for them. And I think that's proven to be right. They can always get on their soapbox and say we've put all this money in. But they've also got it at the right rate.'

Ribot adds News Ltd got 'a sweet deal on the TV rights'.

Having a team in another large Australian city not only improved the broadcast return of the NRL but also attracted national sponsorship partners.

Then–News Ltd chief John Hartigan says,

> There's no question it was Lachlan Murdoch's view, and it's a view that I strongly support, that ... if you went to Victoria, you'd have the three largest eastern seaboard states. And when you go to a national advertiser like Telstra, they're not gunna get out of sorts by not having Western Australia – Perth – and South Australia. But they certainly do want those major areas of population to be serviced. That was the rationale.

Ribot understood all this better than anyone. In coming years commentators and columnists would waste air and print opining Storm should be scrapped or moved to the central coast of New South Wales. News Ltd never contemplated either option. The only way the company would abandon its venture would be to sell it. That was the plan. The problem was: How do you sell a business that is not making money? It somehow had to start making a profit. That's one of the reasons winning was always so important in Melbourne.

Ribot knew that too. So it disturbed him greatly when his team started to fall apart.

Halfback Kimmorley left the club in 2000 for a fatter contract at the Northern Eagles. There are conflicting versions of the Storm Player of the Year's departure. Like many of the start-up players, he was moving into his representative career and rightfully demanded better pay. Says Kimmorley, 'When someone [a club] has success they generally pay a price for it.'

He was initially prepared to sign a long deal with Storm. 'I think it was a four-year deal [on the table at the end of 1999] and things weren't met so they had plenty of opportunity. In the end it wasn't done. Some of those clauses were about others staying at the club. We were pretty close. It was a matter of us all trying to stay together.'

Frustrations about negotiations started to appear in newspapers.

The club rebuffed Westlake for his *Herald Sun* copy. 'I got ambushed a bit by Chris Johns when Kimmorley was deciding on his future – before he signed with the Northern Eagles. Some of the articles that were written Johnsy may have thought I was critical of the club being unable to sign Kimmorley.'

Ribot didn't think he fell out with Kimmorley but he did offer some insight into his methods. 'I had some rules that you could never pull one of my contracts out and say if the coach isn't here I'm not here, if a player's not here I'm not here,' he says. 'That was not negotiable because the biggest thing is ... it's not about individuals. You create that and it should be part of your charter.'

Anderson was dismayed. His son Ben had not been offered another contract. And now his halfback was in the wind. Recalls Anderson:

> They told me for six weeks that they'd have him signed and they hadn't had him signed. I was upset that they let Kimmorley go. The way it happened. Kimmorley didn't want to go. He didn't have to leave. Johnsy was telling me it's done, it's done, it's done for six weeks. But it hadn't been done. If they had a talk to me about it, I could've talked to Brett and we could've done it as a group and had him re-signed. Then they let Ben go without saying a thing to me, without talking to me. They led me down the garden path and it was a lack of respect for what I was trying to do.

Storm management replaced Kimmorley with talented young halfback Matt Orford but in mid–2001 Anderson took a job to coach Cronulla. He would've coached out the rest of the season at Storm but Ribot and Johns didn't want him to.

'I'd done well and I'd enjoyed my time,' Anderson reflects. 'Once it got out they let me go. We all got caught up in the emotion of winning and we didn't have some things in place that should've been in place.'

At an icy press conference with Ribot, Anderson said in 2001, 'I think it got to the stage where it was affecting my performance, it was affecting the team, so it was a good move for the club and a good move for me.' Anderson was also coaching Australia by then. Ribot said, 'To have people away from your administration for anywhere between 12 to 17 weeks or whatever the number is, has an impact.'

Anderson looks back at his time down south with pride. 'I loved it mate,' he says. 'Had a great time. I loved Melbourne. I loved training at Olympic Park. If you're in sport that's gotta be the best place in the world to be stationed. I loved every minute of it. It's a pity it finished like it did but sometimes life's like that.'

Johns rang Mark Murray and asked him to move from Norths Devils to coach Storm for the rest of 2001 (the team finished ninth). Murray stayed until the end of 2002 (tenth). Players from that period did not think it was a particularly gloomy time. They admired Murray. Young men were learning their trade. But there were personality and power clashes between coaches, players and staff.

On Dr Gorgenyi's team cycle-of-life Storm had disintegrated and was now entering the infighting stage.

Johns vented his frustration during that period after yet another player – Ben Roarty – was poached by the Panthers. 'We would have loved to have kept him ... we tried,' he told the press. 'But under the cap restrictions, the number of internationals and current playing roster we have, we didn't have the same money available as Penrith.'

It would only get worse. The Roarty announcement was minor compared to the news favourite son Richard Swain was not being offered a new deal by Ribot and Johns.

The affable hooker had represented Storm in all 125 games. He had topped the NRL tackle count for four seasons. But when the club sacked him, he didn't even get a phone call.

At the time, Swain told reporters: 'They [Johns and Ribot] spoke to some of the senior players today and told them what the decision was but no-one has come to see me face-to-face. They spoke to my manager ... it's probably a bit disappointing, the way it happened. It's the loyalty thing; you expect to be treated a bit better.'

The timing of Swain's axing meant he ended up going to Brisbane for minimum wage. Ten years later, Murray explains, 'Swainy was a terrific player for the Storm and he was great for me and he was the heart and soul of the club. You get managers involved and it all gets a bit complicated.'

There was some backlash for Murray. Storm fans adored Swain for his work ethic and New Zealand heritage. Melbourne's membership has always had a high percentage Kiwi contingent and Richard wore black-and-white in international tests. Here he was being sold off ... for what? Who would take his place?

Cameron Smith.

During the Swain negotiations, Murray almost lost Smith too. He recalls,

> I wanted to sign him [Swain] in the early part and his manager was holding off and we had Smith coming through. Smith had a manager and once Smith had played a couple of games we wanted to sign both of them, but as it turned out the longer it went the more difficult it got and then Smith's manager was saying well if Richard Swain is staying then what are we doing here. He's saying the kid is ready to push into the top grade so it all became very difficult and in the end we didn't have the money to fit Richard into the salary cap, which was disappointing for him, very disappointing for the club.

Johns did the contracts but kept Murray informed. 'There was a bit of a reaction to the club and myself over that,' he remembers. 'It's understandable that the fans would be disappointed and they didn't know Cameron Smith, they'd never heard of him. They'd be more than happy now.'

Murray adds, 'Ultimately I guess, those who could see Cameron coming through – it was a matter of looking after the future I guess.'

Goodbyes become commonplace at Storm.

Not long after Swain left, Chris Johns quit as Storm chief executive to start a car-cleaning business (Ribot took on the dual role of CEO and managing director). Media manager Chris Appleby got a call from a mate in the US and went to work for the Miami Heat basketball team. Westlake had already flown out of Melbourne, having moved back to Queensland to write at the *Courier Mail.*

Then, at the end of 2002, Murray's brief coaching reign was over. He wasn't too disappointed to be sacked. He had liked coaching young players but the older blokes were probably still missing Anderson. Murray concedes,

> I probably didn't handle those guys as well as I could have. If there's any blame you blame yourself 'cause it's your job to make it work. I enjoyed the time there. If that wasn't such a great period on the field for the club I took some satisfaction out of the fact we ... have had a major benefit to the club over a long period of time.

Of course, he is referring to the young players sunning themselves in Brisbane – Slater and co – about to light a match under the National Rugby League.

The next big decision Ribot had to make was hiring a new head coach. That turned out to be easy. He sat down with a man called Craig Bellamy and knew he was special.

PART TWO

CHAPTER 8

A NEW COACH CHANGES EVERYTHING

Bellamy was born in New South Wales, in the Central Tablelands town of Portland, home of Australia's first cement factory. As a child he enjoyed games. If he wasn't playing football he was carrying a cue around a snooker table. There was always a contest.

From his parents he learned the value of commitment to work. His father left school when Bellamy's grandmother died, and worked for many years before being killed in an accident. Norm Bellamy was 51. When a son loses his father, the grief causes an emotional pit impossible to fill. Who is left to teach you the simple things about being a man, a husband, a father or a coach? Bellamy has fond memories of his father playing his guitar and singing around a fire. Norm wanted to teach his son to make music but time ran out.

Bellamy's mother, Betty, encouraged him to play rugby league, just like her father and brother. From her, Bellamy learned to be passionate. His behaviour in coaches' boxes over the decade he was in charge of Storm is proof. Through the windows you can see him in his sanctuary, churning and burning: caring. The swearing he picked up along the way.

As a solid footballer he played for Oberon, where it snows sometimes. He later joined Macquarie United in the Newcastle competition. St George paid some interest in Bellamy but baulked at signing him. The new team in the NSWRL – Canberra – gave him his shot in 1982. He played 148 games for the Raiders and scored 46 tries. Although he experienced some successful years as part of the Green Machine (he was part of the 1990 premiership team as a reserve) his best years were when the team was not as dominant, between 1982 and 1988.

Bellamy stole no headlines during his playing career. Like his father, he was a worker. He may not have realised it then but he was serving the ideal apprenticeship for coaching at the highest level. It is easier to relate to players if you have occupied all positions in sport's pecking order.

Early in his career as Storm coach, Bellamy went out of his way to talk to two players he'd recruited from Sydney. They were previously second-graders and had been in Melbourne for only a few weeks. Bellamy asked them what they thought of their new team. He was not fishing for compliments but seeking their honest opinions. 'You've been at other clubs, what can we do better here? What have you noticed?'

Though the coach was probably interested in the answers, he did not need them. By asking these young men to contribute anything at all, he was sending them a message: we see you, we hear you and we value you. From that moment those athletes would give more of themselves. So began their rapid improvement. Want to know how Bellamy takes 'recycled' players and helps them reach representative level? A few words, eye contact, the right question, can make work life more meaningful. It doesn't sound like much, but it is real.

At the end of 2002 Bellamy had compiled an impressive resume. He had been a youth coach at Canberra and an assistant coach under Wayne Bennett at the Broncos. Trusted friends told Storm boss Ribot that Bellamy would make a fine replacement for Mark Murray.

Wests Tigers also showed interest in Bellamy but Ribot won his signature. The new Storm coach was 43 when he moved to Melbourne without his wife and school-aged children, who stayed in Queensland to finish their formal education.

One of Bellamy's first training sessions in the southern capital is well remembered.

The Royal Botanic Gardens flourish on the southern bank of the Yarra, across the bridge from Storm's home field. The 38-hectare landscaped bush was selected by Charles La Trobe, Victoria's first lieutenant-governor, in 1846. Just beyond the perimeter of the colourful green gardens is a track – The Tan – made of stone aggregate that measures 3.8 kilometres. For decades The Tan has been the training ground for Melbourne people, athletes and casual walkers. Middle-distance veteran Craig Mottram holds the track record at 10 minutes and 12 seconds; no Storm footballers have ever threatened to break it but the footprints of rugby league players are now on the track.

The eager coach lined his team up to 'do The Tan' as a time trial. Storm had done it before, under Anderson and Murray. This time would be different. The players would be required to do it twice and they would be racing Bellamy as well as each other. With hindsight, Matt Geyer suspects Bellamy trained very hard in preparation for the event, determined to make a point. Nothing Bellamy did was an accident. Years later, the coach and his assistants would furiously lift weights in the players' gym. They worked out at strategic times, Geyer reckons, so they could be seen setting a high standard of physical fitness.

The club's best runner, Ross, was injured and couldn't run around The Tan. This allowed the middle-aged Bellamy to win the time trial. He was 20 years older than some of his team. He chest heaved from the effort. It was his first statement as the man on top. In leadership, it is important to make such impressions.

When revered New York mayor Rudy Giuliani took office in the 1990s he was appalled by the city's crime rate. One of his first actions was to boot the repugnant and aggressive car windscreen beggars off the streets. He considered their behaviour – kicking doors and spitting on drivers who refused to give them money – bad for New York's morale and reputation. His officers struggled to find ways of catching the hoods breaking the law. You had to see them doing something wrong to arrest them.

After giving it some thought, Giuliani gave instructions to his officers to book them for jaywalking. It worked. It was a small victory but it was critical in sending a message. Not only did it rid the city of a nuisance, it lowered the crime rate because, as it turned out, most of the washers had been breaking their parole. Giuliani's transformation of the city started from that example of exercising discipline.

Bellamy's run around The Tan was like getting rid of the windscreen pests. Word drifted with the breeze back across the river to the front office staff.

'The coach just beat everyone.'

It set the tone for change. The club needed a lot of straightening out and someone to come in there and give it a clip over the head and that's exactly what Bellamy did. The discipline and no-nonsense approach he brought to the players spread throughout the entire organisation.

In preparation for his first game at Melbourne, Bellamy had to sort through a captaincy quandary. In 2002, Rodney Howe had been given the title, when many thought Robbie Kearns, who had captained in 2000 and 2001, was more deserving. Keen to move past the issue, Bellamy placed the 'C' beside Stephen Kearney's name.

Other line-up uncertainties had to be addressed. Richard Swain's departure had left a void. Without hesitation, Bellamy gave his number nine jersey to Smith. So began their long and fruitful association. Smith, still a teenager, was quiet and laid-back, which helped him deal with the pressure that came with stepping into the boots of one of the most popular players to ever represent Melbourne. The other hooker on the list, Danny Williams, was left on the bench.

Overall, media attention in Storm had waned. Necessary publicity stunts involved inviting AFL players to help promote matches or professional wrestlers or American footballers. Anything. Performances weren't warranting generous coverage. Even the *Herald Sun*'s printed word count was poor despite the guaranteed weekly wrap. But that was about to change. Reporter Karl de Kroo was given the beat and he was a top operator, able to plan stories and follow through. He would become invaluable to Storm in the early Bellamy years. *The Age* rugby league journalists Stathi Paxinos and Mark Fuller were also supportive. They understood the club would give exclusives to the *Herald Sun* but access was otherwise easy.

Crowds had been poor in 2002. The experiment of playing home games at Docklands' stadium, a bigger venue with a retractable roof, had failed. The gate takings would not increase soon. For the next two years Storm's average home-game attendance was less than 10,000.

The club had one radiant source of energy and promise: Bellamy. His commitment was complete. With his family back in Queensland, he gave every hour of every day to the club, relishing stepping out of Bennett's shadow. Olympic Park was his new home and sometimes he slept right there at Storm HQ. The smell must've been comforting to a bloke who lived for football.

After The Tan experience, Bellamy was intent on hill running with the players. Melbourne is not as up and down as Sydney or even Brisbane, but the coach found a course demanding enough. The only problem he had was he could not watch his players run the whole way. He wanted to make sure they didn't bludge so he wandered off to find a place to hide behind trees on a tougher section. From this vantage point he would jump out and startle players he thought were not trying hard enough. Lumbering front rowers were aghast.

Bellamy befriended innovations. He sought counsel at AFL clubs, built relationships within the rival game. Aussie rules coaches taught his team how to jump and catch a ball. Later he would be invited into AFL coaching boxes – sacred spaces in Melbourne – to observe and share ideas.

Sometimes the Storm players dined at restaurants in Melbourne and Bellamy arranged guest speakers. One night it was Randy Couture, actor and former mixed martial arts world champion (UFC Heavyweight). Someone special.

On Monday mornings, Bellamy would chair meetings with club officials – his assistant coach, physiotherapist, doctor, trainer, media manager, strength and conditioning coach and a couple of others – at a cafe in inner-city Richmond, where lattes and baguettes are popular and pricey.

The coach ran the meetings like an army chief officer, going around the table, pointing at each person, demanding answers. Top priority was players' fitness. How were the injuries being cared for? Should we back off or increase workloads? How are we gunna map out their week?

Employees had to be ready to provide an answer because Bellamy was a heavy controller and would pick anything apart.

The intense coach could not wait to start leading his team through the 2003 season.

Storm team V Cronulla, Toyota Park, Round One 2003

Matt Geyer	Peter Robinson
Billy Slater	Stephen Kearney
David Kidwell	Dallas Johnson
Steven Bell	Interchange
Marcus Bai	Danny Williams
Scott Hill	Kirk Reynoldson
Matt Orford	Mitchell Sargent
Robbie Kearns	Semi Tadulala
Cameron Smith	
Rodney Howe	Coach: Craig Bellamy

Bellamy's first game in charge was a tough one. His opposition, Cronulla, was led by former Storm duo coach Chris Anderson and halfback Brett Kimmorley. The Sharks boasted arguably the best fullback in the world, David Peachey, and had finished among the NRL's top four teams in 2002.

Melbourne tried two debutants that day: Billy Slater and Dallas Johnson. Slater had been brilliant in trial matches. In one stunning summer he had replaced the injury-weakened Ross as the club's number-one fullback. Cameron Smith was in his third first-grade game, having been played twice by Murray the previous season.

It was a steamy autumn day.

In the first few minutes of the contest, large Shark Jason Stephens scored a try. Slater tried to tackle him but was too small. He clung like a koala to Stephens's shoulders. Kimmorley took control of the match for the next 20 minutes, arranging three more tries, including a grubber to the smooth-moving Peachey. Slater was out of position.

Cronulla led 22–0. Someone shouted, 'It's a March carve-up.'

Storm's nervous, sliding defence was timid.

Bellamy, neatly trimmed and smooth-faced, sat pensively in the stands. Just when it seemed he would have to wait until next week for his first victory, his world changed forever.

Storm reserve Semi Tadulala was tackled in his team's half. He played the ball and Slater, from dummy half, exactly 30 minutes and two seconds into his first-grade career, picked it up in two hands and ran past Tadulala and his marker. Within four strides he was rocket-heeled. The Sharks were startled, as if witnessing a brazen shoplifter. Who's gunna grab him?

One tackler lunged hopelessly but Slater pushed down hard on the ground with his left foot and changed his angle, swerved, swayed his hips. He was through the defensive line.

The fullback Peachey confronted Slater one on one. It would be a simple shut down. The experienced man would wrap his arms around the youngster's legs, let them slide down to his ankles, like a lasso ... no ... Slater again stepped off his left, this time with more emphasis, in deference to Peachey, who was slow to react and ultimately a spectator to the new boy's agility and speed. Slater looked to stumble as he often does stepping but he kept his balance and Peachey did not touch him on the way past. An open field and a lifetime of happiness – his reward – lay ahead. Carrying the ball loosely in his right arm and pumping his left, straining all the way up through his body and face, Slater scored the try. He was only 19.

It was a snapshot of Storm's future.

Slater's effort lifted his team. The match was a thriller. Storm was trailing by two points with two minutes to go. Shark Kimmorley had the ball ten out from Melbourne's line. He attempted a grubber but it bounced off a Storm player's shin. Peter Robinson picked it up and shovelled it to Steven Bell, who had scored three tries. With only Peachey to beat, Bell passed to Geyer, who fist-pumped the air all the way to victory. Storm had travelled 90 metres. Matt Orford, perhaps the best player afield, converted. Storm won 36–32.

Karl de Kroo wrote a story for News Ltd papers later in the year, after Slater had scored 18 tries in 22 matches and a hat trick against the Eels in August. He quoted Slater. 'Mum and Dad get stopped in the street a fair bit these days. Mum's a bit dirty, up home in Innisfail. They are calling her my mum, instead of me being her son.'

Parramatta coach Brian Smith said of the Storm fullback, 'There are a lot of good, young players in the game but he has had an astonishing first-up season. His coach would tell him he has got some things to work on, but he has some phenomenal speed and tremendous agility carrying the ball.'

Careful to manage Slater's self-opinion, Bellamy pointed out he wasn't so astonishing in July.

'Billy hasn't been on his game the past four weeks,' the coach said.

> I have been a bit disappointed in him and he has been disappointed in himself. He has been going okay but for a while there, he was a bit in denial. He thought he was going maybe better than he was. He got a rocket up him this week and responded really well. It's a really good sign for a player in his first year in first grade to be able to handle a rocket and respond the way he did.

Not to be outdone, Smith won the Storm Rookie of the Year in 2003. He had adapted to the NRL as easily as Slater but with fewer slow-motion replays of his excellence.

Publicly, Bellamy might have been trying to keep egos and expectations under control but in secret he now realised Mark Murray had left Storm's list in better condition than he imagined. From dark days to rainbows they went. Confiding in a colleague one day, Bellamy said of Smith and Slater, 'And they're only just kids, they're gunna be here a long time.' He would build his life's empire around them.

CHAPTER 9

RIBOT'S END

Penrith won the 2003 NRL premiership. Storm's young team finished an admirable fifth, despite having only one player selected on the end-of-season Kangaroo tour: Robbie Kearns. After the Round One win against Cronulla, Bellamy's men were never outside the top eight. In week one of the play-offs, Melbourne celebrated a finals victory for the first time in three years, after beating the Raiders 30–18 at Canberra Stadium. Channel Nine Melbourne denied a club request to broadcast the match live, preferring to show the movie *Heat*, starring Al Pacino and Robert De Niro. If you wanted to watch Storm on Friday nights in Melbourne you had to stay up past midnight. Not much had changed since 1998.

The next week, Storm was flogged and eliminated 30–0 by Canterbury, which had largely held its team together after the salary cap scandal.

By 2004, Ribot was driving flat out with no brakes toward his salary cap cliff. The fines his administration was receiving were relatively minor. Other teams were copping them too. But they were *every* year. And they embarrassed News Ltd. Storm board member and News Ltd company secretary Peter Jourdain was charged with reining in Ribot's spending. It meant butting heads with the club's chief and part owner.

Ribot was tired and restless. It had been an exhausting seven years in charge. One of his gripes was Fox Sports was not even showing Storm matches at preferred times. News Ltd had management rights over the broadcaster but that didn't make any difference. Public support was bottoming out. The club continued to lose millions of dollars every year. The NRL would not allow the salary cap concessions it had flagged. Ribot was being worn down.

Most of these issues were private Storm business. But then, all of a sudden, Ribot was thrust back into the headlines. This time it was for his handling of sexual assault allegations made against two of his players. A police investigation was being held into the conduct of two Storm footballers but Ribot did not tell the league about it. This was a touchy subject, to say the least.

NRL CEO David Gallop only found out about the Storm investigation when a Melbourne journalist rang him about it. Gallop was miffed. He told a reporter, 'I just thought, given what we're going through at the moment [he had been dealing with another scandal, involving the Bulldogs], we didn't really need any more surprises.'

Instead of telling the NRL, Ribot decided to wait for the police investigation to run its course. Typically, he defended himself against criticism of non-disclosure.

Ultimately, no charges were ever laid against the pair. But News Ltd newspapers were reporting the story. Ribot rang his good mate Peter Blunden, editor-in-charge of the *Herald Sun*, to learn what kind of coverage the 'Storm sex scandal' could expect from the tabloid. Page one, Blunden said, but it would not last forever. Just hope that a bigger story comes along soon.

It did. Within days, rape allegations were levelled at two players from the St Kilda Football Club in the AFL. There were marked differences in the public relations performances of club officials in the separate NRL and AFL stories. Ribot was thought by the league hierarchy to have acted wrongly. St Kilda was being praised for its transparency, honesty and respect. Newspaper columnists were promoting the Saints' chief executive, Waldron, as a model sports administrator.

One week after the 'sex scandal' was in the *Herald Sun* – on the eve of the NRL season – Ribot was at his daughter's hockey practice. He took a phone call from Storm coach Bellamy, saying, 'I dunno where to start. What's happening?'

Ribot shot back, 'What do you mean what's happening?'

Bellamy explained that he had just eaten lunch with John Hartigan and Lachlan Murdoch. 'They've told me you're no longer here.'

In the past, Ribot had enjoyed a healthy relationship with News Ltd's top brass. Ken Cowley was the chief executive of News Ltd when

Ribot was running Super League. They had shared heady times and unique experiences. Cowley was Storm's first chairman.

But Hartigan was now the News Ltd chief and he had neither pangs of loyalty nor fondness for Ribot.

Ribot asked the coach if he was serious.

Bellamy said, 'Yeah it's all over.'

Ribot rang Hartigan but missed him; he left a message to call ASAP.

Hartigan rang Ribot the next day. The Storm boss was at the club informing his staff he was leaving them.

Someone called out, 'John Hartigan's on the line.'

Ribot said,

> John, we're all working our way through this and you've let the coach tell me that I'm no longer here and you can't even give me a phone call. You've got a funny way to do business. Look, I'm not gunna talk to you again, we'll get our solicitors involved and hopefully we can finalise this 'cause that's just not the way ... I haven't been selling newspapers on the corner for you ... this has been a tough project and I expected different.

Nine years later, when asked about the sacking, Hartigan said he couldn't remember it. 'No. Oh, well, I'm not sure if I did [sack him]. I think I must have but I can't recall.' This was not a statement of Hartigan's memory as much as his priorities in running News Ltd.

Hartigan officially fired Ribot at 11am. By 4pm Ribot had sold his share of Storm back to News Ltd. He was paid out. He did not cut all ties with his team. News Ltd gave Ribot a well-paid 'consultancy' role. Both parties made an agreement not to throw mud at each other in the media.

Melbourne Storm released a statement saying Ribot had decided to 'stand down' because his 'other business interests have become increasingly more demanding'.

The statement read:

> It is a sad day for me because I have become so emotionally involved with the club and its people. The supporters have been fantastic, their support and that of our corporate partners has been tremendous. The highlight of my involvement with Melbourne Storm has been the loyalty of staff and the lifelong friendships. These relationships have made this a difficult decision.

At the time Ribot and News Ltd denied the Storm boss was ousted 'as a result of the current police investigation involving Melbourne Storm players.'

Today, Hartigan says the removal of Ribot was due to the consistent salary cap breaches. 'If we're 50 per cent partners in the rugby league and our clubs are flouting the salary cap I'd argue that's more embarrassing to us than it might be to a club that doesn't have that affiliation,' he explains. 'It's just a public acceptance that if you've got management rights and 50 per cent ownership with the NRL, you're expected to abide by their rules.'

But back then, Hartigan praised Ribot's role as 'a cornerstone of the club's phenomenal success'. 'John has quickly made Melbourne Storm one of the country's most successful rugby league clubs,' he added. 'The Storm has built up a loyal following of supporters. John has spent his life in football and we are delighted he is staying at the club so the Storm can continue to rely on his experience.'

The new interim Storm CEO was the experienced Frank Stanton, a News Ltd manager, who had been a player, national coach and former chief executive of Manly and North Queensland (acting CEO in 2001).

Melbourne Storm employees were dismayed to see Ribot leave. He was popular until his final day in the front office. But Stanton gave the club stability. The workers liked his no-nonsense approach. Everyone respected him.

The salary cap fines were rarely discussed within the club. They did not seem out of the ordinary. Other teams were getting them. AFL teams had also been sanctioned. Storm getting pinged every year didn't even make snippets in the Victorian daily papers.

The resilient Bulldogs won the 2004 NRL premiership. Storm finished sixth. Again Melbourne won a final, beating Brisbane 31–14 at Suncorp Stadium. But again it lost to Canterbury in the second week of the playoffs (43–18).

After his season ended, Bellamy called for salary cap concessions. In an uncommon public display of self-doubt, he said to the press: 'I don't know how long it's going to take, because we've got some good young kids coming through the place and we've got some good players in key positions.'

Fairfax ran a story on the coach's concessions comments. Mark Fuller wrote, 'Bellamy said that although the Storm had improved in the past 12 months, it was impossible for him to estimate when the club should be a genuine premiership contender.'

While Storm's administration was undergoing upheaval, individual players continued to shine.

Orford had developed into one of the best halfbacks in the competition and was named Storm Player of the Year but did not make the Australian squad at the end of the season. Scott Hill and Billy Slater did.

The team had found another young cult hero: centre Matt King. King originally played for North Sydney but had retired prematurely because of injury. He was talked into giving his career one more chance, firstly at Norths Devils and then Storm – another recruiting success story. While Smith continued to develop as an on-field general, Slater provided the highlight of 2004, playing for Queensland in State of Origin.

It was Game Two in Brisbane. The home team was trailing by two points in the 62nd minute. Maroon five-eighth Darren Lockyer was only 40 metres from his line when he kicked a small left-foot grubber. It looked a peculiar option until you saw Slater, with a mop of curls, charging through. Slater picked the ball up safely in his fingertips – getting there so quickly he must have been offside ... He barely slowed. Having beaten the Blues' defensive line he approached NSW fullback Anthony Minichiello. In an action similar to his debut try, he stepped off his left foot and appeared to stumble but did not. Minichiello was far enough away not to be passed as easily as Peachey was in Cronulla. Slater was 30 metres out from the Blues line. Cover was coming from both wings. The kid, although blazing at full tilt, was being hemmed in.

Elite football is at its most appealing when men resemble boys having fun, unrestricted by coaches' instructions and teammates' expectations. Here was Slater improvising, skating and carefree. He held the ball in his right hand alone. He waited until he was just metres from Minichiello – baiting him.

As Ernest Hemingway wrote for *Esquire* in 1933, 'Anyone can hook a hungry fish who gives him enough line, doesn't backlash and sets the hook hard enough.'

Minichiello was frozen for a moment. It was all it took for him to be outwitted.

Aiming diagonally at the right corner post, Slater dropped the ball to his right-foot instep and lobbed it over his opponent's skull into a pocket of space on the left side of the field, just upon the tryline.

The ball bounced twice before Slater regained it and dived in for what has been described as one of the greatest State of Origin tries. The video ref was needed to adjudge its status. Surely, he was in front of the kicker Lockyer ... But no, he wasn't. Minichiello was gasping. Onlookers couldn't believe it. The crowd went troppo.

Back in Melbourne, Slater's try thrilled Storm teammates and their wives and girlfriends watching it on a live feed from Channel Nine's Bendigo Street boardroom because it wasn't broadcast throughout the state. As soon as the game finished the club started getting requests for interviews with Billy the Kid. He was the first of the young'uns to be a star. Because he was so likeable and unaffected – so natural – he carried the attention with ease.

CHAPTER 10

SAINT BRIAN WALDRON

John Hartigan made a career of writing words and reading people. He went from a 16-year-old newspaper copy boy in 1963 to News Ltd chief executive in 2000 and chairman in 2005. No common man rises like a hot air balloon through the unique atmosphere of Rupert Murdoch's newsrooms and boardrooms. Reflecting on his career, delivering the Andrew Olle Media Lecture in 2007, Hartigan said, 'Journalism took me out of the suburbs and into the big smoke: Sydney in all its raffish elegance, and later, London and New York.'

Hartigan played a starring part in the big Melbourne Storm dramas and decision-making. But he did not perform a role in the day-to-day functions of the franchise. It is important to note News Ltd's structure and how it relates to rugby league.

In the mid–2000s, News Ltd was divided and managed state by state. Sydney-based Hartigan oversaw it all. He also sat above the operations of Foxtel and Fox Sports. Then there were the football enterprises.

Hartigan explains,

> For rugby league we had two positions on the partnership board [NRL], we also had the Broncos, which are a public company, so we appointed a chairman and directors on that board. And with the Storm, I always felt that rugby league, while it was part of the management of our company, I always kept it away from my desk.

Hartigan says he entrusted the management of News Ltd rugby league interests to Peter Macourt, News Ltd's chief operating officer.

Macourt delegated the running of Storm to two other News Ltd officials: Frank Stanton and Peter Jourdain.

It was these gentlemen who were charged with improving Storm's off-field performance, as well as hiring a new CEO.

Jourdain, who is now the CEO of North Queensland Cowboys, remembers Melbourne at the crossroads. 'When John [Ribot] moved on we took a step back and said what's the future of Melbourne Storm?'

He commissioned market research that offered some hope. It found that there were 300,000 people in Melbourne who 'actively followed' rugby league but did not attend Storm games. 'So we sat back and said it's clearly a big market,' Jourdain says. In short, Stanton and Jourdain thought Storm hadn't actually become part of the 'Melbourne fabric'.

News Ltd decided to increase its expenditure on marketing and advertising for a couple of years. It sought to attract a bigger profile. With that in mind, administrators with AFL experience were preferred for the vacant role of chief executive, for their greater understanding of the crowded sports market.

One prospect stood out: Brian Cook, a former Australian rules player who had gone on to become the dual premiership–winning chief executive of West Coast Eagles Football Club (1990–99) and then CEO of Geelong Football Club from 1999. Cook went close to being appointed CEO of the AFL in 2004, eventually pipped by the league's operations boss Andrew Demetriou.

News Ltd executives thought Cook would be perfect. Jourdain and Stanton passed his name up the company tree for consideration. Hartigan was pleased. He recalls,

> He was a quality applicant and he quite obviously was pissed off because there was a very strong push for him to get the job at the AFL instead of [Andrew Demetriou] and it was the late chairman who I understand had the casting vote to ensure that Demetriou got it and not Cook. So Cook put his hand up for the job. He then withdrew at the end.

Toward the close of negotiations Cook baulked at the Storm job because he thought he had unfinished business with Geelong. It was the right call for Cook, who went on to lead the Cats to unprecedented financial and premiership–winning success in the next eight years.

With Cook no longer available, Stanton and Jourdain went to their next best candidate. He was Brian Waldron, the St Kilda CEO, who had performed so professionally during the 'Saints sex scandal' a few months earlier. Since then Waldron had left his job. Publicly, it was stated he had resigned to seek a new professional challenge.

Waldron impressed Jourdain, who remembers, 'He certainly had some qualities that were impressive and he was someone who was prepared to get out in the community and push Storm. At that point in time it was [about] trying to raise their profile and significance in Melbourne itself.' If Storm was trying to lift its profile it could not go past Waldron. Jourdain concludes, 'That was pretty much the reason why we ended up hiring him.'

Jourdain and Stanton made the recommendation to Hartigan. Before Waldron was appointed he would have to impress the News Ltd CEO. And he did, sort of. This is Hartigan's assessment of Waldron from their introductory meeting.

'He's sort of a bloke's bloke,' he begins.

> He's one of those guys – you'd have one of two reactions. You'd say, one, god he's just a boofhead. Or, two, he's a very personable person, almost larger than life. He's in your face. He's constantly all parts moving. And he's a person who was just so confident in his own ability to perform. And that's ultimately the sort of person we wanted: an entrepreneurial person.

Above all else, Hartigan wanted a promoter of his company's team. 'I think that there's certain levels of governance and probity that you look for in their [potential CEOs] backgrounds and in their performance but equally our job was to try to sell rugby league in a town that really wasn't prepared to listen,' he says. 'And here was a person who was like someone [that] had been wound up and could be just let loose. And I found that attractive.'

Hartigan did a bit of homework on Waldron. He says he rang AFL boss Andrew Demetriou, who explained that St Kilda had been turned from a basket case into a thriving club on Waldron's watch. Demetriou added that there was a rumour circulating about Waldron having a relationship with a woman at work.

Hartigan paid little attention to that final piece of information. 'To my mind, it was a rumour but it wasn't anything that I felt should cast negatively against his appointment for the job,' he explains. Workplace relationships happen almost everywhere – including at News Ltd. Why should Hartigan worry about that?

Waldron was one of seven siblings, raised by hard-working parents. His father – Brian Joseph Waldron – held the position of Victoria's auditor-general, parliament's financial watchdog, guarding the public purse. He was a clever student and graduated to become a secondary school teacher.

But in the late 1980s Waldron decided to leave the classroom forever and head toward a career in the sporting field. He applied for a job at the Victorian Football Association. The VFA was the respected second-tier competition behind the Victorian Football League, soon to become the AFL. The position was as a development officer. Waldron missed out. It was explained to him he was not experienced enough.

So he set out to know more about the business of football.

In 1989 Waldron worked for no pay at the Oakleigh Football Club (VFA). When he wasn't teaching, he was helping run the club, including organising fundraisers. This volunteer work was rewarded handsomely when Waldron was appointed the club's general manager. He was 27 years old. He left teaching and did not look back. Those were the days of older administrators, hard men who had played football in the 1960s and 1970s. Among these types, Waldron stood out as a fresh face. It was obvious he would not last long in the VFA.

In 1990, Waldron received a phone call from Richmond Football Club. Promptly, he was appointed that AFL club's junior development officer, in charge of managing the Under 19 and Under 15 programs. Two years later he was promoted to assistant recruiting manager and then recruiting manager. Waldron had made football his life.

Like all other professional sports, 'footy' was starting to provide full-time employment for more and more people in the 1990s. Positions were imagined and then created to take the load off the senior coach and top administrators. It was an expanding industry.

Waldron's ambition burned hotter every year. It was during that period that the game was forever transformed. Player agents surfaced, led by bold ex-footballer Ricky Nixon. *The Age* and *Herald Sun* started covering the game in greater depth than before. *The Footy Show* on Channel Nine was the top show in town. Its host Eddie McGuire, who would later become the all-powerful president of Collingwood Football Club, could've been a pin-up for Waldron. McGuire had gone from being a lowly journalist to a powerful figure in the game by his persistence, will, personality and work ethic. Waldron had some of those characteristics.

As Richmond made rare finals appearances in the mid–1990s Waldron continued to be promoted within the club. He was made football manager and served in that role, overseeing recruitment, playing contracts and all other functions of the team, until 1997, when he was sacked. Internal politics had him booted out. Richmond's numerous coaching changes were always going to be hard for him to survive. Eventually he had to fall out with someone. Staying in a stable position at an unstable football club is as difficult as riding a mechanical bull.

In the late 1990s Waldron became a multi-tasker. He studied and completed a Master of Business Administration. Together with a student he met in his MBA course he created a business: The Waldron Cook Consulting Group. The company offered strategic planning advice. One of his customers was a pioneering athlete management business called Elite Sports Properties. Ever the all-rounder, Waldron then began working for ESP as a football player agent, helping to sign a number-one national draft pick, among others.

Throughout this period, Waldron also took on other casual jobs. He was married with children by then. He acted as a real estate scout for a company where his sister was a general manager. He did some football commentary on the new AFL pay-TV broadcast network. He studied a Graduate Diploma in Business Management. And he wrote some stories for *Inside Football* magazine. Although his copy was clean, it often came in after deadline, frustrating his sub-editors. Perhaps his heart wasn't in it. Certainly he was restless. The Richmond sacking had left him unfulfilled. He wanted to get back into a club environment.

The chance came through former Essendon football champion Tim Watson, who was coaching St Kilda. He called to ask if Waldron would like to be the new Saints football manager.

If there was a less stable club in the AFL than Richmond it was St Kilda. Within a year Watson quit his position as head coach. But Waldron was ensconced and making friends. His comeback was well underway.

Saints HQ could not have suited Waldron better. It was being taken over by a young and cavalier board. No-one really wanted to be a long-term CEO. He had acquired strategic planning skills that could help him climb the ladder, when the time was right.

In his first season Waldron was witness to one of the most famous and shambolic coaching appointments in football. When Watson tossed it in, the Saints decided they wanted to hire two-time Adelaide premiership winner Malcolm Blight, who lived on the Gold Coast. The club sent half-a-dozen players to Queensland to woo him out of retirement. Waldron accompanied the players and officials: new president Rod Butterss and Director of Football Grant Thomas.

Saints historian Russell Holmesby described the incident in his book *Strength Through Loyalty*:

> Peter Everitt [a player] was in the group and had clear memories of the scenario. 'We got up there and Brian Waldron didn't want us to have a beer while we were waiting for the phone call to go to the Chinese restaurant at Jupiter's [casino] and get Blighty as coach. Hally [Barry Hall, another player] and I ordered one and Waldron went nuts. When we walked in, the first thing Blighty said was take off your ties and get some beers. We had quite a few, and Hally let the crayfish out in the restaurant that night!

Blight was eventually hired but would not last long in charge. Everitt remembered a discouraging feeling after games. 'We had a dinner ... [Blight], Brian Waldron and Thommo [Grant Thomas] would be sitting in the corner having a few wines and a few darts [cigarettes] and wouldn't talk to the players at all to have a relationship.'

Blight was never comfortable at St Kilda. He should not have taken the job. Within 12 months he was sacked. The chairman of selectors at the time, Grant Thomas, replaced him.

Waldron was not flustered. He remained focused on making a good fist of his second chance. One day he made a presentation to the St Kilda board. He had drawn up a plan to revitalise St Kilda's playing list, categorising each athlete and formulating what the team needed to start marching up the ladder. The board was impressed. Not long after that, the CEO quit. Waldron was given the top job.

Some people at St Kilda were stunned. They wondered about the chief executive's dependability. How did he go from part-time magazine scribe and boundary rider on TV to CEO of an AFL club within three years? Others didn't bother thinking too hard about it – but it was indicative of how St Kilda was run at the time.

Waldron's first 12 months as chief were tough. Frankly, he was inexperienced and out of his depth. No-one can ever be prepared for the role of sporting CEO in Melbourne. Bank CEOs and captains of industry, with decades more experience managing large workforces, don't face the same scrutiny as heads of football teams. Really, there is no other job like it. Perhaps some front-bench politicians know what it means to be grilled and picked apart and judged by the public as much as football bosses – but not many.

Anyway, Waldron learned on the job and got better.

Dealing with the media during controversy was one area he needed to improve. At times he acted the bully.

When St Kilda player Steve Lawrence crashed his car in 2003, police investigated. The Saint ended up in the Alfred hospital. Melbourne's television newsrooms were frenzied. It is a common occurrence in the city when a professional footballer is suspected of wrongdoing. Lawrence had been in trouble before. Was he drunk again? Publicly Waldron stated, 'It's extremely unfortunate for him. It's fortuitous that no-one else was involved in it and he has our full support.'

One TV reporter rang the hospital to request an interview with Lawrence. It was a long shot, a journalistic box to be ticked by a worker under instructions from a chief of staff. The common procedure is to ring the Alfred's media manager and leave a message with a request for an interview with your name, phone number and network. It's called a 'Hail Mary' because you know it is unlikely you'll get a call back.

The respected reporter received a call back, not from the hospital but from the St Kilda CEO.

'Hello.'

'This is Brian Waldron, from St Kilda Football Club,' he said sternly. 'I've been told you called the Alfred hospital and claimed you had my football club's permission to interview Stevie Lawrence. Is this true?'

The reporter set Waldron straight. But the administrator did not believe him.

'I'm gunna give you one more chance to tell the truth,' Waldron boomed. 'Did you tell the hospital you had the club's permission to interview Stevie Lawrence?'

The reporter was stunned. He was from interstate, did not worship at the altar of AFL and was unaware he was supposed to be intimidated. 'I didn't even mention your bloody club. Are you calling me a liar?'

Waldron repeated, 'I'm gunna give you one *more* chance to tell the truth ...'

Waldron's raised voice was ineffective this time. He could not frighten the journo. No doubt the CEO thought he was standing up for his embattled charge. Anyway, he gave it a go.

St Kilda sacked 'Stevie' Lawrence later that season.

The two stints Waldron had as CEO of big-time sports teams – at St Kilda and later Storm – had one obvious similarity. Both teams were flush with exceptional young athletes when he took over.

Although St Kilda had lacked continuity in the coach's box, it was bound to start improving from 2002. The team had held on to some of the league's best veterans from its Grand Final appearance in 1997. Now it would benefit from recent mediocrity by blooding top draft picks, including once-in-a-generation forward Nick Riewoldt. The AFL's system of awarding the worst teams the best teenagers in the country through a national draft has been the equaliser the NRL never could live with. Attempts to introduce a draft into the old NSWRL were thwarted by court action. A draft can be ruled a restraint of trade, if properly challenged. But AFL clubs do not want it changed. Theoretically, it gives everyone a chance at winning silverware if they make the most of their 'window of opportunity'.

As well as stand-out recruits, Thomas proved to be an effective coach.

The Saints had a large supporter base, mobilised by the winning of matches. When this inevitably happened crowds swelled. And while the bandwagon is brimming it's time to cash in. Improving sponsorship was Waldron's strong suit and he oversaw the club's financial improvement, no doubt. Some people still debate whether Waldron was a well-performed CEO at St Kilda. But the fact is the team and its front office became more successful under his watch.

Then came his downfall.

An attractive and persuasive woman called Trish Medwell was hired as an events coordinator at St Kilda. She had previously worked at Cricket Australia. Waldron, still married, fell for Medwell and promoted her to the position in charge of St Kilda's commercial operations.

Sex in football clubs is not new, not even scandalous. But it makes for hearty gossip and the sports industry has in its ranks hundreds of world-class gossips. Soon, it was widely touted the chief executive at St Kilda was compromised.

The players liked Waldron, although behind his back some of them called him 'Smoke and Mirrors'. One veteran footballer took the CEO's ambition for selfishness. 'He was a good bloke,' the player says. 'He showed some interest in how you were going. A bit of a good old boy. I reckon he was always looking at where he was heading individually.'

Waldron negotiated contracts for a while. He was partial to 'back-ending' them. If a player was worth $400,000 a year, Waldron might strike a four-year deal and pay the footballer annual instalments of $200,000, $200,000, $400,000 and $800,000. Back-ending contracts was a Waldron special. He was not alone in that practice but it did highlight his tendency to shift problems to a later date, put off doing today what he could do tomorrow.

In the end, some players started to negotiate their contracts with the coach, who was seeking greater control of the club.

Coach Grant Thomas was trying to make his position resemble that of an English Premier League manager: omnipotent. In his grab for power, he could no longer be close to his superior, Waldron. Thereafter, St Kilda became a divided club. Only one or two loyal front office staff openly supported the CEO. The rest fell in behind the popular and increasingly successful coach, along with the entire senior team. The relationship with Medwell was isolating Waldron. A player from that era says, 'Having an open affair as a married man ... In terms of leadership it's not a great look. That's not sustainable when you're trying to run a multi million–dollar business.'

Sporting teams talk every day about morals and values. Such idealism is bound to end in disappointment. But they try. By the start of 2004, Waldron had lost a lot of support.

Waldron and Medwell's relationship was not a fling. He would later leave his wife for her. They are together today.

Then came the 'Saints sex scandal', Waldron's finest moment because he proved himself unflappable under pressure, and a leader of composure, loyalty and confidence. In just three years he had come a long way. Media camped on the nature strip of St Kilda's training base at Moorabbin for a long time, seeking truth, making judgements. It is a news dragon that roars in the face of club leaders in Melbourne during football crises. But Waldron was superb under fire.

Advising him was self-styled businessman, St Kilda supporter and media-spin specialist Peter Maher, who would later join the Melbourne Storm board. Maher's first impressions of Waldron were, 'He was very good on his feet, there's no doubt at all about that and he was very good at carrying out direction and carrying out what you wanted done. Once he understood what needed to be done, he was very clever with that. He certainly doesn't lack for intelligence.'

Almost enjoying the challenge of his leadership qualities, Waldron was calm, measured, professional, courteous and approachable; everything that a chief executive should aspire to. From the outside looking in, Waldron was one of the best in the business. He must've felt like he'd risen from football's rank and file to the establishment. If only his personal life wasn't dragging him back down.

Following complaints from staff, the St Kilda board – still Waldron's lunch mates – gave their man a final warning. End this thing with Medwell or you're gone. It did not work. The CEO and his girlfriend were told to leave.

Waldron's friendship with president Rod Butterss, his executioner at St Kilda, endured despite the sacking. Butterss allowed Waldron to say he had quit. Waldron even continued showing up to work at Moorabbin for a few weeks after his axing, acting out a farce that he was still controlling his destiny, while he looked for another job. It worked a treat. Melbourne Storm thought he was a real catch.

News Ltd provided Waldron with its financial spreadsheets as part of the interview process. Waldron gave them to his last trusted colleague at St Kilda, accountant Cameron Vale, for checking. The pair discussed Storm's potential. After much thought, Waldron accepted the job.

Hartigan considered Waldron up to the task. 'I think rugby league needs someone who's a bit of a character,' Hartigan recalls. 'And he certainly suggested that he was a bit of a character.'

In the wonderful world of sports administration – where you are what you say you are – Waldron was still alive.

After News Ltd welcomed Waldron to the family and gave him the master key, the new chief executive made two key appointments. Vale became his chief financial officer; and Storm's new general manager of commercial operations was Trish Medwell. So began the Waldron era of champagne and tears.

CHAPTER 11

THE SPECIAL ONE

Esteemed cricket writer Neville Cardus recalled in his book *Close of Play* spying the talents of all-time great batsman Walter Hammond.

> I first saw Hammond in 1923 playing against Lancashire at Gloucester; he was an unknown youth, and he batted low in the innings, amongst the tail-enders. He drove one four to the off, then got out; but I had seen enough. I wrote half a column in the *Manchester Guardian* about the boy and ventured a prophecy of greatness to come. It was easy to look into his future; there is no mistaking the thoroughbred.

From the cot to first grade, there could be no doubting Greg Inglis was a thoroughbred. Born in Kempsey, New South Wales, Inglis played junior football for the Bowraville Tigers. Inglis was 15 when Melbourne Storm found him in 2002 and enticed his mother to sign a contract. The deal saw Inglis relocate to Brisbane and attend Wavell State High School. By 2004 he was playing for the Australian Schoolboys team and scoring tries for Norths Devils. In 2005 he made his debut for Storm, scoring a try in his first final against the Broncos. In 2006 he played for Queensland and Australia. In 2009 he won the Golden Boot Award for being the world's best. The two previous Golden Boot winners were Cameron Smith (2007) and Billy Slater (2008).

The Storm employee who crunched the deal for Inglis to wear a purple jersey in the NRL – the signing of a lifetime – was Peter

O'Sullivan, who started working for Melbourne after the club's original NSW scout, Theo Burgess, retired. Johns hired O'Sullivan (they were old friends), a productive and resourceful worker. 'Sully' was liked at Storm. Johns said his mate was a stand-out talent hawk. Waldron came to admire O'Sullivan too. But others played down O'Sullivan's abilities, describing his methods as akin to duck shooting: see prey, get prey, do it quickly before some other gun takes aim. Anthony Griffin's words can settle any argument on the subject: 'Recruitment's a bit of a lucky dip sometimes, guys that tell you they know what they're doing and get it right all the time are lying.'

Like O'Sullivan, player manager Allan Gainey was pleased to win the prized signature of Inglis in 2002. Gainey was watching a school seven-a-side tournament at St Marys, Western Sydney, doing what agents do: a combination of star-spotting and crystal ball–gazing. The boy he liked most represented Hunter Sports High School. Beside Gainey stood Penrith player Preston Campbell, a client.

Gainey recalls the moment. 'We were talkin' about this big lanky kid who was out the back takin' these high balls and runnin' like a bloody gazelle. Preston said, "Oh, he's my cousin."'

The agent introduced himself to the Inglis family. He signed Inglis to a five-year management contract, which would become worth more than any agent ever imagines when adding the name of a boy to a long list of maybe-champions.

There were no other agents at the sevens tournament when Gainey met Inglis, but that is not to say managers weren't routinely signing up boys as young as 12 to long-term management deals (up to seven years), in the late 1990s and early 2000s. In 2005 the Rugby League Player Agent Accreditation Scheme was introduced to monitor the practices of managers, some of whom were deemed unscrupulous. From then, agents had to wear identification tags at youth carnivals and tournaments. The minimum age of managed players was lifted to 14. And agents not abiding by a code of ethics would be asked to explain themselves. Its loose restrictions have not diminished the management ranks. There are now more than 100 agents in the NRL.

The NRL website almost warns against agents. It states: 'No player is obliged to have an agent. Clubs don't require an agent in negotiations; but if an agent is used, he or she must be accredited.'

Another player manager, Steve Gillis, saw Inglis play three months after Gainey, who was his business partner. The footballer stuck out as unusually tall and skinny but extremely skilful. No 15-year-old player is a sure bet to make it big in pro sports; more often than not if you sign someone at that age you're wrong. You can measure only so many variables; dedication and determination are hard to recognise from 50 yards. But Gillis said to Gainey, 'I like this kid.'

Gainey replied, 'I've got him under control.'

Peter O'Sullivan and Melbourne Storm also had Inglis under control. Hard-working NRL recruiters track boys as well if not better than any agent.

'The family told me they had signed,' Gainey recalls. 'I can't remember what the deal was. It might have been three years, something like that. Five hundred [dollars], a thousand, maybe 1500.'

Inglis was initially housed by Storm and cared for in Brisbane accommodation with an Indigenous family. Behind the scenes, Ribot made contact with friends at Queensland Rugby League to ensure they knew about the boy and qualified him for State of Origin as a Maroon. It was a clever move. NSW league authorities have been annoyed ever since.

Both Storm and Gainey would not have to wait long for their modest, tall, sleek investment to pay dividends. By the time Inglis was 17 there was no longer any doubt about his value. O'Sullivan upgraded his deal with Gainey. In matches for Norths Devils, Inglis was stunning teammates, coaches, other onlookers and opponents with his try scoring – pushing defenders out of the way with one hand (who were awed by his combination of power and light-footedness) and leaving them lying flat. Like an Olympic sprinter, his leg power drew the eye: thighs pumping, gears grinding up. But when he strode long and hit the gas his boots seemed to barely touch the grass ... That's when you watched his arms, swinging like chimes in a gale. After beating the defensive line, Inglis would routinely reach the other fullback and it would become personal – a bandit and the sheriff, the town's last hope. Tacklers tried to embrace Inglis's hips – somehow – but could never quite make it. Timing a cobra strike with those long limbs, he would often wait for the half-second his opponents were off balance or unsure and stiff-arm them in the face ... then cruise to the line, enjoying the feeling of superiority.

Inglis appeared to be a man in a boys' competition, flipping reality on its head. Storm flew him south for training camps, and had dinner with his parents. Gainey told Melbourne Storm if Inglis was ever homesick he should be allowed to take leave. Waldron and co. gave earnest assurances to take special care of the lad. Inglis was not just a footballer anymore. Like rumbling clouds to the Mallee farmer, he was a promise of prosperity.

CHAPTER 12

FRESH START

Bellamy was frustrated in his first two seasons to be eliminated after the second play-off. But the team was changing, becoming more experienced and cohesive. There was now a sensation of harmony in Melbourne that Anderson's team had enjoyed in 1998 and 1999. The difference with Storm Mark II was that day-to-day happiness had been developed gradually and was still growing. Once again, Storm was starting to feel less like an unpredictable workplace and more like a family household with a big backyard for playing games. Though they may never be mentioned in victory speeches, the assets of continuity and stability are vital to lasting success.

The NRL and AFL have awarded 28 Grand Final trophies in the past 14 years. More than 30 per cent of those trophies have been presented to teams stationed in cities barely interested in their business.

In the NRL, Melbourne has won four Grand Finals. AFL clubs Brisbane Lions (2001/02/03) and Sydney Swans (2005/12) have rushed the presentation dais five times in 11 AFL seasons. Some people will rightly point to the players' wages as a helper in each instance: through salary cap concessions for the Australian rules teams and through secret overpayments to players from Storm. But the clubs' postcodes are also important. Firstly, the outposts provide a distinct home-ground advantage: maybe worth a couple of extra victories a year. This sometimes allows for a less stressful build-up to finals. You can physically and mentally time your run to September better if you're not scrambling madly for four wins in August.

Serenity is another bonus. Not being treated like a celebrity is beneficial to an athlete's humility, which often determines work ethic; and not being called up every other day to have lunch with your mates from school or catch up with family leaves you free to train harder or, just as importantly, rest.

The relationships at Storm, within the team and the staff, have been mostly strong and supportive for 15 years.

Being away from home 'dragged the players together', foundation coach Chris Anderson says. 'We socialised together and we spent a lot of time together and that was an easy thing to do 'cause we didn't know anyone else in town.'

First halfback Kimmorley adds, 'It happened from day one, they did a wonderful job in building the franchise from the start. The players, staff and administration were very friendly to each other. Some of the best friends I ever made out of football were from those couple of years. The partners were very close.'

Club champion Geyer reckons living in each other's pockets bred an unofficial policy that repelled people with disruptive personalities. 'While it's not written on the wall when you walk in, it's almost self-regulating because the blokes who don't fit in – they're not happy – they end up going somewhere else, [and make a] move interstate.'

Bellamy added, 'It's just people that play rugby league in a foreign city I suppose, they gotta rely on each other not only for footy but also their social life outside footy.'

The language used by Sydney Swans players in the AFL is almost identical. Ruckman Shane Mumford recently told *Inside Sport*, 'The only support network you've got is the guys and the people in the footy club, which does create the atmosphere. If you're going out on the weekend or for dinner, it's always with the same guys. It definitely creates a closer group.'

Such team harmony is a gift to any coach.

Bellamy was proving more than a disciplinarian and motivator. He was a fine communicator from day one. He knew players' wives' and children's names. It doesn't seem like a lot. But to an athlete, whose emotions can rise and fall with performances, it means everything – it means he cares. In this way, Bellamy was starting to appear to his impressionable players as a father figure.

O'Sullivan was playing his role, busily acquiring at cut-price rates a powerful pack to drive Bellamy's team forward. About to retire was Kearns, the last of Anderson's original front rowers.

Brett White was one of O'Sullivan's best signings. He was a perfect example of a player, picked up by Storm, who was able to reach his potential only after pulling on purple. White was a self-conscious big man when Sully found him. From a country town near Cooma, in New South Wales, he had left home at 16 to begin a plumbing apprenticeship in Sydney. A bloke he was working with invited him to play for the local team. White thought it was a way to make friends. He showed promise and started making his way through the grades at St George Illawarra. Soon he quit plumbing to become a full-time footballer. It wasn't all he had hoped it would be. He wasn't thriving. Injuries struck. Ankles.

'I didn't really think I was going to be able to crack it,' White recalls. 'I had a couple of players in front of me, Australian front rowers, and I was a young kid.'

Before taking the recruiting job at Storm, O'Sullivan had coached White at the Dragons' Under 20s. By the end of 2004 he recalled the prop fondly and flew him south.

White's induction to Storm was a commando-style preseason program, the hardest task he's ever completed.

The camps have become annual for Storm. In Bellamy's early years the whole squad went through them. Now, only recruits are invited. Hosted by ex-police from the elite Special Operations Group, they are too physically wearing to go through every summer. The first one – in 2003 – became a horror story told for years.

White arrived the year after.

Being from the country, he wasn't worried. He didn't believe it would be all that gruelling. 'I thought oh yeah, go out in the bush for a night and do a bit of training, can't be too hard, it'd have to be a bit of fun wouldn't it?' Nope.

Storm travelled an hour and a half from Melbourne to the west coast, where the Great Ocean Road cuts into the Victorian coastline. The first day the players trained hard. Before lunch they did twice the fitness work they would normally accomplish in one session. Then they trained all afternoon, on the sand, down the beach. Dinner followed. The camp hosts gave the athletes a large feed, allowed them to get all comfy and relaxed. They were still covered in sand, filthy, just waiting to have a shower and go to bed.

The instructors said, 'Get your packs on boys we're gunna go for a walk.' The mood darkened. No names were allowed. No talking at all. No running but it was a time trial. The walk was five laps of a five-kilometre track.

'At about two or three o'clock in the morning, on the last lap ... I remember walking up a hill,' White recalls. The players had all spread out by then. He was alone. 'I thought if this is what it takes to be a footballer I'm done. Guys were bleeding from chafe. Everyone was chafed up from the sand. Your mind really starts to think about a lot of things during that 25-km walk in the middle of the night, in the dark, not talking to anyone.'

White was on the side of a road at one stage. He saw the lights of a car and assumed it was a bus, come to pick him up. At last, he thought, it's over. He saw the lights stop on a rise. The player approached the spot, shining his torch but could not find anything or anyone. Nothing was there. His mind had tricked him.

'That's when I thought I'm going back home,' he says. 'I knew where the highway was, around Bells Beach, and I thought I'm done, I'm outta here.'

White decided the next time he saw Bellamy he would punch him in the face. But when he finally got to the end his mind turned only to sleep. He had made it. The relief you feel when you finish such a torturous ordeal is immense.

The lesson learned was that he was more capable then he thought. Pressed and tested, he could endure almost anything.

White survived, although he suffered night terrors for a week, waking up in sweats. He went on to represent Australia. Playing for New South Wales in State of Origin, he most memorably knocked out Steve Price in a toe-to-toe dust up. Bellamy could forever be thankful his charge did not follow through on his resolution to whack him at the end of his quiet adventure on Victoria's pristine coastline.

Those types of exercises were not entirely original. For decades sports teams have taken their players away to test them. One Storm player says it felt like the club was taking him apart so they could put him back together again. But it was really a tactic of stripping players emotionally and seeing how they reacted when challenged.

In America, legendary coach 'Bear' Bryant took his college football team from Texas into a desert town called Junction in 1953. He trained them on hard ground and disallowed them water, forcing them to practice even if they were injured. He told the student-athletes he had bus tickets home in the drawer of his desk. If they wanted to leave early all they had to do was ask for a ticket – but they would not play football for him that season, or ever. A fine book was written on the story, which perhaps contained some myths or exaggerations. But you can imagine the players lying in bed each night, fatigued and questioning whether it was all worth it – like White did – while listening to the footsteps of their teammates heading into the office to see Bear, asking for a ticket outta there, please sir. A year later Bryant coached his 'Junction Boys' – the ones who stayed – to a national championship. His unforgiving regime had worked.

Things are different now. Or are they?

Storm's camps were not mindless. The athletes were watched closely and given rankings for performing under pressure, helping others and leading. Some players surprised with their scores. Early in his career, New Zealander Adam Blair was considered by teammates to be too carefree. Some thought him uncommitted and wondered why the club was bothering to keep him on the roster.

Years later it was revealed Blair rated second highest of all players at a Storm camp. The Kiwi went on to be vice-captain of his country. Bellamy knew he had it in him, when others did not. The coach put faith in his system and trusted the person. He stuck with Blair and reaped the benefits of another loyal follower.

If 2005, while players like Inglis, White and Blair started complementing the established ball users Smith, Orford and Slater, Waldron was also attempting to make his mark in the NRL.

His most important task was to fix the salary cap problem. Critically, it was stated in his News Ltd employment contract that he should make no mistakes. Former board member Peter Jourdain says that Waldron's agreement with the media company was that if he ever overpaid players, he would be dismissed instantly. 'Simple as that,' Jourdain says. '[We were] very strong. He knows well how important it was to us, to News, as half owner of the game. And it got rammed home at every board meeting.'

This clause should be considered alongside Waldron's actions thereafter. If he broke the salary cap he would lose his second consecutive CEO job and be fighting enormous odds to win another such position. He resolved to do the right thing from that day. But such a standard is hard to meet in the NRL.

The league had fined Storm for salary cap breaches the last four years. The final sanction of Ribot's administration came to Storm after

Waldron took over. It was a $120,000 fine for undisclosed third party agreements (TPAs).

TPAs had always produced arguments between Storm and salary cap auditor Ian Schubert. Previous chief executives Ribot and Johns thought it was reasonable for sponsors and other organisations to pay some players money for promotion of their products. But Schubert had the final say and often knocked back proposals. The club administrators still claim Schubert was being unfair.

'We were continually bumping heads with Schubert because of his archaic bloody mentally,' Johns recalls.

But Schubert was simply enforcing NRL rules.

In any case, the clashes had reached a cessation. Johns had gone into private business. Ribot had been sacked. Debates about salary cap concessions were no longer. Waldron was in charge and was intent on making a good first impression with the league bosses. Schubert wrote to him about past TPA breaches. Waldron wrote back.

10 February 2005
Ian Schubert
Salary Cap Auditor
NRL GPO Box 611
SYDNEY NSW 2001
Dear Ian,

Re 2004 Salary Cap Audit

As requested I enclose Melbourne Storm's response to your detailed report on the Club's 2004 Salary Cap Audit.

Ian, it is clear from your correspondence that the issues you highlight ... are legitimate breaches of the cap. Further to this, I understand your disappointment that these issues have become apparent despite the fact that the responsibility for this can be directly attributed to Melbourne Storm's previous administration.

As you [sic] aware Melbourne Storm's Administration department has recently been totally restructured. It is a commitment of this administration to work within all rules and regulations of the NRL. Personally I am extremely conscious of the embarrassment any further breaches may cause News Limited given their stake in the game.

> Importantly, we have reviewed your 2005 salary cap report and highlight changes in the attached spreadsheets that forecast Melbourne Storm to be $35,010 under the cap this season.
>
> Moving forward let me reiterate that Melbourne Storm is committed to acting with honesty and integrity in its salary cap dealings, a stance fully supported and expected by News Limited executives.
>
> Finally Ian, in the event that the NRL see fit to consider any penalty for breaches attributed prior to 2005, the Melbourne Storm respectfully requests some leniency be demonstrated for the new administration.

Cleaning the slate was a bright start for Waldron. He was also having success in another arena. He had begun lobbying the state government for a stadium upgrade, laying the groundwork for negotiations with Premier Steve Bracks's chief of staff, Tim Pallas. Since then News Ltd CEO Hartigan had joined the push and Lachlan Murdoch agreed to attend a meeting with the Labor government hierarchy.

Present were Waldron, Bracks, Sports Minister Justin Madden, Tim Pallas, Hartigan and Lachlan Murdoch, a fan of rugby league as a sport and as business. Back in 1995 Murdoch Jnr was at the first Super League meeting. He and Ribot (then–Super League chief) signed up key players to start the dispute, which eventually won News Ltd so much control over the game.

Victoria had recently failed in its bid to attract a Super Rugby franchise to Melbourne. Part of its unsuccessful pitch was to purpose-build a rectangular stadium – as unfamiliar in the southern capital as cane toads. When rugby administrators shunned Melbourne and gave the franchise licence to Perth (Western Force) shoulders sagged but not in the halls of News Ltd. The company twigged and said, in essence: Oh well, bad luck, what about a stadium for Storm?

Hartigan looks back. 'Arguably, if it wasn't for the Victorian government's backing of the Victorian [rugby] bid we wouldn't have approached the government and it certainly wouldn't have been built to the timeframe it was built.'

Pallas remembers Waldron being passionate about brokering a new stadium deal. He recalls Hartigan being insistent. A state election was due for 2006.

'So that was the leverage,' Hartigan explains. 'I don't think it was ... certainly not blackmailing them but it was pointing out the bleeding obvious that here was a code that had invested in Victoria – *quid pro quo* from the government to support them. They came back very quickly and recognised the need for a ground ... and pushed the button very quickly. It was a tremendous response, which I think ultimately has just filled out that whole sports precinct.'

Today the unique arena boasts tenants Storm, Melbourne Rebels (the latest Australian Super Rugby franchise) and Melbourne Victory soccer team. It lights up the city's river frontage on cold winter's nights, when there's a game on. Patrons in thick coats park their cars over at the MCG or the other side of the Yarra, next to The Tan, where Bellamy once ran faster than his players. Then they stroll toward the stadium and marvel at its lit-up bubble-wrap exterior. The place looks like a terrific spaceship. After the people swipe their tickets at the entrance, buy a coffee or some hot chips and take their seats, the teams run out and the barracking starts. Children watch the big screen for replays and parents monitor the referees' performance. Each time an athlete pleases, the crowd cheers and the noise echoes – just like it does at Lang Park or Old Trafford.

CHAPTER 13

WALDRON'S VISION

In his first two years Waldron fulfilled his first promise to his employer, News Ltd. Like a butcher's spruiker, he began talking up Storm's future. The club was losing about $6 million a year. The CEO pledged the improbable: to turn a profit within three seasons.

'I've been brought in to get the business right,' he repeatedly said at the time. His News Ltd managers had explained to him the club was 'no longer sustainable under its current structure'. The franchise owner was still reaping the benefits from having a Melbourne team in the competition it half owned. But it needed Storm to start making money if it was ever going to sell it. Waldron was given carte blanche to make changes in the front office. He was afforded a marketing budget over five years that Ribot would have only dreamed about.

Within months, Waldron had cleaned house. 'We had to change,' Waldron told the press. 'The definition of insanity is doing the same thing over and over and expecting a different result. The club has done well to get to this stage but we need to change to go forward.'

Waldron started speaking as if Ribot had never heard of advertising and promotion. 'I don't see us as a mass-marketing operation,' he offered. 'We need to target-market. We will push our brand, but we will do it strategically. Our bottom line was very poor last year. We had the lowest average crowds, a merchandise drop-off of almost 500 per cent in four years.'

Waldron also talked publicly about salary cap concessions.

'All I have heard out of Storm in recent years has been cries for salary cap relief,' he lectured.

> That is like a red rag to a bull at NRL headquarters because other clubs straight away scream, 'Why should they have salary cap relief when they have been regular finalists and have won a competition and we haven't.' To me it is not about salary cap relief. All that does is provide short-term incentives for players to come.

He promised to create an environment similar to the Sydney Swans in the AFL. 'How we do that is by creating a welfare program that is second to none.'

Waldron had unknowingly made a mistake talking about the shortcomings of the Ribot administration. Ribot had a termination agreement with News Ltd that prevented such criticism. His ears were burning.

Ribot recalls, 'I went to Peter Macourt at one stage and said, Peter we had an arrangement here, I don't say anything about you for five years, you don't say anything about me, you're breaching this agreement. There's two sides to every story but your guy is making life unpleasant for me when it's not based on fact.'

News Ltd brass told Waldron to be friendly to Ribot, who was later offered the chairmanship of the club. The board needed expanding. At that point it was a skeleton. It included only Jourdain and Stanton (who both resided interstate) and John Webster, an accountant from the Herald and Weekly Times. Ribot declined the role of chairman but nonetheless made peace with Waldron. Both men were headstrong but understood they would be better off as allies.

The board's overhaul began in May 2005. Peter Maher, who had advised Waldron on crisis management and media relations at St Kilda, was the first non–News Ltd Director at Storm. He began helping Waldron attract others, including leading health official Dr Rob Moodie and Rehame executive Petra Fawcett. Club sponsor Gerry Ryan would later join them.

Waldron's vision was typically bold. His declaration to create a 'welfare program that is second to none' was integral to everything he did in the next two years. He envisaged using Storm players to help develop rugby league in Victoria, particularly at the junior level. This would have two benefits: Storm could convince children to play the game, with the hopes of one day fielding some locals; and the players could earn more cash. In theory, both advantages would eventually increase match attendances, with parents suddenly taken by the sport and fans continually attracted to the world's best players, going nowhere and winning games under a fine coach.

Waldron even met government officials suggesting the state should help pay his athletes for their services to the sport. In return, he would push for future State of Origin matches to be held in Melbourne. Origin was now a centrepiece of the Australian sporting calendar and much sought after. He imagined this would all be done legitimately outside the salary cap. It was all above board with the NRL – at this early stage. Waldron floated his development payment idea with league CEO Gallop, who seemed amenable.

Gallop recalls discussing it with Waldron but denies he officially agreed to it. 'It's not okaying it,' he says. 'It's saying look you need to take that to Schubert. And as long as it's not part of the contractual negotiation and later on you can use some of the development money.'

Waldron told his senior staff he had the green light from the league. He did not write to Schubert requesting permission until the next season.

In-house changes were made to accommodate the plans. Popular football manager Greg Brentnall, who'd been with Storm since 1998, was shifted to the role of player development manager. Brentnall also held a position on the Victorian Rugby League's board. The CEO established a business unit called Melbourne Storm Development and made Brentnall general manager. The club called its program 'Storm Rugby League Development'.

Recruiter O'Sullivan started factoring in the development payments for some of the players. Commitments were made in letters of offer: unsigned documents detailing players' wages and additional bonuses. These letters preceded official NRL contracts.

The third person involved in players' pay (besides Waldron, who approved everything, and O'Sullivan) was the chief financial officer, who managed the budgets. In 2005 this was Cameron Vale, a quiet man, liked by all.

Vale grew up in a housing commission estate in Anglesea, country Victoria. His parents divorced when he was nine. But from such circumstances is ambition born. Vale resolved to become a success.

He loved sport. In high school he had an aim to be a sports journalist. He talked about it with a career counsellor, who mapped out the long, barren road ahead – tertiary study, cadetship at a local newspaper and move up the ranks if you're lucky. It all seemed fruitless and risky. Certainly, if Vale wanted to be wealthy one day he chose wisely against sports reporting. Only Eddie McGuire, morning radio presenter, journalist and AFL club president, and a few others, might disagree.

The boy was smart with figures. He identified finance as an industry unlikely to shrink. He could go into the commercial side of things, maybe even reach partnership at a big firm. Vale chose to study commerce at Deakin University.

After tertiary graduation, he worked at a couple of small accounting firms. His career shot up when Village Roadshow hired him as a financial accountant for three and half years. Then he saw a job advertised at Carlton Football Club. It was his chance to merge a career with sport.

Vale interviewed well for the position and there was no need for a protracted process. He hit it off with the Carlton CFO and was hired after one showing. Again, his ambition smouldered. He thought to himself, if I'm going to get into this industry I'm going to get to the top some day.

As part of the Blues front office, Vale saw the best and worst of professional sports. During the late 1990s and very early 2000s Carlton was a top team. But in late 2002 it was found guilty of cheating the AFL's salary cap. The league commissioner Ron Evans stated,

> Firstly, the nature of one of the breaches revealed a complex and deliberate scheme designed and implemented to hide payments and deceive the AFL. This involved the use of trusts, confidentiality agreements and payments to third parties. The paper trail was carefully followed by our investigations team.

Carlton, historically one of the most successful clubs on and off the field, was penalised draft picks, preventing it from bringing in any talented youth, causing it to suffer a decade of gloom.

Vale was too junior to be aware of any wrongdoings until it was announced in the media (the cheating was revealed after a disgruntled unpaid player turned whistleblower). But by then he was becoming more experienced working in the maelstrom of elite football in a town that is consumed by it.

At the start of the 2003 season, Vale saw another opportunity for professional growth. St Kilda Football Club was advertising a position (financial controller) that would count as a promotion: more cash, more responsibility and a possible pathway to becoming a chief financial officer.

Although Waldron was CEO at the Saints, the person who interviewed Vale was Matt Hanson, another executive, formerly of the Docklands stadium management. Hanson was charismatic and confident. His pitch to Vale was, 'If you come and work here you may succeed me as CFO. You're gunna run finance, not report to someone else, you'll report to me but I'm gunna be hands off.'

Vale landed at St Kilda at 28. He was earning about $80,000 a year, moving on up.

As we've learned, the St Kilda Football Club was climbing the ladder too. The team was young and its coach was a strong leader. And Hanson was true to his word. Vale ran finance. That first year was enjoyable. His friends had told him it was a mistake to leave Village Roadshow, a big corporate player. The wider finance industry didn't understand football's appeal. AFL footy? Is it full time? What do you do in the off-season? But Vale could see the light.

Then Hanson suddenly left the club to take a position at a hotel group.

Hanson endorsed Vale for the vacant CFO role but Waldron didn't promote him. He let him down easily, told him he was young and impressive. 'You'll be a CFO one day, but not yet.' Waldron hired a person from another AFL club, whom he knew.

Vale sought more career advice after that. It was stressed to him that he'd get to a point in his job when it's not about applying for positions in the paper. It's your network. It's not what you know ...

He was disappointed but settled back into life at St Kilda. The only other negative at Moorabbin at that time was the tension and power struggle between Waldron and coach Grant Thomas. Which side are you on? Vale did not believe the rumours about Waldron and Medwell that were circulating at the time. Waldron told him it was not true. There was no relationship. Waldron's denial, publicly and personally, was absolute.

So Vale was on Waldron's side.

In 2004 Vale went to a finance managers' conference and workers from other clubs were talking about Waldron and Medwell. Vale disliked the gossip. 'Yeah,' he replied. 'I've heard that but nothing's going on.' He repeated this often. Back at St Kilda the air was heavy. People were talking about it all the time.

Then Waldron and Medwell were sacked.

Vale became Waldron's confidant in subsequent weeks, following up some things for him, checking his emails. He felt Waldron had been harshly treated. He still believed the rumours were unfair, based on falsehood. Then Waldron came to him with the Melbourne Storm figures. What do you think of the numbers? How does their sponsorship compare to our sponsorship? How do their admin costs compare to ours?

Waldron went to Storm and offered Vale the CFO position. Vale thought it almost perfect. The News Ltd ownership was an attraction. It would help combine his interest in big business and sport. It also involved a substantial pay rise.

Knowing the industry heat was on Waldron, Vale initially baulked at the offer. He asked Waldron straight, 'Is Trish coming?'

Waldron: 'Absolutely not.'

Vale agreed to take the job. Within three months Medwell was appointed too. Immediately Storm staff started asking Vale, 'What's this thing about Brian and Trish?'

'Nothing,' Vale replied.

He never wanted to be a martyr. All he wanted was to do his job, climb the ladder, be respected.

CHAPTER 14

THE ORFORD DEAL

Storm was winning enough games in 2005 to be considered a contender for the title. Bellamy knew his side was making inroads. The improvement was gradual but certain. Keeping the squad together was the highest priority. It was proving difficult.

Steve Bell had signed with Manly and Glen Turner was tipped to leave soon. The coach was nervous. He told a press conference after his side's mid-season loss in Brisbane, 'We're having a little bit of trouble hanging on to players down there for whatever reason. These guys, they're getting real big offers ... it's proving a bit hard for us at the moment.'

Asked again about salary cap concessions, Bellamy said, 'That's been coming up for 18 months, two years and nothing's happened so I don't imagine anything's going to happen in the future. I think it would be handy if they wanted us to be successful down here ... we're out in the new frontier for rugby league and it's tough. We're finding it pretty hard on the same rules as everybody else, but if they're not going to give us any help, that's fine. We'll just get on and do the best we can. Like other out-of-Sydney clubs we've got to pay more to get players – but we'll survive.'

The coach's comments reflected an understanding of his players' value and remuneration compared to those from opposition teams. Of course, he was in constant communication with O'Sullivan. They had to win matches now but also plan for the future. The salary cap was ever-present.

Waldron, with a history in recruitment at Richmond and list reform at St Kilda, didn't have to be told to hang on to the best players. But contracting footballers in the NRL is more cutthroat than he was used to in the AFL because it happens all year every year and your best player – maybe your halfback – can decide to sign with another club smack in the middle of the season. Then he plays the rest of the year with you but it is not the same. He'll soon be bolstering the opposition. Winning an NRL premiership without an ace halfback would be like claiming an Olympic basketball medal without a fine point guard.

Waldron's first contracting challenge had appeared.

Recruited to Melbourne to fill Kimmorley's position at halfback, Orford had become a league star. Storm was trying to re-sign him but sky-high offers were on the table from Manly and South Sydney. Press speculation lasted several months. Where would he go? How much is enough to keep him? What would happen to Storm if he went? No-one knew for sure Cronk would be able to adequately fill Orford's position if the first-choice halfback departed. Cronk was a utility at Norths Devils. O'Sullivan was starting to imagine the former St Laurence's College boy as a decent number seven but could not be sure.

It was up to Waldron to win Orford's signature. Rhetoric would not help him now. He could not blame the Ribot administration if he failed. This was make-a-deal time, knowing the rest of the league was watching very closely and any breach of the salary cap rules would cost him his job.

Negotiations stretched into extra time. Waldron was reported to have offered the small man $540,000 a season. It was the most the team had tabled for one of its players. South Sydney offered him the captaincy and more than half a million dollars too, plus phone calls of seduction from the Rabbitohs' star-power duo, Hollywood actor Russell Crowe and TV interviewer Andrew Denton. Incredibly, Manly offered more. Waldron was losing his prized playmaker ...

During the negotiations, Waldron complained to colleagues that Orford's manager, George Mimis, had told him Manly was offering Orford half a million *plus* the Sea Eagles were going to 'buy him a unit'. The Storm CEO was heard cursing, 'This is fucked. Fucking NRL.' Usually Waldron was unflappable. You could shout in his face and he would smile. But now he was fuming.

Waldron told Vale, whose office was nearby: 'Manly are cheating the cap. This is ridiculous.'

Everyone at Storm was talking about the unit allegation. Even Sydney-based director Jourdain heard about it. Rightly, he points out, 'It doesn't mean it was true but yeah I heard about it. All you can do is raise it with Schubert and let him investigate.'

Such speculation and rumours are everywhere in professional football and should never be taken as fact. Often such things are invented and pedalled by players or agents – or clubs – to manipulate the bidding.

Orford went to Manly.

Storm released a painfully long statement for the media stating that Melbourne's 2004 Player of the Year had signed with the Sea Eagles for a four-year stretch.

It quoted Orford. 'Obviously one of the reasons was commercial,' he said.

> But [there was also the] thought that life after football needed to be planned, and I think the options in Sydney are going to help me to do that. I've been away for five years. I grew up on the beaches up there so it's just a great opportunity for me to go back and plan for life after football.

Bellamy reacted, 'At the end of the day, we're very disappointed. I can understand his reason and I've got no problems with that.'

Ever the optimist, Waldron chose to be gracious and remind people of his fantastic franchise.

> The people of Melbourne and the people in other markets have to understand this is the nature of the game. People get opportunities because of the rules to actually further themselves. We reckon we've got the best coach in the game. We reckon by 2008 we're going to have the best ground to play at. But Matt has to make a decision that is a long-term decision for himself now. Whether he's made the right footy decision, time will tell, but he's comfortable with the decision and we support that.

Schubert investigated Orford's contract. There were other rumours about the deal. Some made it into the press. Fairfax journalist Roy Masters wrote a story revealing the league looked into reports a businessman provided $100,000 to the halfback. There were never any sanctions against Manly.

Masters finished his report with the line:

> The Storm, who claim Orford waits one hour in the office for a refund of $12 petrol vouchers and $6 parking fees, are ridiculing suggestions Orford accepted a reported $450,000 per year for four years from Manly, sacrificing $360,000.

At the end of 2005 the NRL fined five clubs for breaching the salary cap. They were Canberra, St George Illawarra, Newcastle, Canterbury and New Zealand. The Warriors were stripped of four competition points and fined $430,000 at the start of the 2006 season. The team was reported in the New Zealand newspaper *Sunday Star-Times* to be $800,000 over the cap.

Gallop said, 'I certainly think this sends a very strong message. Not that the message needed to be sent: that the salary cap is a very important part of our game and the loss of competition points before the season starts is going to heavily impact in their season.'

Warriors chairman Maurice Kidd said he did not agree with the NRL's decision to deduct competition points.

'We haven't committed a crime in 2006,' he said. 'You can't be punished for a crime you haven't committed. No doubt there should have been a fine, but there shouldn't have been a stripping of points.'

Player agents George Mimis and Jim Banaghan were reported to have broken rules in arranging deals for players. Both denied wrongdoing.

The chief executive of the Accredited Player Agent Scheme, Paul Osborne, said, 'I can't comment beyond saying I have spoken to the player managers concerned and will report to my board. It is up to the board to determine whether they will suspend, cancel or take no action against the managers.' No penalties were given to Mimis or Banaghan.

In September 2005, Bellamy again felt the anguish of ending a season in the second week of play-offs, losing to North Queensland 16–24 at Sydney Football Stadium. In his final year at Storm, Orford was the team's leading scorer for the fifth consecutive year. At Manly, he would go on to win the 2008 Dally M Medal for being the competition's best player, finishing two points ahead of Slater.

Emerging Cameron Smith, who signed a four-year deal with Melbourne the day after Orford left, was Storm Player of the Year in 2005. White was Rookie of the Year.

A new television rights deal was struck by the NRL at this time. Fox Sports and Channel Nine paid $500 million over six years, a 65 per cent increase in direct TV revenue. Part of the contract was a guarantee of live Grand Final coverage in Melbourne 'with a commitment to work with the NRL to improve scheduling of major events in Victoria and other states'. News Ltd and Waldron could smile at that achievement.

Waldron also crowed that he had softened the blow of losing Orford by signing Queensland State of Origin player and Australian representative Michael Crocker from the Sydney Roosters. Crocker had a mediocre 2005 due to injuries and poor discipline but he was 24 years old and a premiership player. His agent Banaghan said, 'Melbourne always told Michael he was their number one choice ... and that was very important to him.'

Internally, Storm felt 2006 was going to be another year of improvement. Externally, there were doubts.

Bookies rated Storm down with the competition plankton as a contender for the 2006 title. Centrebet manager Gerard Daffy said the long odds (paying $26) were based on a glaring weakness as halfback. 'Orford's gone and so are the Storm. For all these teams it's crucial that you have a class halfback and Orford's in a class of his own and that's probably representative of them drifting out and Manly [$21] drifting in.'

Some knew better. O'Sullivan started urging Bellamy to try Cronk at halfback. Masters, using his experience as a former coach, wrote the following: 'Cronk is an ideal replacement for Orford – tough, resilient, strong and, if slightly slower than Orford, only by a fraction.'

In fact, Cronk was Orford's equal. And Cronk had the bonus of being in sync with Smith and Slater. The boys from Queensland would finally run a first-grade team together, using their strong sense of each other.

Waldron's behaviour in attempting to keep Orford was telling. He was under pressure from all parts of the business to keep the star. But he offered not one more dollar than he could afford under the rules of the game. And he lost out. What toll did it take?

The salary cap pressure would build. The development money was committed to some players. But Schubert still hadn't given written approval for it to be paid outside the cap. If only they would win a premiership soon.

CHAPTER 15

2006 GRAND FINAL

Coach Bellamy's purpose never changes. 'I work really hard and I'm very disciplined in playing my role for the team. I've got a role to play and I try and do that the best I can,' he explained to ABC television's 7.30 program, in one of his more relaxed moods.

> It's the same as a player or any person in any walk of life, whether you're a doctor or a butcher or you own a store, whatever it is, you need to have [the right] mentality to work hard. We all want to be successful at what we do, whether you're a plumber, an electrician, a solicitor, everyone wants to be successful and the difference is: how hard are you willing to work to be successful? If you want to be a good coach, you need to put the time in.

In the same interview Bellamy was asked how he handles losing players to other teams. His answer reveals a pragmatist: 'The first step is not to worry,' he said.

> We know it's happened. We need to make the best of the situation now. You pick the guys who are gunna take their place or take their position. You just start that process of making sure those guys are disciplined and determined in what they need to do, you make sure they work hard. And you show 'em what they need to do, tell 'em how they need to do it. I give 'em the resources to be able to do that job, and off they go and we start building again.

> If you sit back and worry that they've gone, well that's not giving the guy that's comin' and takin' their place a fair go and that's where it all starts again. Hopefully that guy is gunna turn into the next Inglis or the next White or Dallas Johnson. It comes back to making sure you're doing the best you can for that player.

That's how he approached the loss of Orford.

In 1970 the satirical movie *M.A.S.H.* was released to critical and popular acclaim. Its star was Donald Sutherland, who played the lead character, 'Hawkeye', a chief surgeon. After the film was nominated for five Academy Awards, a television series of the same name was produced. But Sutherland would not be playing Hawkeye. How could the TV series be any good without him? Then Alan Alda brilliantly auditioned for the part. It was Alda who made the role of Hawkeye one of the greatest ever. In 1983, after leading the cast for 11 years, Alda directed the final episode of *M.A.S.H.* – breaking the United States viewership record (125 million).

Cooper Cronk was Storm's Alan Alda.

Injecting him into the Melbourne line-up was like placing the final battery in a torch. Everything was brighter after that.

In his first season (2006) Cronk was named the league's best halfback. That year saw Storm win 20 from 24 regular season matches, setting a club record of 11 straight wins between rounds 12 and 23. Smith was named hooker of the year and won the Dally M Medal for the league's best player. For the first time, Bellamy was awarded NRL Coach of the Year. The club finished on top of the ladder, no less than eight competition points clear of the second-placed Bulldogs, to be awarded Storm's first Minor Premiership.

In the first week of the play-offs Melbourne pipped eighth-placed Parramatta 12–6 to earn a week off. In the preliminary final two weeks later Melbourne beat St George Illawarra to qualify for the Grand Final. During that match Cronk chipped a kick across field that Matt King caught high above his head for a try. It was this type of spectacular play that made Melbourne favourite to win the Grand Final. The team had found a wonderful balance of efficiency and flair.

Its premiership decider opponent would be Brisbane.

Waldron was not only feeling more secure in his job, he was thriving. The CEO was performing exactly as News Ltd had asked him to: raising his team's profile. Twenty-four-hour sports radio station SEN – heard by mostly AFL addicts – made him a co-host on Friday mornings alongside Australian rules hero Kevin Bartlett. 'Wally' jousted with talkback callers and almost always won them over with his blokey banter. Listeners considered it one of the best sports segments on air. Most football identities and officials in Melbourne are formulaic in speech and manner. They give little away. Many are frightened of upsetting anyone or causing controversy. Waldron was colour in the drabness. His language was more like the people he was talking for. He made jokes and had fun. His common touch was perfect for the medium. Bartlett, an ex-Richmond man, seemed to enjoy his company in the studio.

During the football finals the AFL announced it was going to spend $100 million in Sydney and Brisbane to win over fans' devotion and money by making new franchises on the Gold Coast and in western Sydney. So badly did they want to take supporters away from the NRL, the AFL planned to convert brilliant rugby league players into Australian rules rookies for promotional purposes. Waldron was interviewed on the national sport television show *Offsiders,* hosted by Barrie Cassidy and Gerard Whateley. Waldron was asked about the AFL's spending spree.

He replied, 'We're doing a similar thing down here ...' When making a point, Waldron streamed sentences together, his words surfing a very long wave.

> Certainly this year the impact the Storm's impact had in so many areas is a direct result of the fact that we've put some money, energy and effort into actually growing the game at grass roots. This is a generational approach that takes a long time but I don't think the NRL are doing anything different in Melbourne than the AFL are doin' in Sydney and Brisbane.

Whateley challenged, 'They're not spending a hundred million dollars, Brian, in Victoria to grow the code.'

> Well it depends on where you spend the money and how you spend the money it's a very different market. I mean Sydney's a totally different place to Melbourne, I mean you can get lost and think that the whole of Sydney's gunna get engrossed in what's going on with the Swans and they are. But it's for a brief period of time it's a niche period of time I mean ...

Like a door-to-door salesman wanting to finish his pitch before you shut the fly-wire in his face, he raced on,

> I understand now what this is all about: this is a generational approach – what we're doin' in the market down here is not about tryin' to get bums on seats now, it is nice that we do, but it's about growing the game long term and getting your niche in the market, it is a generational cultural change that needs to take place. But we will never be any more than a niche player here in Melbourne and I can tell you the AFL will never [be] more than a niche player in Sydney or in Brisbane because there are religions up there called rugby league.

The days leading up to the 2006 Grand Final were some of Waldron's best in charge. He was emboldened by Storm's position as a competition heavyweight.

The above conversation is a perfect example of how Waldron ran Storm's front office. Former Storm employees say they could walk into his office to raise a problem or cast a query and be psychologically somersaulted into thinking his way. He always argued superbly.

This book's author spent a week at Storm headquarters in the lead-up to the 2006 Grand Final. The team was at ease in its environment, uncorrupted and hopeful. Players moved among dedicated supporters at a fan day, signing autographs in the sun. In the frightfully guarded environment of professional sport, here was an exception.

Inglis said, 'Seeing all these cameras and media out here today, we haven't seen this all year, but we live in an AFL community, so y'know, doesn't faze us one bit, gets us out of the limelight a bit. We just concentrate on what we gotta do day in and day out.'

'There's a unique bond that we have here that the Sydney boys probably don't,' Slater said, 'and hopefully we can use that to our advantage.'

Winger Steve Turner added, 'We keep everyone together as a family and it's just a great bunch of blokes and we do everything as a family.'

Geyer's wife Belinda was interviewed. She and her husband had moved to Melbourne after Geyer departed the disbanded Perth Super League franchise. He didn't want to go to the southern capital. Now they had three children and 200 NRL matches to boast of. Belinda said, 'It was hard but you make the most of the situation and now I've made lifelong friends down here and all the partners are in the same situation so we just help each other out.'

Indeed, the girlfriends and wives at Storm got along exceptionally well.

King found a neat comparison for Storm, at its happiest since 1999. 'I grew up in a town of about ten thousand people and it's got a lot of the family values that I had in the footy club up in the country. Everyone brought their kids along and there'd be a barbeque after every session, a couple of beers. And it's just got that feel and I love it.'

Bellamy was interviewed during this week. He looked fit and relaxed, perched on the seat of a dilapidated grandstand. 'I suppose if someone had have said at the start of the year we'd win this many games we'd have been surprised and perhaps wouldn't have believed it all,' he said. 'But the consistency of the young players has been tremendous and that's why we've won as many games as we have.'

The coach was masking his anxiety well.

During an extended interview, Waldron sat cross-legged in his office, a refurbished corporate box at Princes Park, overlooking an oval field with rugby league line marking and posts. The chief executive wore a light-purple shirt, no tie and an air of delightful confidence. Pressing his fingertips together like a priest he claimed credit for the successful reformation of Storm.

'We're a business first and foremost,' he began.

> We've just got a terrific product. You need to integrate business principles into what you do and that's pretty simple – good people, y'know, good planning, good structures. Because you are a business but you do have the product [used air-quote marks] – which is sport – and it's a matter of leveraging that in the marketplace.

Waldron had recovered from the Orford loss impressively. His contracting success rate had picked up. Another player had tried to leave Storm but Waldron helped prevent it. Steve Turner was a stand-out junior footballer and made his NRL debut for Penrith before crossing to Melbourne in 2003. By 2006 he had become an elite try scorer. The Gold Coast Titans lured him north. Turner's manager David Riolo agreed to a deal that was going to see his client represent the south-east Queensland team for three years from 2007.

When Gold Coast made the announcement, Waldron somehow quickly convinced Turner to change his mind. All of a sudden the footballer wanted to stay in Melbourne. Gold Coast insisted it had a legally binding agreement (an email from the player's manager). Waldron guffawed: 'For what? People need to understand the rules, he hasn't signed a contract, he never signed a thing.'

Gallop sided with the Gold Coast club and was making threats. 'I can't force him to play for the Titans but I can make sure he is not registered to play for Melbourne.'

Waldron seemed almost pleased to be having the stoush. In August he released a statement to his club supporters.

> No-one is denying there may have been some arrangements in place for Steve to go to the Titans, but the fact is these arrangements were never consummated and no legal contract was ever entered into nor letter of intent signed.
>
> Now, who is to blame here? The player did not at any time receive any verification of any deal with the Titans so understandably he starts to question the Titan's [sic] commitment to him. He now admits that the idea of going to the Titans is not a good one and agrees to a new three-year-deal with Storm.
>
> Melbourne Storm and Steve Turner are the innocent pawns here, the player wanted to secure his career and the Storm wanted a top-class back to remain on their list. We at the Melbourne Storm will vigorously defend our rights to conduct our business in a proper and professional manner. We will not adhere to the business principles of others.

In the end, Storm had to compensate the Titans. Turner got a pay rise. Bellamy was pleased to keep his strong winger.

The whole episode was a chance for Waldron to be an aggressive leader. Gone was the passive Waldron from the Orford deal.

But by the time the Grand Final came he could only sit and watch. You can't bluff your way to success on the field. Not against Wayne Bennett's Brisbane Broncos.

Storm team V Broncos, Grand Final 2006

Billy Slater	David Kidwell
Matt Geyer	Ryan Hoffman

Matt King	Dallas Johnson
Greg Inglis	Reserves
Steve Turner	Adam Blair
Scott Hill	Jeremy Smith
Cooper Cronk	Ben Cross
Antonio Kaufusi	Nathan Friend
Cameron Smith (C)	
Brett White	Coach: Craig Bellamy

It was the first NSWRL/NRL Grand Final since 1908 that did not feature a team from Sydney. Storm was favourite to win its second premiership but faced a team with an impeccable Grand Final record. The Broncos had won five titles since 1988.

The television coverage on Channel Nine broke records. There were 100,000 more viewers from Melbourne than Sydney.

At the beginning of the telecast a mop-headed Slater, standing beside the Yarra, flanked by Geyer and Inglis, in full costume, said in his North Queensland drawl, 'Down at the Storm we don't care much about history, all we care about is now.' He pointed awkwardly at the lens.

About 80,000 people filled Telstra Stadium. They saw INXS and Hoodoo Gurus perform live.

'I love the way you talk, you walk ...'

NRL administrators were tense about staging an event with no home team. The same emotions dogged the AFL when the MCG hosted Brisbane versus Port Adelaide in 2004. But neither competition hierarchies needed to worry. Grand Finals hold up, always.

Storm was inexperienced in the last game of the year but had beaten Brisbane four of the last five times. Broncos boasted a mature pack. Loved Queenslander Shane Webcke, like Glenn Lazarus for Storm in 1999, was about to play his final 80 minutes. Melbourne original Scott Hill would also bow out of the NRL, win or lose. (He was bound for London Harlequins next season.)

Underneath the stadium, in the dressing rooms, where you can most accurately measure a man's composure quite simply by seeing his face, the youthful Storm players appeared tight and fearful. All were seated on plastic chairs. No talking. Slater was jittery, getting up and down a lot. Inglis was topless and sitting in front of a fan, eyes shooting a volley of glances. Only Geyer and Hill appeared to be men at work. At the same time, Brisbane was running through passing drills, building up a necessary sweat, like a pugilist about to march with his entourage into the music and darkness of the one-shot roped square.

Bellamy gave his final instructions, his polo shirt hanging loose, imploring them for effort and concentration. The coach looked tired. Injured recruit Michael Crocker stood leaning on one crutch. When Bellamy's speech ended the Melbourne men stood and gave each other pats and half-hugs, using the touch of teammates to calm themselves.

Smith led them out of the tunnel. On reaching the grass and tumult, he turned back to his mates and said earnestly, 'C'mon boys.'

The team ran through an AFL-style banner, which read: 'Victoria's brothers Storm in to claim the Holy Grail in a purple reign.'

Slater caught the Darren Lockyer kick-off and was hit by three tacklers. Both teams were efficient in the first few minutes. Cronk seemed to be organising his team in attack and defence. He wasn't flustered. Unsurprisingly he made the first attacking flurry, throwing a successful dummy at the rushing Bronco line, running 40 metres before losing his footing looking for support that wasn't there.

Dallas Johnson was hungry for toil. Smith stole metres from dummy half. Inglis took five minutes to touch the ball. Brisbane defended its citadel without panic. King made the first error, a knock on. Hill conceded a penalty. Then Slater unfairly stripped Shaun Berrigan on the line and Lockyer scored two penalty points. Replays showed the Broncos were lucky, Slater wronged.

Brisbane 2–0. Ten minutes gone.

Cronk kicked the ball long into touch from inside the 40-metre line, advancing his team and keeping possession, another sound decision made by the calmest player in purple.

Bellamy sat mute and stared at the match with concentration, as if he were trying to use an old Jedi mind trick to influence the play.

Smith and Inglis charged at the line. Hill took advantage of the field position, carrying the ball and spinning, delivering a one-handed pass to Steve Turner, who scored a try on the sideline. Smith sprayed the conversion. Storm 4–2. Lockyer kicked a high ball. Storm error – Steve Turner knock-on. On replay, Brisbane appeared lucky again. Ten-metre scrum. With Storm's line flat footed, Justin Hodges eased through and scored an easily converted try.

A classical Slater 50-metre kick return – *left foot step* – caused excitement and an opportunity to score at the other end. But Storm was not composed and couldn't manage precision. You can't fight the pressure. Only time can help you handle it. Still, Storm pressed. Broncos held on out wide. If only Melbourne could settle. Bellamy's team was too quick for Brisbane, which was scrambling. Half-time gave the northern club some relief, as it was still leading by four points. 8–4.

The second half Bellamy watched with arms crossed. He was frustrated his team was not playing the way it had all year. There was no structure. Simple roles were not being performed.

Brisbane carted Melbourne around the park until Inglis caught a bomb and sublimely sprinted through broken play for a 50-metre gain. Smith looked a chance to score when felled by Hodges, through a high shot that fetched a penalty. Smith was injured in the tackle. Storm forwards boiled at the sight of their hooker going down. A fight seemed imminent. King scored a try two tackles later but Smith was so crippled by the Hodges hit he could not take the conversion, which Geyer missed.

The Grand Final was a joy to watch. It was one of those games that compels onlookers to read the shifts of momentum. It would be easier to read tarot cards. On the field, it just felt close. An error here, a run there, a charge down, some luck ... Something unpredictable would decide it.

Slater was penalised for a high shot at the other end of the field. The call was wrong. An obstruction call was missed. The penalty should have been Storm's. Brisbane hit the lead. Still smarting, Melbourne was slow to shut down a Bronco passing exchange ... Tate scored in the corner. Bellamy winced.

Brisbane 14–8.

A hobbling Smith persisted but not for much longer.

Cronk wobbled a high ball and landed it perfectly, just near the posts, the ball spilling from Hodges's hands and Ryan Hoffman's head into the grasp of King, who touched down. On replay it looked a try. The commentators thought the game would be levelled. But the video ref denied the four points. A minute later Storm was mistakenly called for a knock-on after Slater dazzled in a run down the right side: three bad decisions in a row against Melbourne.

In the 70th minute, Smith retired from the field. The captain was spent. His example of courage and effort would reward his team in later years but not today.

In the end, the game was won by experience and chance.

Shane Webcke powered up the middle and the champion Lockyer slammed a darting 45-metre field goal. Brisbane 15–8. Storm tried for the last seven minutes to find points. Bellamy rubbed his forehead, knowing he would have to wait another year. Hoffman sat on the grass and sobbed like a toddler. Later he said of the disallowed try, 'I've got no idea whether I touched it. I just jumped up for a ball and it bounced off something. It doesn't matter anymore.'

Smith stated in the dressing room, 'We played nowhere near our potential against those blokes. We went away from our game plan and that got us into strife.'

While sadness pervaded the team, Storm had built foundations in the defeat that would make them hard to beat from then on. Blisters from shovelling rock all day develop harder, surer hands; so would Smith and co. benefit from the 2006 Grand Final. As Bellamy said to the ABC, 'I don't think I'm smarter than anybody else, as far as footy tactics or anything like that. I'm probably not as smart as some guys but one thing I've grown up with and one thing that has been proven to me over the years ... if you work hard, at some stage you'll get lucky.'

A loss would make his players hungrier. His best players were his youngest. The rugby league world was at Storm's feet. But nothing is so simple in the NRL.

In the second week of the finals series, Waldron eventually wrote to Ian Schubert requesting permission to remunerate some athletes outside the salary cap for developing the game in Victoria. The money was to be paid by a charity called the Unity Foundation, which was now running the Storm development program.

Waldron proposed to pay five players a total of $130,000 per season. Inglis was to be the highest paid ($40,000 per season, increasing to $60,000). These were big numbers for charity work.

Waldron did not tell Schubert the money was already committed to the players through their deals.

Schubert did not allow the payments. Gallop says, looking back, 'They [Storm] were actually making the promise of development money part of the contractual negotiation.' That was against NRL rules. 'So it was just the fact they didn't do that the right way and didn't get approval beforehand.'

It mattered not that Waldron had previously flagged it with Gallop.

Gallop explains, 'I never agreed to that kind of thing. I only ever said, "Look, it sounds like it might be okay but you need to take it to Schubert."'

Waldron had made an error. He had told people in his executive the league had already approved the payments. Now the CEO was stuck. How was he going to pay the players what they were owed? He could not pay them legitimately (directly through Storm's finance department). That would show up on the NRL audit and Schubert would fine him for being over the salary cap. He would be fired, as per his employment contract. It was like he had taken one step into quicksand. Pressure was coming from all sides. With star players due for pay rises, he was about to face cap pressure anyway. How could he possibly keep this team together long enough for it to win the premiership that Bellamy and his football department craved?

Waldron decided to take the risk he would not be caught by Schubert. He instructed CFO Cameron Vale to go ahead and pay some of the money promised to players in their letters of offer, through the Unity Foundation. The charity offered training programs and could use high-profile Storm players to aid their charity work.

Vale was still loyal to Waldron and believed what he told him, that Schubert had 'screwed them' on the development deal, broken a promise, left them with no choice. Vale knew it was wrong to pay the players outside the cap but agreed to help Waldron avoid this small pothole. They were mates, after all. And Vale perhaps felt indebted to Waldron for bringing him across from St Kilda, fast-tracking his career.

Unity Foundation was a totally above board charity dedicated to improving the lives of disadvantaged Indigenous youths. It was founded by Aboriginal former St Kilda footballers Xavier Clarke and Allan Murray. Its chief executive was Peter King, a mental health nurse and psychotherapist, who helped organisations run self-improvement programs. King had helped establish St Kilda's player welfare committee. He had mentored Clarke and Murray, who in turn wanted to help children.

Unity's programs were carefully planned. 'We spoke to a whole lot of homeless agencies,' King says 'and found their model didn't quite fit the young people we wanted to treat so I developed a model for the boys [founders] on how to treat homeless youth.' The new charity contacted local councils – Bayside and Frankston – and were able to pay minimal rent on two houses. They hired four qualified carers to work at the accommodation.

King explains, 'And then we put young people through the houses. We identified through contacts in the Aboriginal community young people at risk and offered them a home.'

In the next few years Unity Foundation attracted donations and grants, including $440,000 over two years from the Department of Education, Employment and Workplace Relations, to help teenagers survive their damaged lives.

St Kilda Football Club's player welfare program was excellent. It was so successful, Waldron decided to copy it at Storm and poach St Kilda's welfare officer, Brian Phelan. Once Phelan had settled at the rugby league club, he contacted Peter King and said, 'Can you give us some support and some education and all that sort of stuff on how to deliver community programs on behalf of Storm?' Waldron subsequently asked King if Unity Foundation wanted to be Melbourne Storm's charity partner. That's how the relationship began.

Storm's aim was not simply to assist people in the community. It was to develop players' communication skills away from professional sport. By teaching athletes how to talk to, and work with, young people, the club could broaden its employees' perspectives. Life experience helps people mature and ultimately become better contributors to society. A spin-off benefit is that expert communication skills help footballers excel in games and at training.

Phelan and ex–Storm player Peter Robinson, who also worked at the club in a welfare role, became involved in organising players to go through Unity Foundation training.

King says training involved,

> how to communicate, what the skills are, what the programs are and how to deliver the programs. Everything from decision-making, how to talk about your own story without getting too personal, how to identify when a young person is getting too personal and going beyond the scope of the program. I think it was a good eight weeks or something. It was a fairly intensive program.

Waldron talked to King about how much it would cost. A small fee was agreed upon for players who worked for the charity, made school appearances and attended special events, including a charity ball.

Inglis and Cronk worked on Unity Foundation programs. King says Inglis shone in the company of youngsters looking up to him. 'When he has the Indigenous boys around him he certainly does. He has a big presence.' Inglis later took part in a government-paid Indigenous cadetship, worth up to $15,000.

Many other Storm players were involved in Unity Foundation activities during 2006 and 2007. After that, Waldron decided the club could better educate its charges and the charity provided no further training.

King paid all Storm players – those who worked on programs – a total of $134,000 over two years, which is a relatively small sum considering Unity had staged ten-week courses for other organisations that attracted funding of $50,000. The money came through Storm's finance department and was documented as 'donations'.

Once Vale paid King, Storm had no say over the money.

'I was told the money was for the charity,' King says. 'Part of that process was that we would employ the players to deliver programs and services and they would do that on behalf of our charity but also they would be doing that in setting up Melbourne Storm in the community.'

King never distributed other funds on behalf of Storm. 'Definitely not,' he explains. 'I can guarantee you that's not true. We definitely were paying the players. It's part of the community program [but] I couldn't pay someone if they're just sitting there doing nothing.'

The players' photographs and names were used to promote events in inner-city schools, which was beneficial to all involved. 'We got a number of principals raving about how valuable it was,' King says. 'It gave us a pretty good name in delivering programs before all the salary cap stuff happened.'

The community benefitted from Storm's contributions. But the players still needed to be paid what their deals stated. With athletes having to work for their cash from King, not all of the promised 'development money' was going to reach them through the Unity Foundation.

Inglis's manager, Gainey, for instance, later complained his client only ever received about $5000 of his promised development money, which was supposed to be many times that amount.

Other agents pressed for their players to be paid. Melbourne Storm had to find another way. Waldron started asking around. TPAs were an option. He talked to sponsors. Making contract variations was another ploy to hold the team together until it could win silverware. All the players Melbourne had developed – Cronk, Smith, Slater, Inglis, White, King, Johnson – were becoming the best in the league. And they had not won anything yet. Their prices would soon go through the ceiling. If only the club could keep them together for one more season ... Or maybe Waldron should go to Bellamy and tell him to choose a couple to get rid of.

Waldron's dream run in the job was coming to an end. He was now at a crossroad. For two years he had run Storm well. In 2006 he was a finalist in the Australian Sports Administrator of the Year awards. A ceremony was held at the ritzy Crown Casino Palladium Room. Australian Rugby Union CEO John O'Neill won the gong. But Waldron was now in the company of the best, chatting to some of the most powerful people in the country, sitting right up there with them on the top shelf. It was a long way down.

PART THREE

CHAPTER 16

STORM HQ

Melbourne Storm was a small but vibrant workplace, full of young people on the make. Waldron called the club a family. He also talked endlessly about 'culture'. 'You can't buy a culture, you gotta create a culture,' he used to preach. 'And it's the people that you bring together that make the culture.'

The family was made of two parts: football department and front office.

Morning tea was often a source of merriment for front office staff. Workers were regularly given the task of making some snacks or refreshments for all. Colleagues rated each other's performance based on taste and presentation. It was a good laugh, typical of the team-building practices Waldron encouraged. Almost all Storm employees were aged between 20 and 40 years old. Most worked weekends throughout the season. They shared more hours with each other than their *real* families. The club was their life. The team represented not only itself: it trained and played games on behalf of its support staff and front office. Therefore, it wasn't only the players who suffered and benefitted from the emotions of winning and losing. Everyone was committed.

Storm social functions were very popular. Staff mingled with corporate partners and sponsors in a uniquely relaxing way.

Number-one celebrity ticketholder Molly Meldrum (Australia's most famous music guru, former host of TV show *Countdown*) personified the fun. Wearing his signature cowboy hat, Meldrum used to turn up to the President's Club lunch with his dog. No-one said anything. That was just Molly. Olympic Park was a difficult venue to stage social events. It was old and cramped but Waldron and his staff made it work. There was smiling, dancing and drinking.

Storm people from the Waldron era still catch up to talk about those days. They know they will never work in another environment like it.

The front office workers did not adore Waldron but they respected his zeal. He was a polarising manager. Some say he was unpredictable and overbearing. Others defend his assertiveness, explaining he necessarily held people to high standards.

In his better moments he could be the most nurturing, caring person. At other times he could yell his staff down.

There is no debate about his ability to host functions. As a master of ceremonies, he was universally admired. With a microphone in hand he was articulate and sold the Storm message to anyone who came. In the media, whenever you heard from Waldron, he was talking about Melbourne Storm and the NRL. He did a tremendous job to be heard in a town obsessed by AFL. He instilled pride in his franchise.

Other NRL CEOs called him 'Hollywood Waldron'.

Socially, Hollywood could be charming. At dinners and fundraisers 'Wally' worked the room endlessly. When he talked to people, he shook hands and made eye contact. He was truly engaged. It gave visitors a feeling of warmth that this powerful executive would use their name and really listen to their words. But in no time at all he would move onto the next person, leaving the last conversationalist wondering what had just happened. Waldron was like an outback willy-willy, spinning and twisting his way through the crowd.

The CEO had a workplace Achilles heel. His relationship with Medwell was disliked by almost everyone in the front office. 'I think he [Waldron] took too much direction from Trish,' an ex-staffer says. Others said Trish had too much power.

Medwell's career was sailing at impressive knots. She had graduated from being an events coordinator at St Kilda Football Club to General Manager of Commercial Operations at Storm, in a relatively short time.

Along the way, she had impressed some important people. News Ltd director Jourdain recalls her achieving high marks in marketing and sponsorship. Even now, he considers her contribution to the club's improved image through Waldron's early years as significant.

But Jourdain was based in Sydney. He was not privy to Storm's office politics, which were coloured by the Waldron–Medwell liaison, or, more particularly, the constant, fervent denials they were together.

The relationship was not visible. But it was always present. And *most* people secretly knew about it. Collusion was a common word in the Storm front office. It was used to describe any whispered conversations about Waldron and Medwell. Collusion could get you fired, or so it was rumoured.

Waldron's News Ltd superiors found out about the office relationship but decided there was no cause for intervention. (If any company knows about intra-office love, it is News Ltd. Countless romances have flourished in newsrooms across the country for decades.) No-one said anything. Medwell was being judged on her work.

Jourdain recalls,

> That became known at some stage but then we just sort of sat back and said well lets evaluate her on her own performance. And to be fair I thought she was a very good operator and did a lot of good stuff for the Storm. It wouldn't have been fair on her to evaluate her on anything other than how she was performing.

Other key administrators were becoming important to the club's improved brand. Medwell's second-in-charge was Christine Finnegan, who had worked at Tennis Australia and ACT Brumbies. She was a trusted and admired figure at Storm, a peacemaker who had a strong relationship with the football department, particularly coach Bellamy and retired player–cum–ambassador Kearns.

Every workplace gives its employees reasons to smile or moan. At Storm, the boasts outnumbered the gripes. Being near the top of the NRL helped. Winning feels good. Moving into the 2007 season, no-one wanted to be anywhere else.

However, that was about to change. Vale was the first to start searching for the emergency exit.

One day the chief financial officer went by Waldron's house to pick him up for a meeting. He saw two cars in the driveway. They were both Hondas ... Sponsor cars. Vale's mind and heart raced. He was one of the very few people who did not believe Waldron was in a relationship with Medwell. He had trusted Waldron's denials this whole time. They were more than colleagues. Waldron had been at Vale's wedding. They were close friends. The CFO had defended his boss against the awful rumours over several years.

Now the two cars made him feel uneasy. He wrote down the number plate on the car that he knew did not belong to Waldron. Back at work, he matched it with the records he kept for the company vehicles – it belonged to Medwell. Although Vale tried to imagine all sorts of legitimate reasons for her car being at Waldron's house at 8am, the relationship was now undeniable. Vale considered it a humiliating and personal betrayal. He asked himself: How long has this been going on? Was it happening back at St Kilda? How am I going to look?

Significantly, the discovery redefined Vale's view of Waldron, personally *and* professionally.

The CFO could not bring himself to challenge his boss over the truth. And he let the lie fester. For months he thought about confronting Waldron but it was not in his nature. Then at a board meeting in Sydney, arranged for the convenience of interstate directors, Waldron approached Vale and told him to wait outside.

'You won't be coming in for the first few minutes,' he said. Waldron was going to talk to the board about Medwell. By then his marriage was over. He wanted everything out in the open. 'It's Trish and I – we're an item. I'll talk to you about it later. I know you're gunna be disappointed.'

With that, Waldron left Vale to sit by himself and stew. The young executive's embarrassment was complete. Why had he been so naïve? Was he really blinded by friendship or did ambition block his view?

Waldron subsequently called a meeting back at Storm headquarters. Everyone gathered in the boardroom. Matter-of-factly, the boss announced: 'I've spoken to the board, Trish Medwell and I are together.' He added that Medwell would be leaving the club. He was staying. The popular Finnegan was being promoted to General Manager of Commercial Operations.

While the rest of the front office silently smiled, Vale glowered. He now resented Waldron. He no longer felt obliged to be loyal or protective of the man who had once impressed, inspired and mentored him.

The CEO did not offer any further explanation. He didn't owe Vale anything more than he had given him. He had come clean. Now it was time to move on.

But their relationship was damaged irreparably and it would have consequences for others. Without his rose-coloured glasses, Vale started to see everything at Storm differently – dispassionately – including the club's new attitude toward its payment of players.

CHAPTER 17

THE EMAIL BRAWL

Up until now, Vale had relished fixing and revitalising Storm's budget. Waldron knew little about finance and had handed over control of the books. Like any ambitious accountant, Vale found it enjoyable to get in, clean it up and prove his credentials. It was not difficult work for someone with enthusiasm and expertise.

The NRL salary cap was his most difficult task. It was different to the AFL's cap. It was more complicated: there were bonus payments for State of Origin and test match appearances, and a carry-over system of shifting money from one year to the next.

In the beginning, Vale found it helpful to meet Schubert and discuss the peculiarities of the league's rules. Schubert mixed with accountants from all clubs at regular finance conferences. He also came to Melbourne to talk to relevant Storm staff. Sometimes he would socialise with club officials over lunch or a few drinks. They talked about salary caps, measuring the NRL against the AFL. Often Schubert would complain about his lack of resources. Waldron and some of his department heads at Storm underestimated the salary cap auditor. He was a riddle they never solved. They knew he once played a bit of footy (in fact, he played nearly 15 years in the NSWRL) and they wondered whether he had any professional audit training. He had plenty.

As Storm's wages started to blow out, Vale was increasingly contacting Schubert for rulings on potential payments. This would lead to angst in the football department.

Vale's relationship with O'Sullivan was already strained.

O'Sullivan largely ran his own show at Storm and rightly so. His passion, work ethic and nous had landed Storm many fine players; he was finding them young and they were developing into league standouts. No doubt the elite football programs at Norths Devils and Storm were assisting his list of successes. But he was now one of the best scouts in the business. O'Sullivan's latest triumph was signing a boy called Israel Folau. The winger had surprised everyone by playing well in trial matches, even though he was only 17. A first-grade debut beckoned.

O'Sullivan liked to sign players using a standard letter of offer, a deal between club and player, which was *not* the NRL contract, then he would discuss the implications with Vale.

A letter of offer is not necessarily scandalous. It serves a legitimate purpose. NRL contracts take time to be approved by the league. A contracting agreement needs to be in place so players and clubs can plan for their immediate future. Only when a letter of offer does not mirror the NRL contract is it likely to be breaching salary cap rules.

Vale first found a discrepancy with one of Melbourne Storm's playing contracts (aside from the development money) in 2006, when a smart footballer went to the CFO to ask about his wage. Vale explained to the athlete his contract and how it worked. He did not have to. The player knew exactly what he was owed – and he had been shortchanged. Vale extracted from his files the player's NRL contract. 'You see?'

'That's not the contract, look at my letter of offer' he said, handing a copy to the finance chief. Vale had not seen the player's letter of offer.

Vale was surprised to see the player produce a Storm letter of offer different to the player's NRL contract. The CFO did not think much about it. He assumed an administrative mistake had been made. He phoned Schubert and conceded the error. It was corrected. No further action was needed. No harm done.

From that day Vale made sure to keep track of all the letters of offer. Sometimes this led to squabbling with O'Sullivan. O'Sullivan was trying to keep the players happy. He was conscious of providing them with enough incentives to stay in Melbourne. Not one of Storm's athletes was from Victoria. The young men longed to see family during a long season. A couple of flights here and there were not unusual offerings in the national competition. Anyway, this type of thing was no headache inducer for Vale. He controlled the spending. He and

Waldron had to lodge the salary cap summaries. If he didn't want to pay certain things to players he could tell O'Sullivan it was not allowed. Vale thought Waldron would back him up if a dispute arose between the CFO and the head of recruitment. This was not personal. It was a critical part of the business.

By 2007 Vale knew about several letters of offer that did not match the NRL contracts. They were not surprises and they were not O'Sullivan's wrongdoing. Most of them involved the development money. Vale had commenced paying donations to Unity Foundation as he had been instructed to do. The charity was paying players for work but only in small instalments. One of the players had a deal, struck in 2005, for $60,000 over two years. It was described in his letter of offer like this: '$30,000 League development payment for work in the Victorian rugby league.' This commitment had to be serviced, despite the NRL's refusal to allow it to be paid outside the cap.

The shortfall was enough to start causing restless nights within Storm's front office executive. But the development money was no longer the only thing causing wage pressures.

There were other troublesome letters of offer hanging over Storm. Vale knew Cameron Smith had an agreement for the 2006–2009 seasons, which stated in an unsigned letter of offer that he was to receive an undisclosed third party amount (TPA) of $50,000 per year (the club had promised the cash without specifying where it would come from). Crocker had also been promised a $50,000 TPA. His offer also included his agent's fees of $20,000 per season and various flight allowances.

Seven other players had signed NRL-approved contracts in 2006. Some of them were on long-term deals. For instance, Ryan Hoffman wasn't a cheap youngster anymore. White's salary was increasing by about $40,000. And Inglis had just had his contract extended and inflated. His manager had negotiated Inglis's salary to rise by $150,000 in 2007 and $140,000 in 2008. It was declared to the league. This was as it should be. Inglis was improving at a rapid rate and Storm was reaping the benefits.

On top of all of this, Storm needed to negotiate with Slater. His management wanted a large, long-term deal. The squeeze was on.

Vale could not ignore it any longer. He raised the alarm internally.

On 1 February, 2007, Vale sent Waldron and O'Sullivan an email with a spreadsheet identifying the discrepancies. The CFO flagged he wanted to talk about the 'discrepancy between offers and contracts'. His spreadsheet projected a salary cap breach of $167,667 if the NRL contracts and letters of offer were all paid up.

The three men met to discuss the figures and solve the problem. Storm had several options. It could have owned up to the development money debacle and suffered a likely fine from the league. It could have resolved to cut loose one of its stars, therefore making room under the cap to rearrange its commitments. Neither of those options was on the table. The season was about to start. Storm's best players had been developed, not bought. Why should they be given away? Storm believed other clubs were cheating the salary cap. It was not a hard decision to admit nothing to the salary cap auditor and try to wriggle out of the bind.

Instead, Waldron resolved to carry out contract variations (shifting money from that year to the next) with seven of the club's top-paid players. This shuffling of dollars would reduce each man's 2007 contract by $15,000 and increase all seven contracts by $17,000 in 2008. It shifted more than $100,000 of payments into the next year. This was a legitimate tactic.

The players were agreeable to the variations because it wasn't a lot of money. And they wanted so badly to win the premiership. They did not fancy losing any of their teammates. If they did not agree, one of them would be offloaded immediately; a second player would be booted later that year. Waldron explained this. The players saw the sense in the variations. They knew salary cap pressure was mounting.

A day after the variations, Storm lodged its preseason salary cap declaration for season 2007. The club stated it expected to come in $71,233 *under* the salary cap. Waldron signed a statutory declaration verifying the figures. Vale was not required to sign a declaration. It was clear to him now that Waldron was ready to keep paying players outside the cap to hold the team together.

Two days after that, Storm blitzed Canberra Raiders 32–16; prop White and fullback Slater the best players. No off-field talk would distract the players in this stage of imminent dynamic balance.

The salary cap discussions continued between the front office and football department.

On 17 April Vale sent another email to O'Sullivan and Waldron. Attached was another spreadsheet – a further warning. He wrote it was 'not pretty reading as you would be aware'.

Vale had calculated Storm was going to be over the salary cap in 2008 by $150,000, excluding the troublesome letters of offer payments. Slater had not yet been re-signed. A week later he was. The wages were going up and up. But the salary cap was staying the same.

Waldron, as tireless as ever, was at that moment raging against the NRL and television scheduling. He criticised Channel Nine for playing only two Storm games on primetime – Friday night or Sunday afternoon – in the first 11 matches of the season. 'It's a major concern, the lack of exposure for us on free-to-air,' he said. 'It isn't as if we're not an attractive proposition.'

These comments show remarkable drive from the CEO to push his team into the national spotlight. Not satisfied with being in charge of the best team in the competition, he was still making demands, beating the drum. Perhaps it also indicates how much pressure a News Ltd manager endures when he is failing in his one true aim: making money. News Ltd was now more interested than ever in selling the franchise. The club was serving its purpose to help the league attract national sponsors. Waldron's stewardship had slightly improved the brand. There was no reason for News Ltd to own it much longer. Waldron would soon be encouraged by his employer to keep an eye out for would-be stakeholders. He was the club's agent-in-chief.

As important as it was to improve the financial situation at Storm, News Ltd also desired to keep its public image, which was about to take a major hit, respectable. When the NRL released its annual salary cap sanctions list in 2007 (fines for the previous year) Storm was on it for the first time since the owner had appointed Waldron. The league fined Melbourne $63,266 after Schubert detected overspending, not related to TPAs or development money.

It could have meant the end for Waldron, who had signed a News Ltd employment contract with a salary cap clause. But the team owner chose to allow their executive one slip-up ... It was decided Waldron could stay on. On balance, his performance as CEO was more important to the owner than the payments misdemeanor. At the same time, the NRL also fined Cronulla ($5000), Brisbane ($30,000), St George Illawarra ($62,427), Newcastle ($19,260), South Sydney ($28,573), Canberra ($173,203) and Wests Tigers ($21,250).

In that company, Storm was just another name and number. Except it was not. News Ltd had already made it clear that its clubs' breaches were not acceptable, primarily because it also half-owned the competition. That's why Ribot was sacked, News Ltd says. That's why the clause existed in Waldron's contract. A fine in excess of $60,000 was at the medium–high end of breaches. Such a fine does not involve insignificantly small change.

Waldron was not sacked. Rather, with the sanction in mind, News Ltd–appointed director Jourdain spoke at a Storm board meeting, attended by the club executive. He ordered all measures be taken to avoid further salary cap fines, big or small. He stated the company would no longer tolerate any mistakes, adding that any proposed method of payment to players needed to be approved by Schubert in writing. Waldron did not seem frightened. He never did. He promised Jourdain to keep his record spotless from then on. All others at the meeting nodded. Jourdain had made his point. The directive was a relief to Vale. He could now use it to clean up some improper practices.

Jourdain recalls making such a statement. He says he did not know about any extra salary cap breaches at the time. He was merely issuing a warning on behalf of News Ltd.

The director's words inadvertently triggered an internal spat between the front office and football department that revealed the club's attitude toward the salary cap.

In mid–2007 the club proposed to pay some players through a unique method. It involved redeeming points from credit cards and transforming them into vouchers for household items. One player had received such a benefit when Vale questioned whether it was against NRL rules.

The CFO wrote an email to Schubert and his assistant Jamie L'Oste Brown on 19 June.

> Ian/Jamie,
> Hopefully a minor query this time.
>
> We redeem credit card points on various club credit cards for voucher [sic] – e.g. Harvey Norman vouchers.
>
> Can we use those vouchers redeemed for players with relocation in the contract, subject to them buying items of a relocation nature (fridge, basic tv, washing machine, etc [sic]) and having the documentation? It allows us to fulfil the contract, but save cash and greatly reduce the flow of paperwork. We still ask the player give us the receipts once redeemed so we can check for FBT (fringe benefits' tax) purposes the items are relocation.
>
> FYI & Accounting wise – it is very handy accounting/cash saver.

I book $2k in revenue from the voucher, while football [department] then wears the $2k cost it has already had budgeted for in relocation. But obviously no cash changes hands. A win all round.

Regards,
Cameron Vale
Chief Financial officer
Melbourne Storm Rugby League Club

Schubert's frank reply came within two hours. It was a refusal.

Cam

Relocation [money] does not include items of a capital nature such as the assets you note – these are a benefit and are an included item [in the salary cap]. If you provide the vouchers to the players for redemption, the value of the vouchers is included unless such value is deducted from the players after tax.

Regards
Ian Schubert
Director
Registration and Salary Cap Auditor

On receiving the response from Schubert, Vale tried to contact O'Sullivan to tell him about the ruling. O'Sullivan wasn't available to talk. So Vale passed on Schubert's rejection to the chief recruiter via an email at 6:50pm that evening. He copied in Waldron.

Sully,
As per board directive on having all issues in writing resolved by Shoey, I put to him what we were proposing to do (and did with one player) in redeeming vouchers to offset for relocation costs.

Effectively, below [pointing out Schubert's response, which is included on the email] he is not treating items like washing machines, furniture, etc [sic] to set up new players as relocation.

Therefore from today onwards, only legitimate relocation costs re transporting belongings should be claimed by players for relocation and not capital items.

I trust you will communicate this to managers when making contract offers.

Cam

The email read like a challenge. Certainly it was without warmth. It hinted at tension between the two managers.

That same night Peter O'Sullivan wrote a long and emotional reply. It was sent at ten minutes to midnight. And it was written not only for Vale. The following was copied to Brian Waldron, Craig Bellamy, football manager Dean Lance and assistant coaches Stephen Kearney and Michael Maguire. O'Sullivan wrote:

> Cam,
> He has never picked up on that ever.
>
> Why would you bring it to his intention [sic]?
>
> With all good intensions [sic] you are making it more difficult by the day to keep our squad together and keep our good young kids in our system.
>
> I am at a loss to why we are self destructing ...
>
> The BOARD would have no idea on relocation etc. and when the BOARD see [sic] us loosing [sic] players because of flights and furniture etc who will explain.
>
> I fight a daily battle with Craig [Bellamy] on players [sic] income and loosing [sic] players because of our success but I am loosing the drive to try and hold this squad together. I am frustrated as when I started here and Craig took over we were within an inch of the club going under but due to a lot of hard work and planning we now have a team and club to be proud of.
>
> If you want us to slip back to mediocrity keep the current thought process and we will suffer.
>
> I am at a complete loss to know what to do as I want our club to blossom and shine but you have no idea of the suffering we went through to get to this stage and I see it coming undone so quickly, You [sic] have seen nothing but success on the field in your short stay at the club and have no idea of the pressure and finger pointing that was endured before you.
>
> Be under no illusion that this club is staging a remarkable comeback from being a laughing stock on the field due to the worst coaching ever in the history of the NRL to potentially a super club.
>
> We can't cheat like other clubs so we need to be creative and bold in our attempt to hold our squad together and if you think

that players will stay at our club and come to our club because of the Melbourne City you are off with the pixies.

We as a team have created a wonderful environment for success and I am very concerned that this is quickly being evaporated. Look at St George and there [sic] current standing and you will see how quickly you can go from the penthouse to the sh#t house.

I am frustrated to the maximum and perhaps you should do the next ten contracts and I should sit back and be critical and watch you loose [sic] nine players to other clubs and sit in on the coach and your meeting when you explain why so many players are leaving?

As I stated before you have no idea of the level of mediocrity and pressure that was endured before our current status in the game and the ability to slide from the current position to cellar dweller is real. In 2008 we have some super stars coming off contract and 2009 we have the games [sic] elite of the elite coming off but in the mean time we need to hold a group of players around them to ensure success.

When the BOARD have questioned me at the loss of Ben Cross and the prospect of loosing [sic] Jeremy Smith when we are over the cap imagine the outfall [sic] at loosing [sic] a SMITH or INGLIS or FOLAU.

HELP ME PLEASE!

By the way it is me and Brian who face the players next Monday to describe WHY we are loosing [sic] players and with no support from Coaching and finance our predicament will worsen.

I implore you to help me with the small things that may keep a player and I implore the coaching staff not to lumber [sic] a decision to release a player so we stay under the cap on my shoulders. If we go into 2008 500k over it will be Brian and ME looking for a job and the Coach starting the premiership on minus 20 points and where will you be looking for income?

Kind regards

Peter O'Sullivan

General Manager List and Recruitment

The email, half-plea, half-tirade, was frightfully passionate, a rare insight into the pressures of life inside the professional football bubble. The reference to daily discussions with the coach revealed the constant frustrations and deepest fears of the football department. It also highlighted the franchise's desperation to keep the best players in Melbourne. After losing the 2006 Grand Final, Bellamy had an even greater intensity to extract from his roster the premiership he believed was deserved, against the unbeatable opponent of time running out.

O'Sullivan's recollections of the mediocre years was also revealing. O'Sullivan had been at the club since 2001. He understandably felt the club had earned its position and rosy future. But his appraisal of Mark Murray's coaching performance was unfair. Murray inherited a squad divided and depleted. When he was removed from the role, to make way for Bellamy, Murray left behind a field rich with diamonds, namely Smith, Slater and Cronk.

O'Sullivan's next paragraph was perhaps the most educational of all. It summed up the long-serving football man's approach to player payments at that time. Despite discrepancies in the letters of offer and NRL contracts, O'Sullivan did not believe he was doing anything wrong by offering 'small things that may keep a player'. He also had a genuine belief other clubs were breaking the laws of the game.

This belief was standard in rugby league and remains so. Rumours of overpayments are as unavoidable as a common cold during unforgiving NRL seasons. Players and coaches move between clubs. They know the system better than administrators. They gossip. Agents know more about payment options than anyone (except Schubert, whose knowledge is necessarily incomparable, even if he sometimes falls short of finding the evidence he seeks to prosecute). Some managers peddle half-truths to achieve better deals. They also know the game's dark secrets. And to those who dismiss the speculation, the facts must surely speak louder.

At the time O'Sullivan wrote his email to Vale, the NRL salary cap, as it was, had been running for seven seasons. The league had fined 14 clubs for breaching the salary cap. It had handed down more than 50 fines totalling $3,134,430. The NRL had a policy of discounting fines for teams that own up to overspending. So the $3 million–plus in fines only hints at the real overspending during that time.

The final section of O'Sullivan's message painted a state of something approaching panic. 'HELP ME PLEASE.' Mentioning the shaky futures of 'Brian and ME' showed an acute awareness of consequences for paying players over the limit. But complicating this was his thought that the club needed to 'hold a group of players around them [elite players] to ensure success'. It did not. The club only had to encourage Bellamy to do more with less. He was capable of building up role players around his top men. All Bellamy had to do was back his department and its methods, trust the development of Smith, Cronk, Slater and Inglis.

By copying in Bellamy and the entire coaching staff, O'Sullivan seemed to be trying to intimidate Vale. The coach was the undisputed boss of the football department. The CFO was renowned for being non-confrontational. Most people at Storm were in awe of Bellamy's growing status in the game. Waldron was not one of those people. Neither was O'Sullivan. But Vale wasn't likely to relish a discussion with the coach about his players. Or so O'Sullivan thought.

In fact, Vale lost his temper when he received the email the next morning. He fired back an email response at 8.43am. He did not copy in anyone. It was between Vale and O'Sullivan. It read:

> Sully,
> Because of the unprofessional & gutless way you are approaching this issue and didn't wait to discuss face to face on Monday, we now have a major fu*cking problem. We didn't before this morning, now we do.
>
> I am not going to hit send on my response which I want the coaches to see until Brian has read the email.
>
> But since you have dragged others in on this, I will be responding in due course.
>
> Cam

Fifteen minutes later, O'Sullivan responded coolly via email:

> I have sent to Craig for you mate.

Vale was shaking at this point. He had hoped that Waldron would back him. But from interactions that morning it was clear the CEO would be of no help to him. Waldron told his CFO to calm down, let it go.

Vale was alone. He had no-one to turn to for support. So he emailed his wife. Electronic records say he wrote to her at 9.47am.

> Sully and I are at war, Coach has been brought in, Brian is telling me to back off.
>
> Have a read –
>
> Cam

He attached O'Sullivan's message from the previous night. Vale's wife Samantha wrote a 19-word reply that was comforting. With tenderness, she typed:

> Sounds like fun ...
> Try not to get too angry. keep [sic] it professional
> Good luck
> Keep swearing to a minimum!

Vale later wrote to O'Sullivan what may have seemed to the recruiter a surrender message:

> I am not good enough to take on the whole football department so you win, I will step aside and allow you to control the process as you see fit.

With all his major work relationships shredded, Vale was in a tight spot with no easy solution. He was all but isolated. But the young man who had forged a career from modest beginnings was not without resilience.

CHAPTER 18

THE INDEPENDENT DIRECTORS

The need for contract variations and the e-brawl threatened a period of destabilisation, if not disintegration, for Storm. But no-one was willing to revamp the club's list of players beyond a tinkering. A premiership was at stake. So the tension around the salary cap crisis went on.

Like all thoughtful coaches, Bellamy places enormous importance on harmony. It would have been upsetting to know the bridge between the football department and front office was burning. Internal fights and injuries were the only things capable of beating his side in 2007. The coach's defence against any distraction has always been to work harder and harder at finding a winning edge. He was happy striving. So he concentrated with all his focus on the fundamentals of success: everyone performing a simple role in a challenging and fun environment.

The team was now functioning better than ever. The players were highly motivated; not only were they determined to beat their opposition, they were competing with each other for positions. It was a coach's nirvana. And if the talent and drive of Inglis, Smith, Cronk, Slater, White, Johnson, Hoffman, King, Crocker and Turner were not enough to ensure a premiership, then the unfathomable rookie season of Israel Folau would lock it in.

He was first mentioned at a board meeting.

'I'll never forget it as long as I live,' recalls former director Peter Maher. 'O'Sullivan was sitting in a board meeting at the end of one year and we went, "Have we got anyone for next year?" And he said, "Have we what … we've got a kid called Israel Folau". With a name like that, we thought, if he can play he is going to be a superstar.'

O'Sullivan had scouted and signed the rangy Folau at the 2004 Australian Schoolboys Under–15s tournament in Toowoomba, Queensland. Folau's subsequent physical development was startling. The teenager grew up and filled out. He suddenly had thighs as powerful as Mal Meninga, yet he changed direction and accelerated as nimbly as Slater. After an eye-popping preseason, Folau was given his chance in first grade. He scored a try on debut and 21 for the season, breaking Slater's record for number of tries (19) in a first year. In October, he would become the youngest Australian representative ever.

Maher recalls Bellamy's handling of Folau. 'He was a big shy lad – perfect for here [Melbourne] too,' he says. 'He came from a very close family and walked into here and Craig [Bellamy] is so good with those sort of young men and he was perfect for him – he couldn't have gone to a better place than here.'

As Bellamy prepared his team for finals, Maher and the other directors were starting to enjoy their role as the club overseers. The board's reformation, which had begun two years earlier, was now complete. News Ltd executives Peter Jourdain, Frank Stanton and John Webster (who would soon leave his post) had been joined by four so-called Independents, appointed but not employed by News Ltd. And they were now busying themselves with making Storm more appreciated by its hometown.

Maher was the first Independent. He is a rich, well-connected businessman, with an ocean-deep voice.

In the 1980s, Maher was a salesman of many things, including amusement machines and billiard tables. Then he worked at the old radio station 3XY in marketing.

He hurt his leg playing cricket one day, and couldn't get up and down stairs. He spent his idle time working out how to make money. After a couple of different ventures, including running cricket camps with his cousin, former Australian all-rounder Simon O'Donnell, Maher hit upon a better idea. He would record radio and television content and sell it to anyone concerned. He started with very basic equipment.

'We recorded everything from home from cassette recorders and videos until they ran out,' Maher explains.

> You would listen to it and log it and then cold-call everyone. It was pitched to clients as news and information, 'Did you realise this was being said about you?' A lot of the large corporate organisations, especially the internationals like Ford and GMH were already aware of this type of service. So that's how that all started.

Maher's company, Rehame, became a leading media monitor. It sold in 2006 for a fortune. Maher stayed active in the media as a radio presenter for 3AW.

Like many football-loving businessmen, Maher was drawn to his favourite team – AFL club St Kilda. Like many money-craving football clubs, St Kilda enjoyed Maher's expertise.

'They knew of my support and then I would give them a hand as far as their media crisis,' Maher explains. That's how Waldron knew him.

When Waldron took charge of Storm he approached Maher to be a director. They both went to Sydney to talk to Jourdain at News Ltd's headquarters.

Jourdain says Maher fitted the description of the new Storm way. 'We were of the view that we needed a strong presence in Melbourne so you needed Melbourne businesspeople and Melbourne board members to make that happen. So it was just then the process of how you found those people and who was interested and gradually as you get board members on ... who they knew and introduced you to.'

Maher was given the nod. He recalls: 'We went away and then they [News Ltd] came back after we got settled in and got rolling, they said anyone else that you think would be worthwhile.' There was. Maher suggested Dr Rob Moodie might be a top boardroom signing.

Moodie was not an obvious choice for a football director. As chief executive of VicHealth, he was one of Australia's leading health officials. He knew Maher through their commitment to the Premier's Drug Prevention Council.

Moodie was initially reluctant to accept the offer. Although he had played rugby league as a child, his preferred code was rugby union; his father, a mining engineer, had played for and coached the Melbourne University team. Moodie, a big, strong bloke, later played for the same club and even represented Victoria. He has been associated with the Melbourne University since he was five. The professor gave

Maher's suggestion some thought and concluded it would broaden his understanding of public life. He was particularly interested in News Ltd's presence as owner.

'I thought it'd be really good – 'cause News Ltd owns it – to understand News more,' Moodie says. 'They had such control over public commentary.'

While Moodie warmed to the idea, Maher worked on convincing News Ltd that the gentleman who travelled all over the world lecturing and advising governments on public health would be good for their footy team. Jourdain and Stanton were not sure about Moodie.

Maher explains,

> They kept suggesting that he won't know enough about the business and everything else. I was adamant that he would be good. First of all he had entree into most of Melbourne as far as Government was concerned, was probably as respected a Meboournite as you could meet. He was Victorian Father of the Year and he was the sort of person who went and sat down at meetings in a manner that was completely easy to understand and comprehend.

Eventually Moodie was accepted. Immediately Stanton and Jourdain were won over by his character, personality and intelligence. 'He completely changed them dramatically from how they viewed how footy clubs should run and who should be on footy clubs,' Maher explains. 'He was the one, more than any other, that started that. The other thing too, it wasn't easy for coaches and players, they'd never seen anyone like him. Rugby league football clubs had never had anyone like him on their board.'

Jourdain says,

> To get someone of his calibre involved at that level on the Storm board – we were really making some inroads, getting into the Melbourne society, the Melbourne public and Melbourne itself. To me, as a long-term objective that was more important than winning premierships. It's great to win premierships but if you can get that calibre of person – who's a Melbourne identity and so well regarded – involved the club is going to make it long-term and that is what the whole aim of it was.

Moodie developed a mutually respectful relationship with Bellamy and many others.

He was made chairman in 2007.

The third independent director to join Storm was Maher's former Rehame colleague Petra Fawcett, a respected and forthright businesswoman, who specialises in sales, marketing and core business management. Storm was one of Fawcett's former clients.

She recalls of her appointment: 'They explained where they were coming from with memberships, subscriptions, brand management. They wanted to get more expertise. Like most clubs, money doesn't go into those areas so they needed more support.' Fawcett was pleased to be the first female board member at Storm. 'It was a good reflection of the board and how progressive it was,' she adds.

The fourth and final Independent was Gerry Ryan, founder of Australian company Jayco. Ryan had interests in cycling, basketball, horseracing (as owner of a Melbourne Cup winner) and show business (investor of *Walking with Dinosaurs*). He was a long-time sponsor of Storm and remains so.

'I did it purely as a marketing exercise, not because of my love for sport,' Ryan says. He is considered a 'fan' because of his seemingly endless support of women's basketball, football codes and cycling (he now owns the Orica GreenEdge professional team, which contests the Tour de France). But he adds, 'Any sponsorship for sport has got to have a commercial ring about it. Everyone thinks I'm sports crazy. I try and buy sponsorship that is going to give me value.'

Like many people at Storm, Ryan had spent time at St Kilda Football Club. He was finance director at the AFL club and vice president in its darkest days. Ryan is still seen by some St Kilda club veterans as one of the people who saved the team from extinction when it was penniless in the 1980s and 1990s. He paid star players directly because the club had run out of funds. Unlike some wealthy people who attach themselves to football clubs but rarely fork out much money, Ryan is prepared to give cash to his teams.

Initially, he was not a rugby league devotee. 'Even though I followed Storm I wasn't a regular goer,' he explains.

But then Ryan became close friends with John Ribot and *Herald-Sun* editor-in-chief Peter Blunden. The three men enjoyed attending matches together.

In 2007 Maher and Moodie approached Ryan with an invitation to join the board. Ryan said, 'Look, I haven't got time.'

They pressed. 'Just assist us with marketing and network.'

'I knocked them back and they chased me for a few months and I gave in,' Ryan explains. He was up-front and said he could not attend all meetings. True to his word, he attended fewer meetings than other directors. But his directorship gave the board more punch. Gerry Ryan was a big name in Australian sport.

Waldron was mighty pleased with all the appointments. It broadened his network and elevated his status, even if the high-achieving professionals had some question marks over his workplace style. Fawcett says Waldron operated as an 'old-school' manager. 'It was a small business that needed a lot of bringing into the 21st century with corporate procedures, HR policies ... none of that existed,' she explains. 'I think he was an excellent leader. I think he was a great orator and got people on board and very amiable and a nice guy.'

'He could be very charming and was associated with success,' Moodie says. '[But] you knew some of the ways he handled staff wasn't the best by any means.'

Storm board meetings touched on all parts of the business. Directors oversaw specific tasks. Sponsorship gave the directors the most pride. Membership was a tougher nut. Publicly made predictions for growth in that department were always brighter than the board really thought was possible but they reflected their aspiration and hope. Waldron was always present at board meetings, as were his executives. A representative of the football department would also attend meetings – football manager Dean Lance (later General Manager of Football Operations Frank Ponissi) or Bellamy.

Reports about recruiting were often exciting. Maher was the board member assigned to the football roster. A subcommittee was also formed, involving executive management and the football department. The comings and goings of players were always discussed. The value of individual footballers was weighed up constantly. Salaries were mentioned. No-one made any decisions about player retention or movement without Bellamy's approval.

'As far as who we recruited and who we didn't recruit, I didn't have any say in that whatsoever,' Maher concedes.

> The only thing you'd ever give an opinion on was at the end of the day, if you think he's a better bloke or got a better character, let's go with the guy with the better character. That's all it was. There would be lots of discussion about let's keep him, let's let him go – it was different from AFL, without the draft – it's such an amazing thing, it never stops. Whether you are trying to get someone from the higher end of the market or the bottom end of the market, you are constantly fishing.

The Independents helped schmooze potential recruits. Maher recalls a meeting with Crocker:

> Craig in particular wanted him. He reckoned he would be good for the place and he had faith in him as well. Bearing in mind, if we wanted players to come here then, if you were a name, we would bring you down with your manager, wine and dine you at the Stokehouse [a well-regarded bayside restaurant] and whatever else.

But Crocker wasn't taken to the Stokehouse. Storm wanted to woo him privately. So they took him to the greyhound races at Sandown Park. 'We didn't want the world to know he was here,' Maher explains.

> He came down in an off-cream Richie Benaud suit with his fairish complexion and I thought Christ, what have we got here? He had his manager, Banaghan, with him. We didn't bring players down to turn it into a drink-a-thon or anything. Craig and the others did the signing and everything else, I organised the day at the races.

Waldron was an asset on those occasions. Maher adds, 'He would rub a lot of people up the wrong way after they got to know him a bit, but he was always good at that first point of contact.'

As O'Sullivan indicated in his email to Vale, player salary discussions were often, if not regularly, held at board meetings. Negotiations with players had to start a year or 18 months out from the contracts ending. There was never a moment wages were not considered in the running of the club.

Waldron always reminded people there were non-negotiables. By now he valued above all else the positions of fullback, hooker, halfback and five-eighth. He called them 'the one, the nine, the seven and the six'.

Even for a man reared on Australian rules it was obvious how important the playmakers were. Less than ten years before, Anderson had spent most of his budget on larger bodies. 'You can't win without them,' he said, and that was still true. But Waldron and any other people not steeped in the history of the code would wonder how hard it was to find big bangers who weren't required to offload the ball – just play the percentages, execute a run-n-bash role. Carry it up, take the hits, go forward, get knocked over, get back up. If there was more to it than that, why was Waldron paying some of those players the minimum wage – the salary of a fourth-year apprentice plumber? No, it was the athlete who could pass the ball the width of a traffic lane and kick it to land on a patch of grass no broader than a footstep that needed to be maintained.

Slater. Smith. Cronk. Inglis. The Big Four were untouchable. The CEO often boasted he would do whatever he could to keep them from leaving. Likewise, the football department could not stomach losing any of these athletes. Storm's motto was – *we keep The Big Four, always*.

Storm finished on top of the ladder in 2007, as it had in 2006. Bellamy's men faced Brisbane in the first final. It was tempting to expect another classic confrontation between the two teams. But much had changed since the last Grand Final. Melbourne had improved. It was now almost flawless. The score was 40–0. Two weeks later Melbourne beat Parramatta 26–10 in front of more than 30,000 people at the Docklands stadium. Manly was the only other team in Storm's class that season. The Sea Eagles had thrashed South Sydney in the first week of play-offs and North Queensland in the preliminary. A great contest was expected on 30 September at Telstra Stadium.

CHAPTER 19

GATES OF STORM

Like the late Jack Gibson, Bellamy orates the words of others to reaffirm his teachings. Quoting people and recalling historical feats helps long-serving coaches stay surprising to players. It also helps the football bosses to stay interested in their trade. Researching – or observing – inspiring feats feeds the desire to be exceptional and maintains the passion to lead. Nothing is more motivating than an unwaveringly passionate coach.

Bellamy doesn't simply trawl sporting biographies for his intellectual fuel. He enjoys a fine historical novel, as much as any text. The book *Gates of Fire* was given to him. Written by Steven Pressfield and published in 1998, it is a fantastic recreation of the Battle of Thermopylae (480 BC), between the Greeks and Persians, perhaps the most famous in European ancient history.

Gates of Fire tells the story of the 300 Spartan soldiers who held out a suicide mission for seven days against the marauding Persian army. The Spartans were warriors with sons, to preserve their bloodlines should their fathers perish in combat. The Persian king Xerxes demanded the Spartans lay down their arms. Spartan king Leonidas defiantly shouted back: 'Come and get them.'

Almost all the ideals and imagery central to the novel could be reasonably adapted to rugby league.

On page 78, Pressfield wrote: 'The Spartans say that any army may win while it has its legs under it; the real test comes when all strength is fled and the men must produce victory on will alone.'

Bellamy's favourite character was the platoon commander Dienekes. When it was said to Dienekes that the Persian archers were so numerous that their arrows would block out the sun, the Spartan soldier replied, laughing: 'Good, then we will fight in the shade.'

The book is used for inspiration the world over. Famously, it had been required reading for the American military cadets at West Point. Bellamy was taken by it. His Storm soldiers became his Spartans. Bellamy's system of defence demands that if you go out to play – you play for your teammate.

'This is my shield,' goes the saying in *Gates of Fire*.

> I bear it before me into battle but it is not mine alone. It protects my brother on my left. It protects my city. I will never let my brother out of its shadow nor my city out of its shelter. I will die with my shield before me facing my enemy.

Bellamy tried to have some of his players read Pressfield's classic. The book club didn't really catch on. A coach's job is to distill information and deliver it in words easily understood, forget the prose.

The mentor's other strength as a speechmaker is his ability to generate resentment toward the opposition, to urge extra effort. It is commonly called the 'us against them' mentality. For instance, when the team played Canberra, Bellamy would remind his players the Raiders' former coach Matt Elliot was the one who started complaining about Storm's grapple tackling.

'Hey, this is where this shit started,' he would snap, almost snarl, every time they went to the nation's capital. 'These are the blokes that fuckin' whinge about us.'

After the Grand Final loss in 2006, some Storm players ran into a couple of Broncos in a social setting. The triumphant Brisbane players were flashing their premiership rings at their vanquished opponents. It was fat on Bellamy's fire. When they went back to Brisbane, the coach brought up the incident and challenged his men with the memory of that taunting.

This type of psychology usually wears like oft-trod carpet. But Bellamy was able to freshen the message by altering the gripe and picking his moments. He didn't do it always. And often he would counterbalance it with humour. Once he tried to tell his players a game of rugby league was like a cooked breakfast. The teams were the animals, which contributed to the meal. One was a chicken. The other was the pig. The chicken *contributed* the eggs. But the pig *committed* himself to the cause. He wanted his players to be the pigs. This pregame address had the Storm athletes laughing. But it mattered not. Sometimes it is better for players to be more relaxed than too emotionally stimulated. There is no one-size-fits-all mental formula in football.

When in doubt, Bellamy went back to the most reliable method. Us. Against. Them. Understand boys?

It was not hard to find a sore point. Storm was criticised for its ownership, its geography and winning habit. There was never any shortage of sledging to draw from. Perhaps after a while Bellamy actually believed his team was the underdog – the Spartans of the NRL. It was easy to feel that way in Melbourne. But who was the enemy? Other teams? The Sydney press? Maybe it was *everyone* else. The only problem with that theory was Storm had powerful News Ltd's backing: Bellamy was actually in charge of a crack Spartan-like squad with the strength and riches of the Persian army in reserve.

More likely Bellamy is a man of humble beginnings, with insecurities like anyone, who trained himself to overcome his doubts. He found a line of work that suited his inherent enjoyment for learning and teaching. And he was determined above all else to finish what he started. Only Manly stood in his way now. It was time to win the NRL.

Storm team V Manly, 2007 Grand Final

Billy Slater	Clint Newton
Steve Turner	Ryan Hoffman
Matt King	Dallas Johnson
Israel Folau	Reserves
Anthony Quinn	Matt Geyer
Greg Inglis	Jeremy Smith
Cooper Cronk	Michael Crocker
Ben Cross	Jeff Lima
Cameron Smith (C)	
Brett White	Coach: Craig Bellamy

Prematch, Storm players moved with vitality and purpose around the change room, as the experienced Broncos had done a year before.

The team was on its feet. No eyes were glazed. There was still fear in the room. The pressure to win was immense. What would happen if they let another chance slip?

A week earlier, in the change room before the Parramatta game at Docklands, the players had each spoken about the journey they were taking: what it meant personally to be a part of this team. It was like a counselling session, creating stronger, calmer connections during a tense time. The theme of the year had been 'together'. At these moments, the players knew and cared about each other well enough to give everything they have to their teammates.

Storm players might have likened being in Melbourne to being a member of an outlaw bikie gang, minus the lawlessness. The comparison is valid. In everyday life a man says he would do anything for his mate but he actually has limits. In bikie organisations the members really would do *anything* for each other. In the mind-racing minutes before the 2007 Grand Final, Storm footballers felt as if they would die for the team. Such is the rush of the fantasyland of professional football.

Now they were touching each other silently through hugs and handshakes. Crocker was there again but this time in his playing uniform. He bounced on his toes. Slater seemed full of urgency. Smith flexed his jaw.

The air was dry and Manly appeared nervous, their faces tight, as captain Matt Orford led them out to fireworks and cheers from 80,000 people.

Smith ran out and through the banner, his mates following. The reigning Wally Lewis Medallist (best State of Origin player) had been made sole captain during the season. The hooker had grown into his promise. Bellamy had helped transform the relaxed duo of Smith and Slater into players worth following by constantly empowering them, including them in his decision-making. He had been assisted in the early days from the examples set by veterans Geyer, Kearns and Hill.

In *Gates of Fire* (page 127) a trainee Spartan says,

> I could not stop staring at the faces of the warriors I had known and watched in drill and training but until now had never looked upon in the blood and horror of battle. Their stature in my mind, already elevated beyond the men of any other city I had known, now rose close to that of heroes and demigods.

Boos drowned out the applause. Vanessa Amorossi sang the national anthem. Clint Newton, a Storm mid-year recruit from Newcastle, started laughing. Perhaps he was thinking how fortunate he was to be standing where he was. Hard man Dallas Johnson had his head strapped, exposing only one ear.

Manly had scored the first try in its previous 17 matches. Storm's hierarchy wanted to start well.

Slater's first kick return resulted in a penalty for Storm after Jamie Lyon picked the fullback up and drove him head-first into the long grass. A fight ensued but no-one was maimed. Another tackle dazed Johnson. Cronk's first kick was expertly measured, placing the Sea Eagles in danger, forcing a line drop out.

Standout football leaders not only do the right thing all of the time but they demand the same from others. They instruct and urge and cajole, just like Cronk was doing now. Smith was the skipper and Slater his lieutenant. But Cronk was the most effusive leader and possibly Storm's best.

Manly was soon defending again. But Storm made an error. Orford picked up a spilt ball and ran 50 metres. Only one man could catch him – five-eighth Inglis, who followed his first tackle with another seconds later.

Forward Ben Cross started hungrily. He made many runs and tackles. Two nights before, he was declared unfit for the match. But he shook off his ailment and was now performing brilliantly. Johnson was dazed by another tackle – a knee to the head.

Bellamy, wearing spectacles, sat motionless. Manly coach Des Hasler was jittery, his team brutal.

Brett White was concussed. There were increasing worries about Storm's line. But they had trained for this. A month before the play-offs the club executed a mini-preseason to toughen the athletes mentally. There were no bushwalks, rather relentless, boring, grinding training. Ten minutes into a decider, when things are going awry, reserves of self-belief were needed.

White, who knew what it was like to walk 25 kilometres with bloodied thighs and debilitating fatigue, was prepared. Seconds after he was made rubbery-legged by a Steve Matai bullet tackle, White fronted up and tackled again, his head flailing but his arms strong.

Smith *went* to grubber kick. Manly's defence compressed, to disallow Storm players running through easily. But the captain held the ball back. He shifted it left. Slater was a decoy, which confused the Sea Eagles. The ball went out the back to Inglis, who passed to Anthony Quinn. The winger scored a try without being touched. It was a plan executed with ease.

Manly knocked on. Its anxiety was palpable. Hasler winced. Bellamy injected his bench players. Jeff Lima and Michael Crocker were cannon-balls in reserve.

In the 23rd minute Smith, 5 metres from the Manly line, took the ball from dummy half and shovelled it to Cronk, who laid it back to his number nine. Three Sea Eagles were watching Slater, lurking on the right side but the ball went to Inglis, 10 metres behind, who stepped and straightened. He was not looking for a gap in the line. He was going through them. Four opponents could not stop him. Strongman Anthony Watmough was cast aside like a junior. Try. This was Inglis at his finest.

Melbourne reached dizzying heights of team harmony in the next hour. Slater ran and swerved. Johnson battered forward. Folau demanded attention every time he touched the ball. Each man had a clear mind. Inglis tackled as well as anyone could. Manly hung on through will and determination. It even scored a try to make the score 10–4 at half-time. But Melbourne Storm was stretching an elastic band that would soon snap.

Bellamy puts trust in his charges. To define roles within the team he asks them questions. What are you going to do? Do you understand what's expected of you? Both players and coach know the right answers. The athlete is happy to state the obvious. He and his coach share an understanding. Lesser coaches don't ask. They tell and tell and tell until the player stops listening.

Melbourne players enjoyed the reinforcement of their roles at half-time.

A minute after the restart courageous Manly fullback Brett Stewart was knocked out by a Crocker shoulder charge. It sickened Stewart's teammates. Melbourne was emboldened. Three minutes later Crocker ran unchecked through the defence and celebrated a try. Bellamy was growing restless in the coaching box, bobbing and weaving like a middleweight. Manly's tacklers were flat. Storm, without pressure, organised its decoy runners and ran angles to benefit its big backs. Matt King received a Slater pass and scored a try. White offloaded to Inglis minutes later. Inglis was on his 40-metre line.

This is the Inglis to remember when he can run no more. He bolted into broken field, away from two tired chasers, approaching the fullback. With the ball lodged in his left hand, he readied the right – here comes a fend ... It was effective and he scored a try. Inglis opened his mouth like a kid taking a ride on a fast rollercoaster as he dived to the ground to complete the performance. It must be fun when the rollercoaster is you.

Smith's poor goal-kicking was the only blight on a Storm romp.

The last 15 minutes were without time for the Melbourne players. No hurry. No worry. Just playing the game as they had done since they could walk. However, the coach did not relax.

Manly scored a try from persistence. Quinn fluffed a try. Newton got one. His famous father – ex-golfer Jack – raised a plastic cup of beer in the grandstand. Quinn mugged Lyon in a one-on-one tackle and ran over for the try he missed five minutes before. The final score was 34–8. Bellamy had set a record for winning more matches in a two-year period than any coach, including Bob Fulton or Jack Gibson. Finally he smiled.

He said: 'It's a lot of hard work for the boys, some of these boys have worked hard for five years. Everyone was saying we were gunna choke again this year. These guys are great. They've been a credit to the club. Just desserts today mate.'

Inglis won the Clive Churchill Medal, presented by Churchill's wife, Joyce. He thanked his coach, teammates, fans and family.

During the celebrations, which lasted an age, teammates embraced and their smiles glowed like sparklers in the night. They floated around the field's perimeter. Wives and girlfriends shared the moment. The coach and captain hugged and were drenched in sports drink. Satisfaction and relief gave way to bliss. Cronk said it was the best time of his life, adding he did not have children. The birth of one's child and a premiership is a comparable sensation. Sharing the spoils of victory is the big difference. Doing something remarkable with all your mates can make the sporting milestone more thrilling. An athlete's skin tingles in victory. Watching an offspring enter the world is a moment that warms from the inside: the joy lasts longer. But Cronk didn't know to compare.

Waldron strolled among the players and talked on his phone to his children. He was an anonymous suit in the parade around the arena, feeling special too. It was his first premiership in more than 15 years of club administration and it felt as good as he imagined it might. He could afford at that moment to forget completely the burden of the premiership, the rising cost of his players, how he would pay for all of this happiness.

CHAPTER 20

VALE BAILS AS THE ROT SETS IN

When a team wins a premiership and its best performers are nowhere near retirement age giddy fans nod and say: 'This is the start of a footballing dynasty.'

Storm's list of players was sound, indeed. But change was taking place in the management of the franchise. O'Sullivan decided to leave. The recruiter had been with the franchise since Chris Johns was chief executive. With names such as Inglis and Folau written in bold capitals on his resume, O'Sullivan was offered a job at the Sydney Roosters. Waldron and O'Sullivan had a subsequent discussion. The CEO would not match the Roosters' offer. By the time the bubbles went flat on Grand Final celebrations, O'Sullivan had left the state.

Another key member of the administrative team now increasingly desperate to depart was Vale. The CFO has been personally hurt by his clash with the football department over the salary cap. His colleagues expected him to lighten up once O'Sullivan left. But Vale was still morose. He was uncomfortable with the salary cap rules being ignored. Worse, he was now being asked to actively manage the overpayments.

The problem was growing by the day.

Each morning the CFO would sit in his office, log on to his computer and scour employment websites. Through recruitment agencies he even organised to be interviewed for more than half a dozen positions at non-sporting companies. He hated them all. He really wanted to go back to the AFL.

Vale was not as fortunate as O'Sullivan. He had no work offers. And he lived in fear of being asked the question: Why do you want to leave Melbourne Storm?

He sought counsel from a well-connected CEO in the AFL, who was helpful. The CEO told Vale he had two choices. 'You can either rebel against your boss and really go one-on-one with him [over salary cap issues] or just make sure that if he ever asks you to perform a task, that it is in writing.' Email is an effective way to create an audit trail. That way nobody can later deny knowledge of wrongdoing.

Vale did not want to challenge Waldron. It was too confronting and possibly career-damaging. It was unthinkable that he gambled his future to fix a problem someone else created. He was no longer reverential of Waldron but he did consider his boss very influential – not only in the sports industry but at News Ltd.

The choice Vale made was to leave Storm quietly, as soon as possible. He would spend the next few months scouting the work horizon, like a sailor on the crow's nest, ready to jump ship as soon as a sturdier vessel came into view.

During that time he was asked by Waldron to facilitate more deals to break the league rules. He did so. And it was all recorded. His electronic breadcrumbs were left strategically so he would not be later blamed as the operator of the ruse. Rightly or wrongly, he believed Waldron capable of saying: 'My CFO did it.'

Vale drafted two more expansive emails in 2007. The first was dated 24 July. It was addressed to Jayco Managing Director Gerry Ryan, copied to Waldron, and outlined several methods of payments to Storm players outside the cap.

Ryan, a sponsor and now club director, had agreed to help. He says he thought it was all within the rules.

The options, as proposed by Vale, were:

- Melbourne Storm invoicing Jayco for an amount for 'sponsorship' of $150,000 in 2008 but not receiving amount.
- Companies related to Jayco invoicing the Melbourne Storm after paying the players.
- Melbourne Storm invoicing Jayco for an amount for 'promotional costs' of $150,000 in 2007 but not receiving the full amount.

As a sports-business pragmatist, Ryan's role assisting Storm meet its commitments to players was not surprising.

In 2012, it was revealed two-time Melbourne Cup–winning leading jockey Damien Oliver was being investigated by Racing Victoria for gambling on races. The people who had employed Oliver to ride their horse in the Caulfield Cup panicked, fearing public scorn from moral crusaders. The rider was sacked. Few others wanted to touch Oliver that spring. But Ryan, unafraid of the conservative social commentary in Australian sport, sensed an opportunity. He employed Oliver to ride his champion horse Americain in the Melbourne Cup. The wealthy businessman did not try to coat his decision in sugar.

'Damien's record speaks for itself and we believe he can get the job done,' Ryan told the press. (Oliver was later suspended from racing for 10 months.)

There is stronger evidence of Ryan's uncomplicated view of sport in his cycling investments. He has recommitted to help fund Australian cycling through the Australian Institute of Sport until at least the next Olympics in 2016. Ryan is spending tens of millions of dollars on a sport whose image has been dynamite-blasted by an unveiled history of performance-enhancing drugs and farcical denials by athletes and authorities.

Not long after Lance Armstrong made his confession to Oprah, Ryan announced he would continue backing cycling. He held a lunch and press conference at one of his hotels (he also owns popular Melbourne bars and pubs) and sat beside Tour de France veteran Stuart O'Grady and Olympic champion Anna Meares, who praised Ryan's 'contribution' as 'critical'.

Ryan appeared typically avuncular in his grey suit and polar-white shirt, his casual blue-eyed stare. Each time he spoke, people stopped clinking cutlery. Experienced journalists asked soft questions, not willing to risk offending the cycling royalty by mentioning doping directly.

Then someone summoned the bravery to say: 'Gerry, when a crisis hits a sport, sponsors can do one of two things, they can run or they can stick. You've chosen to stick. Why?'

Ryan replied with a rising passion:

> Well, the sport is a great sport. Ah, what happened back in the past, I think if you look over the past six years and what programs

> they have implemented, the [blood] passport system, it's probably one of the cleanest sports, or most tested sports in the world.
>
> We spent two hundred thousand euros in testing at Orica-GreenEdge. I'd like someone out here to tell me, from the media, what other sport tests as much as cycling does and has the programs in place?

He paused to look around the room. Reporters hate questions coming back at them. Ryan swam in the awkwardness for four seconds that seemed like an age. Then he continued.

> Y'know, what happens in the AFL? Huge drug problem. NRL? That never gets printed. Y'know, blood doping. In NRL it's accepted, or was accepted. In terms of EPO [a performance enhancing drug] in AFL football teams? Cocaine? But that doesn't get printed.
>
> What the media has brought up, and it's great, out of every crisis comes opportunity, here's the opportunity for this sport to get out and tell the world that we are heading towards a clean system. The ones that will cheat, and you always will have cheats, they'll get caught.
>
> But I think it's great that its all come out and so we can put it behind us and move forward. At Orica-GreenEdge we hope to wrap up our investigation and review of our policies. We're very confident, and me personally, as an investor in the sport, not only the AIS but Orica-GreenEdge, it's got a great future.
>
> I'd like to see some more positive stories coming out about what we are doing regarding drug policies. Unfortunately good news doesn't always sell.

Ryan's spontaneous address, particularly his seemingly random comparison of cycling with football codes, seemed like buck passing. Not long after his statement, the Australia Sports Anti-Doping Authority and Australian Crime Commission announced they were investigating widespread use of performance-enhancing drugs in the AFL and NRL.

News Ltd's relationship with Ryan was multi-faceted throughout his time as Storm sponsor and director. Firstly, the businessman had an ongoing commercial partnership with the media company. Each year Ryan sponsored the Jayco *Herald Sun* Tour, an elite cycling race. More significantly, News Ltd had long viewed Ryan as a future owner of Storm.

Peter Macourt, News Ltd COO, explains, 'We would [have] liked to have sold the Storm to someone who wanted to own it for a long time. There's no reason for News Ltd to own it really other than we were funding it.' Of Ryan, Macourt says: 'Well he had money. He was very keen on the Storm and he had a lot of money so he was clearly a potential buyer.'

The caravan king says he was pleased to assist Storm with third-party sponsors.

> I had meetings with Brian [Waldron], I think Cameron [Vale] was there, in terms of looking for potential third party sponsors. That's what they would've come to me for. Who can we go and get [for] third party sponsorship?
>
> Third party agreements in most codes happens. You'd be very naïve ... we were led to believe they were being sealed and signed off by the NRL.

He says the deals made outside the salary cap should have been legitimate, anyway. 'If they were lodged, they wouldn't have been a problem. Simple as that.'

Ryan doesn't think much of the NRL salary cap. He uses the analogy: 'So you're allowed to take 5 per cent of drugs and that's okay but you get busted at 10 per cent. So it's okay to be a quarter of a million dollars over or half a million, what's the difference?'

He says his son Andrew handled all the Storm sponsorship for Jayco. 'I never negotiated any sponsorships,' he explains. 'That was his role. In terms of third party, well once again we weighed up the benefits of utilising the club or the player on a market value.' He thinks Schubert's 'discretion' was too inconsistent. 'I've been around all football codes and there are third party agreements happening. How is that classified as legal or illegal? We weren't aware of it as directors.'

As well as the email to Ryan, Vale wrote another damning document. He sent it to Waldron on 12 December 2007. It was entitled: '*Contract Variations Required to Get Back Under 2008 Salary Cap*.' Storm was going to be over the cap by more than $300,000 if something drastic wasn't done. He proposed Storm ask Inglis to move $100,000 of his pay from 2008 to 2009 and several other players to vary their contracts so a considerable load of wages could appear to be diverted to the following season. The players would then be paid the real money by Ryan or through Unity Foundation, Vale wrote.

The proposal was haphazard. Inglis's manager, Gainey, shook his head. He replied the largest variation he could make for his client was $40,000.

Another scenario carried out by Vale was cobbled together by Waldron. Inglis would accept the $40,000 delay, three other players (including Slater) would be involved in variations of more than $30,000 and several others would cop variations of $17,000. That sounded better. But would the players go for it?

Perhaps not wanting a verbal confrontation, the front office proposed these variations via notices in the footballers' 'pigeonholes'. The premiership heroes, still enjoying their victory buzz, were peeved and affronted. The players revolted, bound together and refused the variations.

Waldron was left with his title-winning team grimacing and bursting at the seams. The club was about to leave for the World Club Challenge, to play Leeds Rhinos in the United Kingdom. The 2008 NRL season was not far away. A salary cap declaration had to be made to Schubert. Storm had run out of time and options. Again, it was critical the franchise cut loose a front-line star, one of The Big Four, no less. But that emergency parachute was still being ignored. Neither the board, nor the football department, nor the front office was willing to make the hardest call of all.

Waldron, feeling bullet-proof from the premiership and the likelihood of another one soon, concentrated instead on finding another way to pay the players their 'overs'. And then he found one.

On 11 February, Vale met an official of a company called McManus Presents, owned by music concert promoter Andrew McManus.

Waldron had arranged to hire McManus Presents as its entertainment services provider. Previously the club had paid another provider, Great Big Events (internationally renowned for its contribution to the spectacular Sydney Olympics), to host functions and stage match day music and fireworks etc.

Now Great Big Events was out. McManus Presents was in. The new provider would do fine work but also help make payments to Storm players with News Ltd's money.

On Waldron's instructions, Vale would identify players to be paid. McManus Presents invoiced Storm for consultancy services regularly. Storm would honour the invoices and then McManus Presents would pay the players. At first the amounts would be small. For instance, Vale immediately sent a list of eight players to McManus Presents to receive $17,000. But then the payments would increase in size.

This *was* an adventurous new step to cheat the salary cap. Within one year, Storm had gone from considering itself being 'creative and bold' to being creative beyond measure.

Initially, only Waldron and Vale knew how the McManus Presents option functioned.

Vale carried out Waldron's wishes without fuss, for he had found his rescue ship and was mentally out the door. Privately, he had secured a job at North Melbourne Football Club in the AFL, in the role as chief financial officer under the stewardship of respected CEO Eugene Arocca.

Amid the salary cap scrambling, Vale told Waldron he was leaving. Waldron did not try to talk him into staying. Their relationship had gone cold. Waldron called a former colleague from St Kilda and offered him the CFO role.

Waldron's only request to Vale was that he serve out his time – three months – and do him one last favour to ease the salary cap pressure ...

The club was going to be over the 2008 limit on its legitimate NRL contracts alone. Those contract variations (the ones the players objected to) were still needed. It was frustrating for Waldron that the footballers were unwilling to agree to the shifting of pay. They had been amenable to it in the past, when there was a premiership to be won. But the spoils of victory had been experienced and a professional reality existed. They wanted the money they had been promised.

On 13 March 2008 Storm went ahead and varied the contracts of its best players, including Smith, Cronk, Inglis, Slater, Hoffman and Crocker for sums averaging $35,000 per player. This was done *without* permission from the footballers. They would still be paid those amounts but through McManus Presents, silently and strategically.

Past caring about Waldron or rules or anything other than getting out, Vale agreed to notify Schubert of the variations via email on the same day the club lodged its preseason salary cap declarations. Original copies of signed variations were promised to Schubert. Waldron had told Vale he would in fact get the players' permission. He just needed more time. 'I'll take care of it,' he told his resigning employee.

Storm stated to the NRL that it was under the salary cap for the coming season. Waldron and Chairman Moodie signed a statutory declaration to verify it was true.

Moodie did not know about the secret wages of his club's players. He assumed News Ltd audits were keeping track of the spending. His trust in his executive and club owners, their systems and procedures, was always absolute.

In April 2008, Vale finally walked out of his Storm nightmare and re-entered the warm embrace of the AFL. It had been a long and painful journey. By the time he freed himself from Waldron's employ, he was an emotional wreck. It would take months, even years for him to recover.

He would always look back on his final year at Storm with sadness. But he felt his decision to leave the way he did was sound. Vale didn't want his career ruined by a problem he did not create. The CFO understood other people might one day judge him and say: 'You know what, a bigger person would've done the right thing and challenged Waldron and not worried about the personal ramifications.' He could cop that because he made a clear choice to get out as quietly as he could and leave an electronic record of events for self-protection.

The only thought that nagged Vale on his departure was News Ltd's position regarding salary cap breaches. He would have had that opportunity to quietly tell Jourdain what was going on but baulked because he thought News Ltd either knew about the salary cap breaches or deliberately turned a blind eye to them. After all, the club had internal auditors going through the books twice a year. It was not a forensic audit but it was an audit.

Also, Vale was never directly asked about the salary cap.

In short, he did not want to hand a problem to a News Ltd executive who might hold it against him. In hindsight, it shows his inexperience and paranoia. It is also evidence of the communications disconnect between the owner and its franchise.

News Ltd's executives did not ask Vale why he was heading out the door.

Although he was based in Sydney, Jourdain was News Ltd's financial point man on the Storm board during Vale's three-and-a-half-year stint as CFO. He is now the CEO of North Queensland Cowboys in the NRL. He observes

> I still don't know why Cameron ended up resigning. I was disappointed that he wouldn't have been able to come and front us with it because we were continually asking the question ... to make sure we're under the cap. And then he left and still it didn't come out.
>
> I'd guess he was under a fair bit of pressure from others in Melbourne and I guess he had two choices, and I would guess with Cameron either of them was going to be confronting for him. With his personality, you just wouldn't think he would be involved in anything like that. I think he's a quiet guy, nice guy, hard worker, obviously diligent.

Jourdain reckons the salary cap *was* a major ongoing concern for News Ltd. 'It was [spoken about at] every board meeting and we required a report at every board meeting,' he concludes.

It was Jourdain's directive in 2007 that caused the email spat between the CFO and O'Sullivan.

Vale's final act as CFO of Storm – telling Schubert about the varied contracts of star players without their permission – caused no apparent unrest at NRL HQ. But did it ring alarm bells for the auditor? Perhaps. It would not be long before Schubert started to investigate the suspicious happenings at the country's best rugby league team.

Vale experienced some misgivings about handing over his post to an unsuspecting new financial officer. He must've felt like he was parachuting from a plane about to strike a mountain. Some letters of offer from previous years were still current (the contracts Storm had signed were for two, three, sometimes four years). The arrangement with McManus Presents had been set up. And the 'elite of the elite' (as O'Sullivan called them) had yet to be contracted beyond their mid-twenties. The overspending on players for the 2008 season was bulging. The years 2009 and 2010 ... well, no-one wanted to think about that.

As it turned out, Vale knew his successor. It was Matt Hanson, who had hired him to work in the finance team at St Kilda Football Club several years ago. He had not heard from Hanson for years. There was a change over period but Hanson didn't really need training, beyond trying to understand the complexities of the salary cap. Hanson had much more business experience than Vale. They were very different personalities. Ex-colleagues describe Vale as 'nice' or 'a quiet sorta bloke'. Co-workers called Hanson 'smooth' and 'charismatic' – 'more like Waldron'.

Vale's parting words to Hanson were: 'Be careful, Brian's doing stuff with the salary cap.'

Hanson replied, 'Doesn't worry me, I'm only staying three months to help him out.'

Vale felt better knowing that. And then he left, never to return.

Not long after, Storm was picked up again for breaking the salary cap rules. A breach notice, as per the NRL rules, was served upon Melbourne at the end of April. A fine followed in June. This time the figure was $13,917. Once again Schubert had found an overpayment to the club's top 25 players. Other clubs sanctioned for breaches in the 2007 season included North Queensland ($5000), Brisbane ($10,000), West Tigers ($46,800) Canberra ($45,813) and South Sydney ($70,135). Canterbury failed to provide Schubert with access to 'player information', but was not forced to pay any money.

Maher recalls Waldron being sorry for 'going over' in 2006 and 2007, though he did not know about the real wages situation. 'I remember we got fined and I was fucking filthy,' Maher says. 'Filthy with Brian and the department for it happening. It was certainly mentioned at board meetings and whatever else and certainly in front of him as well. He freely admitted we should have done that better.'

Maher says nothing led the board to believe the club was breaching the cap beyond the NRL penalties for the previous two seasons. 'As far as we knew we were in constant communication with Schubert, he knew exactly where we were,' he explains. 'We were talking about him in all these different things we were doing and whatever else.'

Again, News Ltd was in the position to sack the CEO for allowing the club to be fined.

News Ltd COO Macourt says his attitude to the cap had not changed since the days Ribot ran Storm. 'You can't have a company [half] owning the NRL with the salary cap as part of its rules and regulations and having a team owned by the same company breaching those rules and regulations.'

News Ltd maintained going over the cap was intolerable. But Waldron was *not* terminated.

Macourt explains: 'They [Storm's breaches] were probably very small and they were probably what I term disputable items.'

Just as clubs sometimes disputed Schubert's absolute discretion, so did News Ltd. Macourt was on the board of the NRL. Even he could see why the salary cap rules might be unclear sometimes.

'There are some things in terms of player benefits where the clubs took the view that things weren't a breach; and the NRL auditor took the view that they were,' Macourt says. 'You'd have to look at each one [breach] and say was there a reason the club might think that was not a breach and if there was ... for a relatively small amount of money, sacking a guy [Waldron] who you perceived to be otherwise doing a good job was probably a bit harsh.'

Macourt liked Waldron's energy and knew the team was winning. He also had empathy for the CEO's task of selling rugby league to Melbournians for the purpose of making a profit, which was, after all, his primary role.

CHAPTER 21

THE FATE OF AN HONEST MAN

Club and NRL administrators constantly discuss the merits and faults of the salary cap. Barely an in-season day passes without some mention of players' contracts in the rugby league press. Some stories demand big headlines, particularly if they are different and involve the voice of an insider breaking the game's code of silence, a fellowship as staunch as the best defence in the NRL.

The email inboxes on all NRL club CEOs went ding at about the same time. A lengthy document had been sent to them. Written by a former Newcastle Knights CFO, it alleged salary cap cheating and a cover-up.

Nothing like this appears on the football landscape without soon being leaked to the nation's biggest news outlets. Reactions are sought from club executives. Damage control ensues. Before you know it you're reading the stories under banners like: 'Knights deny salary cap claims' or 'Newcastle denies explosive salary cap allegations'. Sydney newspapers ran it big.

The email sent in 2007 to all clubs from an ex-Knights accountant was an offering of information about Newcastle's past. It included information and a call to arms. It detailed claims the Knights paid out a player's mortgage, issued sponsor-supplied cars and even shifted $200,000 in payments from 2002 back to 2001 (described as Grand Final bonuses on advice from the league) to avoid breaching the cap.

Knights CEO Steve Burraston immediately responded. He looked into it and said the claims were investigated by the NRL years ago and were baseless. (Burraston was new to the top job at Newcastle and had not been working at the club during the years the email referred to.) 'It couldn't be investigated any more thoroughly than it was back in that time,' he told the media.

The NRL sent another email to all clubs, stating:

> Any suggestion the NRL had failed to act in those investigations or that it has failed to act consistently or appropriately, is completely false. The NRL salary cap auditor had received pieces of correspondence from the employee in 2003 and had treated each seriously. The issue of the Grand Final bonuses in 2001 was investigated and addressed by the NRL – there was no breach of the rules.

Records show Newcastle did breach the cap several times from 2000 to 2003 and was fined: once for being $369,108 over the limit, another time for making an undisclosed payment of $115,000, and a third for paying $85,000 into a player's company.

The ex-CFO, author of the widely circulated document, believed the club should have been treated to heavier scrutiny. The question asked by NRL clubs on receipt of this spectacular document was: 'Who is this guy?'

His name is Brad Newton. Though he did nothing wrong, Newton has spent the past ten years trying to clear *his* name. Speaking publicly about salary cap cheating has damaged his life.

When Newton began working at the Knights in 2002, it took him six months to understand the salary cap. By then the top-of-the-ladder Bulldogs were stripped of competition points and heavily fined. 'When I checked our own books, I thought, hang on, we're not squeaky clean here either,' Newton explained. He spent the next six months striving to correct what he reckoned were imperfections in the Knights' practices. It caused internal conflict. Newton ended up resigning his position.

The Knights management did not wait for Newton to serve notice. He was ejected from the workplace. He spoke to the press about his concerns. On 6 July Fairfax journalist Danny Weidler wrote a story. It read:

> The former financial controller of Newcastle Knights has warned that the club could suffer a similar salary cap fate to the Bulldogs.
>
> NRL boss David Gallop admitted that the Knights situation was being looked at after some information was presented to the league six weeks ago ...

The NRL heard Newton's allegations. It investigated. But the league did not prosecute all Newton's charges. And Brad Newton could not let it go unanswered.

Newcastle is not a big city.

When Newton quit the CFO position he had backed himself to quickly find another job. He'd never been out of work. But no other local business would employ him after the Knights debacle. Professional and personal hardship followed.

'I was doing a bit of part-time consulting work, earning $300 a day at a place here and there to put food on the table,' he recalls. 'But I wasn't able to pay my mortgage. So the bank, after six months, wanted to foreclose on the mortgage. I had to access about thirty grand out of my super to pay the mortgage.'

Job seekers need references from two previous employers to find a job through an agency. The Knights hadn't given Newton a reference. He had applied for 22 positions and was awarded 11 interviews, without success. After six months of toil, Newton swallowed his pride and wrote to Newcastle's board of directors, pleading for a 'fair go'. He was written a reference. Almost a year after he was ordered from the Newcastle football club premises, Newton took a job in Fiji, as a financial controller at a resort. He was there for 10 months, sending money back to his family.

'It [the Knights experience] probably set me back about ten years,' Brad estimates of his career decline.

Newton's family life suffered too. Typical of people who believe an injustice has been ignored, Newton became obsessed, difficult to live with. His bright view of life was now obstructed. His marriage became strained. His children could not understand why he would cause them to be teased in the schoolyard. They came home in tears. His son once said: 'Dad, all my mates are saying, "Why is your dad making up all these lies about the Knights, he's just trying to get the Knights in trouble and get kicked out of the NRL."'

He was still trying to get 'closure' when he sent his document in 2007. It coincided with a league CEO conference. Every official in the competition began discussing it.

'The only way I was going to get closure was if the truth was out there and people said, "Hang on, they did rort the cap, and that guy wasn't just a whistleblower trying to upset the apple cart".'

Ironically, Newton singled out Brian Waldron as one of the chiefs most likely to join his fight for honesty and full disclosure. Newton wrote to Waldron separately:

> Dear Brian
>
> Further to my email of last Thursday which seemed to just push the Knights and NRL further into denial I wish to make the following points and seek your advice. I firmly believe there are only probably 2 NRL clubs of the 16 that I think would really care about the preferential salary cap treatments – I would suggest yourself and Denis Fitzgerald *would be the only two I would single out as wanting to*, and having the balls to, make a difference to how the cap is, in my belief, inconsistently applied. Firstly I must state that I still stand by every one of my allegations and always will as they are all true and I would swear this on the lives of my four dear children.
>
> ... I don't know you personally Brian, but I understand you to be a consummate professional administrator and a decent but tough man with ethical standards ...

Waldron did not reply personally to Newton, who would suffer several more years of personal indignation over his claims the NRL did not do all it could to address salary cap cheating.

But perhaps it was Newton's letter that prompted Waldron to talk to Gallop about it this time. He told the NRL chief he should hold a salary cap moratorium so every club could come clean and start again, abiding by the rules from then.

Gallop confirms, 'Yeah, I do remember that. I'm sure he did suggest it to me but I would've said, "No we can't do it", the days of moratoriums finished when we put the Bulldogs back to last in 2002.' Gallop was often told overpayments were rife. 'That kind of conversation happens all the time,' he explains. 'The only answer to it is: Bring forward the evidence, give it to Schubert.'

A decade after working for the Knights, Brad Newton still wonders whether it was worth going public with his views.

Would he do it again?

> I probably would – but I don't know if too many would be so stupid because I was never going to gain anything from it other than having the truth known. The members didn't give a shit. I suppose, how stupid was I thinking they would? They just want their team to win. And rightly so, they're sports followers. And I think the media make a lot more out of it than the public do.

The one thing that still burns is how isolated he felt, how unsupported by his colleagues. 'All it would have taken is one of these men to stand up,' Newton says, shaking his head. 'But no.'

Newton's experience is a cautionary tale. If you speak out what difference will it make?

CHAPTER 22

SUN & STORM / BELLAMY STAYS

Ten years after Storm played its first match it had become a well-established franchise, a two-time premiership team. All the major bigwigs had played their part. Waldron was leading an increasingly successful front office team. News Ltd continued to hold up its part of the deal, providing its team with money and newspaper coverage. The *Herald Sun*, under the editorship of Blunden, had been unwavering in its support.

By now Blunden had been promoted to managing director. A new editor-in-chief had been appointed. He was Bruce Guthrie.

Guthrie was no lover of scrums and tries. But he understood News Ltd's partnership with rugby league and he realised his readership's devotion to sport. On the same weekend Storm beat Manly for the NRL 2007 title, Geelong had won the AFL flag – its first premiership in decades.

The *Sunday Herald Sun* covered the Cats' breakthrough but there was still a lot left in the story for the Monday paper.

As Storm was beating Manly on the Sunday, Guthrie went into the newsroom, and attended a 'news conference' and 'picture conference'. He had to decide what to run on page one the next day. His decision was to lead with the Geelong celebrations, despite Storm's victory. Those types of AFL front pages sell tens of thousands of extra newspaper copies if done right. Guthrie had a discussion with his trusted deputy John Trevorrow about how to handle the Storm story. They decided to run a pointer (a mention and guide to further coverage) on page one and spread Bellamy's boys' win over several pages inside the sport section. Guthrie saw the paper on the Monday and thought his editorial team had nailed it.

No worries. Or so he thought.

Several months later Guthrie found out almost by accident that Storm was playing in the World Club Challenge and one of his photographers was assigned to cover the match. In journalistic terms, Guthrie considered the match 'marginal'. It was never going to compete for page one or even the back page. It seemed a strange assignment. He was then dismayed to learn the photographer's trip was being paid for by the Melbourne Storm.

'I remember at the time thinking this was a newspaper equivalent of cash for comment,' Guthrie says. 'And if you accepted this and applied it across the entire paper it meant our resources could be rented out.'

Guthrie asked his sports editor what it was all about, only to be told Peter Blunden had approved it. The editor-in-chief sent an email to his managing director.

'I remember using the phrase like, I don't want to be Joan of Arc mate but I need to sleep on this one,' Guthrie recalls. 'When I got in the next morning all hell broke loose. It started off with a couple of really intemperate emails, written in capital letters – so he [Blunden] was even yelling in his emails. He thought I was being ridiculous.'

Guthrie rang Blunden to ask why he was so angry. He says he was met with 'invective and vile'. Blunden took the opportunity to criticise Guthrie's coverage of the Storm premiership almost five months before, pointing out 'we own the club'.

'I've been in newspapers for a long time,' Guthrie says. 'On the Richter scale it was about a ten.'

Today, Blunden stands by his criticism of Guthrie's handling of the Storm victory. He says it was a bigger story than the editor-in-chief realised.

'I just think if a Melbourne [team] wins the second biggest sport in Australia it deserves some prominence,' he says. 'It's got some news value.'

He wouldn't have replaced the Geelong story on the front page. But he adds, 'The AFL Grand Final had been on the Saturday ... it [Geelong and Storm] could've been combined [on page one].'

Guthrie didn't understand until that moment Blunden's fondness for rugby league and Storm. The new man in charge of the *Herald Sun* had received weekly invitations to Storm matches and functions from Waldron but ignored them. 'Frankly I was too busy with the paper to go,' Guthrie says. And he was an Australian rules devotee.

He folded on the fight with Blunden over the photographer. Blunden attended the World Club Challenge – as a fan. Storm was without several key players for the cold match on the other side of the world and lost.

When Bellamy arrived at Storm he had been a first-time coach. He came with impressive wraps as an assistant to Wayne Bennett in Brisbane. But there were no certainties he would be successful as a boss. Often the best deputies cannot make a successful jump to the top job. The desire to be adored by players – as assistants often are – is the noose that strangles insecure coaches in higher office. Bellamy was seemingly different. He made it appear he did not need to be liked by his footballers; he wanted only to be respected. In turn, he was loved. He had made the finals five out of five years. Now, for the first time in his life, he was a champion.

And he was soon out of contract. He was not the only one. But he was the most important, in contracting terms, because all the stars revolved around him.

In 2008 the Broncos tried to lure Bellamy back to Queensland by offering him the senior coaching role he once coveted. Bennett was finally moving on, heading to St George Illawarra for a pretty sum and a new challenge. While Bellamy weighed up the offer, players were uncertain about their futures. Smith was 'coming off'. There was talk Inglis might go someplace else for richer reward.

Bellamy and his manager did their negotiations for a new contract with Waldron. The coach and CEO had a decent working relationship but were not too friendly. Both had strong wills. They had vastly different backgrounds. However, their professional relationship was based on enough mutual respect to operate the best football club in the land without major incident. Occasionally they would argue over differences of opinion. But ultimately they shared the same aim: providing a first-class environment for players.

Bellamy was tempted to leave Storm. His children were still in Queensland after all this time. He missed being close to them. Brisbane wooed Bellamy with a strong desire. He went very close to signing, but baulked at the last moment, after the Broncos' management became obviously impatient and insisted he hurry up. Bellamy, not pleased with the ultimatum or the way it was delivered, gave Waldron his signature.

At the time, he told the newspapers,

> One of the real positives is the type of club we've got here. It's got a great culture at the moment and I really admire the playing group – not only as footy players but as people and that was real attractive for me staying here. The footy and administrative staff are very committed to making rugby league work in Melbourne.

His deal was reported to be worth $2 million. The Portland workaholic was to be paid as handsomely as his best ball players.

CHAPTER 23

WALDRON TEETERS / QUESTIONS OF LEADERSHIP

News Ltd considered denying Waldron another contract as CEO of Storm. It was long discussed at board level and in the halls of power at the media company. It had nothing to do with the salary cap. It was more his style as a manager.

Ex-director Jourdain explains, 'Everyone has their strengths and weaknesses and there was a significant internal debate when his contract came up for renewal.'

Waldron had been brought in to increase the club's profile and increase sponsorship. He had been successful in those areas. But, as Jourdain says, 'There were other areas of his management that probably ... there could be improvement.'

News Ltd CEO John Hartigan still liked Waldron, despite his flaws. 'He was a person who would embarrass News from time to time by saying things that I felt didn't reflect the truth and tried to make a bigger man of himself,' Hartigan recalls. 'On occasions I had to pull him up because of it but it wasn't things that rang alarm bells. It was just a person who was over-enthusiastic, in my view, and gilded the lily a bit.'

News Ltd's position as Storm backer had been buoyed in recent years due to improved performance on and off the field. It was still losing millions of dollars every year but it *was* finding traction in the Melbourne sporting market. Its eventual sale no longer looked pie in the sky.

'We wanted to ensure the longevity of the club, not just to walk away from it,' Hartigan says. The owner wanted to make the club financially self-sufficient. That way, it could sell the team and continue to reap its advertising and broadcasting benefits.

Ultimately, the decision was to keep Waldron going for another term. He was no longer a gamble. The owner knew the man they were trusting once again to drive their vehicle. It valued his strengths and would live with his shortcomings. No new management procedures or safeguards or compliance standards were introduced.

There were key changes to the club's structure and personnel during this period. Jourdain left the board. He had served for six years and was replaced by a Melbourne-based finance man: Herald and Weekly Times accountant Craig Watt. (John Webster had also departed by now.) Watt and Stanton were now the two News Ltd–appointed directors. Moodie (chairman), Maher, Ryan and Fawcett were the Independents.

Another key appointment was Frank Ponissi.

After the departure of O'Sullivan (and football manager Dean Lance) a large void needed to be filled. Ponissi, the same man who spent six months in Victoria developing rugby league in 1990, was hired as General Manager of Football Operations. Ponissi would become the club's calming influence, a conduit between the footy department and front office, not unlike Mick Moore in the early days. Ponissi was much admired at Storm and still is.

When he was offered the newly created position in Melbourne he sweated over it. The only negative for Ponissi was Storm's recent premiership. Football leaders want to start new adventures with teams that need improving. Otherwise, what are you striving for? But this team was yet to discover its best, or so it was believed; its best players were still very young.

Ponissi made his decision based on Bellamy's reputation and first impression. 'I'd had a couple of bad experiences in rugby union overseas where we didn't have a strong leader and I thought, I'm not going to go with a weak leader,' Ponissi says. 'I wanna go with someone who's strong. Craig Bellamy was a major attraction.'

Ponissi took the job. On arrival in Melbourne, Ponissi asked what Bellamy expected of him. He immediately detected Bellamy was a person he could be 'up front with'.

'It was just so clear cut,' Ponissi remembers. 'I left that meeting, I knew exactly how he saw my role and what he expected of me so that made it really easy. There was no grey area.'

Ponissi's role was to support Bellamy by carrying some of his load. The game was expanding. Media requirements were increasing. Recruitment needed an overseer. The front office needed dealing with, massaging sometimes. Player managers were constantly calling, trying to extract more pay and benefits. Often they rang the coach. Bellamy told Ponissi, 'I just wanna coach. The other stuff, I just need someone to rely on and look after that.'

A man called Darren Bell was hired as the recruitment manager. Bell had spent the past 16 years involved in junior and senior rugby league in Brisbane. He proved to be an outstanding operator. Ponissi's new position included facilitation of all recruitment and retention of players, overseeing Bell's work but answering to Bellamy, as football department boss, and Waldron, as club head.

'So that was a bit all over the place,' Ponissi recalls. 'In terms of who's responsible, the final charge.'

Being 'all over the place in terms of who's responsible' is common in some Australian professional football departments, which are morphing and growing every year. It is also problematic, as Melbourne Storm would find out.

The former CEO of Telstra Ziggy Switkowski examined the inner workings of AFL club Essendon in 2013, amid a scandal over supplements given to players. He found, 'There was a lack of clarity about who was in charge of the Football Department.'

The same was true at Storm. Ponissi was a 'general manager' but his experience was in coaching and development. And he was initially Bellamy's junior. Switkowski wrote in his Essendon review:

> The position of GM, Football Operations is an especially difficult one given subordinates and peers, eg. coaches, can be charismatic alpha males who carry the weight of supporters' expectations on their shoulders. But this is a critical appointment requiring a strong capable individual who had the respect of the football staff and the support of the CEO.

Football clubs value having flexibility in their departments, wrote Switkowski. He warned this workforce approach needed discipline and 'clear expressions of changed accountabilities, updated job descriptions, confirmed reporting lines'.

Storm's board was trying to address governance issues in the commercial department. But not enough was being done to modernise processes in the football department. There were forever fuzzy lines of responsibility (as Switkowski neatly called them in his Essendon review).

For instance, Ponissi had been given the job to run recruitment and player contracts but within months Waldron was handling the best players' deals.

But if GM, Football Operations was a difficult title to bear, what must it have been like to be the CFO?

Vale's replacement, Matt Hanson, was confident and capable. By any standard he was over-qualified, though nothing could possibly have prepared him for the path his life would take after reuniting with Waldron.

From his earliest years, growing up on Victoria's Mornington Peninsula, Hanson was a hard-working, high-achieving individual. He excelled at football and racing off-road cars, and competed in his first representative Australian rules match at an inter-school carnival. After graduating from high school, he was invited to train with AFL club St Kilda by the revered scout John Beveridge, a kind recruiter, an industry legend, with a computer-like memory for names and faces

There were more than one hundred Under 19 players at the first night of training at St Kilda. There were only 50 spots on the squad and 21 on the team. To impress, Hanson blitzed the 4-kilometre time trials. Beveridge pulled him aside and said, 'Right, we're going to get you in the gym son.' He was so skinny. But he made the team as a wingman.

Hanson attended university and after obtaining a Bachelor of Commerce he applied for six-week summer work placements at accounting firms, which often lead to full-time employment. After a long interview process that required him for the first time in his life to wear a tie, Hanson was awarded a position with Ernst & Young. He dutifully, if not delightfully, examined companies' finances. He was 22 years old and it introduced him to many more people. It helped his grounding in business and his networking. His next difficult step was to become a chartered accountant, another box he ticked through dogged application.

His career became his absolute priority. He was employed by leading Melbourne businessman Ian Collins to help correct the finances of Colonial Stadium, the city's new retractable-roof venue. The stadium's business plan had been a disaster. Originally modelled on costing $390 million, it ended up requiring $460 million. Hanson began taking minutes at the board meetings, featuring heavyweights like Kerry Stokes, Mike Fitzpatrick (AFL commissioner), Julian Clark (managing director HWT) and Ross Oakley. This gave him a front-row seat to the corporate big time.

Hanson's finance boss at Colonial departed not long after he arrived. Collins promoted him to CFO – he was 27 years old. This saw Hanson working day-to-day with Collins on a gruelling schedule. They worked up to 20-hour days to fix the venture. Some days the younger man would go home only to have a shower and put on a clean suit. Collins said to him, 'You can't buy this experience you're getting now.'

A couple of years later the stadium's finances improved. The grass (which was an ongoing problem) was knitting, the AFL draw was improving and the funding issues had been sorted out. Hanson was being paid top dollar. One day, a former Ernst & Young colleague rang Hanson and said, 'You're gunna get a call from Brian Waldron, the new CEO of St Kilda.' Waldron was reshaping the St Kilda staff.

It became apparent Hanson would have the opportunity to return to the club he once represented and always cheered. Waldron offered him a significant pay rise to manage St Kilda's finances.

One of the board members at St Kilda took Hanson aside and mentioned: 'There's every chance Waldron won't work out as CEO and we see you as having that sort of potential, should things not work out with him.' This was early in Waldron's tenure, before he grew into his job.

Hanson and Waldron worked effectively as colleagues and were comfortable in each other's presence, despite their different styles (Hanson was used to wearing a stiff collar and tie; Waldron was an open-neck, feet-on-the-desk type of executive). Hanson's first job was to relieve the financial department of four people and bring in new blood. One of his subsequent hirings was Vale, a terrific nuts-and-bolts accountant.

After a year at St Kilda, Hanson was offered a job by Ray King, a Saints director. It was a classically St Kilda move, a board member poaching his team's key financial staffer to help fix another enterprise. King was chairman of the Taverner Hotel Group. Hanson was all of a sudden earning an impressive wage. He was 32 years old when he crossed to Taverner. He was a CFO but circumstances saw him soon become for a brief time the acting CEO of the business 100 per cent owned by private equity. As part of its restructure, Taverner management was offered a chance to invest in the company before it was sold. Hanson scraped together what he could and bought up. He and the rest of the executive multiplied their monies by 11. Hanson was 35 years old when he left that position, and relatively wealthy.

His next job was assisting the same private equity firm called Catalyst Investment Managers, which was in the process of buying 49 per cent of the fruit and vegetable retailer Moraitis, owned by family patriarch Nick Moraitis. For this Hanson moved to Sydney and was making four times the wage he was on just a few years earlier at Colonial Stadium. He would have stayed longer and perhaps sought a promotion but a personal issue brought him back to Melbourne. He kept racing off-road cars all this time and won the Australian Championship in his class. His father was with him to celebrate.

It was 2007. Hanson bought a house in Melbourne and looked for work. There were no rainbows beaming above the financial markets and private equity positions became scarce. At the start of 2008, Hanson's phone rang. It was Waldron. 'Do you want to become CFO of Melbourne Storm?'

Hanson replied, 'Not really mate. How many staff?'

'Three,' Waldron said. Hanson had managed 70 employees at his last job.

Waldron tried to sell his old workmate on the merits of rugby league. Waldron could always sell well, but this pitch fell flat. Hanson didn't think much of the sport.

But Waldron kept ringing. 'Just come and keep the seat warm, while you keep looking for something else,' he said. Hanson wasn't struggling for cash but he had no other prospects. It is not impressive to potential employers to be sitting on the professional sidelines too long. Eventually, Hanson successfully negotiated with Waldron more money than the Storm position was worth.

In his second week on the job, Hanson went to one of his favourite restaurants with Waldron and Ryan for lunch. Nearing the end of the meal Waldron asked Hanson if he and Ryan could 'have a few minutes'. Hanson had to go and stand outside. Later, Waldron apologised and said, 'We were just talking about a bit of stuff for players and payments and stuff.'

'Whatever,' Hanson said. He didn't care enough to worry about it.

CHAPTER 24

'550 WOULD BE BETTER'

In 2008 the re-signing of Inglis became a major issue for Melbourne Storm.

Inglis was the most exciting prospect in Australian sport. Three months earlier he had helped his country beat New Zealand in the Centenary Test at the Sydney Cricket Ground. In doing so, the quiet 21-year-old created a memory that will outlive him. It happened five minutes into the contest. Inglis ran underneath a precise Jonathan Thurston kick, bobbled the catch and then, falling over the dead ball line, bent his lean torso into a horseshoe and tossed the ball softy over his head into the lap of a teammate for a try. It looked like a stunt from the *Matrix* and was so unprecedented the television commentators needed to watch two slow motion replays before comprehending what Inglis had done. He smiled humbly.

TV commentator Matthew Johns gushed like a burst water main. 'You'll see that on the highlight reels for as long as the game's played.'

After that, the press began speculating that Inglis had outgrown the NRL and could be tempted to fulfil his true earning capacity playing football overseas, where there was no cap on wages. Newshounds and columnists were chin-scratching about whether Inglis might want to sack his manager, Gainey, and sign on with younger agent and boxing promoter Khoder Nasser, who had become a friend.

Gainey received a call from Waldron, who said, 'We're keen to extend Greg's contract. When can we get together to discuss a long-term deal for Greg at the Storm?' Waldron had decided to do the deal, instead of General Manager of Football Operations, Ponissi.

There was a quiet understanding between Waldron and Gainey. Both had been quoted in the press as saying they were not worried about Inglis leaving Storm. But still ... just to be safe. Neither wanted to even contemplate the star heading overseas. Gainey replied, 'Quite happy to do so.'

At that time Inglis had a decent contract: $420,000 (2009) and $450,000 (2010). Gainey knew any extension would mean a pay rise for player and manager.

Waldron phoned Gainey again two weeks later. This time he was more specific. He explained Melbourne Storm had concerns about the speculation that Nasser and prizefighter Anthony Mundine were telling Inglis he was undervalued in rugby league and could get more money from French rugby union – just like dual Kiwi international Sonny Bill Williams.

He sounded determined to make a deal. Gainey liked the tone of Waldron's voice. He offered empathy. They both wanted the same thing: to keep Inglis, a jewel of Australian sport, on their books.

Several meetings were held between Gainey, Inglis and Storm. Before one of the earliest meetings, Gainey spoke privately to Inglis about his asking price.

Gainey said, 'I think you should go for 500 to 550.'

Inglis instructed, '550 would be better.'

'Fine.'

Five hundred and $50,000 a year – a good place to start.

Waldron sat down with them later and opened with a curious statement. He said he had been told by the NRL that he must do whatever it takes to secure the future of Inglis at the Storm and in the NRL long term. Gainey took Waldron to mean that he had been empowered by the NRL, News Ltd and the Storm board of directors to negotiate whatever it would take – that he had totally free hand to keep Inglis in the league.

The CEO proposed a four-year deal.

Inglis had been contracted to Storm for 2007–2010. His performances were improving and his stature in the game was growing at club, state and international levels. Gainey said, 'Greg will need a financial package of $550,000 per season to extend his contract to represent his true market value.'

Waldron nodded and said he didn't think that was a problem. But he added the package would have to include third party agreements and mentioned the possibility of a federal government program for outstanding Indigenous athletes. Gainey says he thought Waldron meant the NRL would approve any increase in salary and perhaps involve its sponsors in some legitimate side deals.

Gainey spent the rest of the meeting chasing up extras. Inglis wanted a sponsor's car to drive and he wanted airfares for his family. The agent also mentioned money owed. Inglis had still not been paid promised money through the league development scheme. Also, there was $40,000 outstanding from a contract variation.

The world's most exciting player had not spoken much during the meeting, letting his agent go to work.

In wrapping up, Waldron concluded that he would seek the endorsement and ratification of the board at Storm and get back to Gainey.

As everyone was leaving Inglis said to Waldron, 'Is there any chance of getting a boat for Dad?' Not even Gainey knew his client was going to make the request.

Waldron replied, 'When you're ready I'll give you a contact person and they'll look after you. Up to a maximum of $30,000.'

The boat order was unusual enough to be subsequently spoken about at the football club.

Ponissi says he heard about it. 'I was aware of a request for a boat,' he recalls. 'A player and his manager will always want more and more. I was not aware of what was delivered.'

A week after the Federation Square meeting, Gainey and Inglis caught up briefly at Manly Pacific Hotel. Storm was playing the Sea Eagles at Brookvale the following day. The agent and footballer itemised the terms for extending Inglis's contract. The list read:

$550,000 per season
a motor vehicle
payment of the outstanding $40,000 from 2007
a boat for his father
$33,000 Unity Foundation cadetship balance
incentives for Dally M/Clive Churchill etc. awards
family airfares

Inglis liked the look of the items and numbers. 'I'll stay if you can get that deal done,' he said. Then Inglis flagged, almost as an afterthought, his desire for Storm to provide rental assistance to his parents should they relocate to Melbourne (they were planning to do so). Gainey said he would try to include it. He left the meeting experiencing relief and satisfaction.

Manly hosted Melbourne the next night. It was a critical match. The teams were atop the ladder. Within one minute there was a fight between ex-Storm halfback Matt Orford and his old teammate Matt Geyer, then 35 years old, approaching the very final stages of his career (he would retire after the play-offs).

Three minutes had gone when Crocker wrapped his arm around Brent Kite's throat and punches were swapped. The air pinged with hostility. Storm pressed and the Sea Eagles shot out of the defensive line hoping to maim. But Melbourne was not intimidated. In the eighth minute Smith was at dummy half, home on the field. He passed to Cronk, who passed back inside to Slater – *left foot step* – one hand flick. Geyer ran in for a try.

Storm moved the ball swiftly, trying to find Inglis and Folau in space. Inglis, playing five-eighth, looked a picture of fitness. He defended and attacked on his toes.

But the Sea Eagles were no ordinary opponents. They were physically strong and hyped-up, eventually scoring a try through Glen Hall. Slater was being tackled fiercely. Storm absorbed another Manly swell of attacks. The captain, Smith, appeared shaken by the force of the resistance. He played conservatively.

Manly was a title contender but Melbourne was harbouring a dream of winning an unprecedented three Minor Premierships in a row. It would not move aside. Just before half-time Cronk chipped a kick midfield, Slater picked it up on the half-volley and passed right to Folau, who made long strides to score. The crowd fell silent, as if it had witnessed a car crash and not a celebration of football at its purest, a wonderful merger of instinct and training.

In the second half, Cronk barged past defenders like a front rower to put his team up 16–6. David Williams went over for a try in the corner at the other end. Then Inglis hurt his ankle. He had to be strapped heavily and appeared in pain. For the last few minutes of the match, Storm held on through grit and will. Such was the tension, Slater made mistakes – a missed field goal and a knock-on. It was a terrific defensive effort to prevent the Sea Eagles winning. Manly appeared to be at top flight, in dynamic balance no less. It was the match of the year. When

80 minutes expired, a handful of Storm fans were drowned out by the locals' boos. The score was 16–10. It seemed inevitable from that point the two teams would meet again in the Grand Final.

If Manly improved from this performance it would be difficult to beat again. Storm needed everything to go well from that point if it was going to win consecutive titles.

A few days later, Waldron telephoned Gainey. He said, 'I have arranged a meeting with the NRL to discuss third party possibilities available to Greg.' The meeting was scheduled for 11am on 26 August. Waldron said he could not attend but Ponissi would escort Inglis on behalf of Storm.

The meeting with the league went ahead at NRL headquarters in Sydney, the morning after Storm beat Penrith 40–6. Present were Greg Inglis, Allan Gainey, NRL chief executive David Gallop, NRL marketing manager Paul Kind, NRL community relations manager Matthew Francis and Ponissi. The men discussed potential third party agreements for the footballer.

Gainey says the discussion with the NRL representatives centred on NRL sponsor Telstra, Indigenous programs and funding from NRL media partners. 'Paul Kind and Matthew Francis both said they were confident that the NRL would be able to assist with third party agreements,' Gainey recalls.

> Kind spoke in particular about Telstra using Inglis to promote the broadband network in outback regions. Gallop said very little, deferring to Kind on most occasions.
>
> It was absolutely extraordinary in my experience for a player's contractual negotiations to directly involve the NRL at the highest level. To me, the presence at this meeting, arranged by Waldron, of Gallop, Kind and Francis and the active role they played demonstrated the truth of my inference that Waldron's authority to keep Inglis in the NRL came, in part at least, from the NRL itself and reflected his enormous importance to the code as one of its biggest drawcards.

Asked about that meeting five years later, Gallop says he does not recall being there.

Pressed on whether it was appropriate for the league boss to assist an individual player attain TPAs, he defended his record. 'As long as they're within the rules. There's a misconception that there's some ban on third party agreements. There isn't, but they have to be within the rules. And they have to not form part of the contractual negotiations and be guaranteed by the club.'

Ponissi did not think it was a special meeting and was not aware who instigated it. 'I don't know whether it was called by Waldron in saying we need some help to keep this bloke,' he says. 'Or I dunno whether it was the NRL calling the meeting saying what's going on, we can't lose this ... I don't know, I just don't know.' He remembers a positive meeting, 'with no guarantees or anything like that'. He adds, 'To me it was a real initial meeting to get the ball rolling, a starter meeting rather than a decision-making meeting.'

Waldron subsequently rang Gainey and arranged to meet him in Sydney, at Sheraton on the Park Hotel. The CEO and the agent went through Inglis's list and made one change. After the meeting Waldron said he would prepare an NRL contract.

Four weeks after the brilliantly violent match at Brookvale, Storm needed to win by 26 points in the final round at Olympic Park against South Sydney to gain yet another Minor Premiership. Inglis had been under personal strain. His father was sick. But he made himself available for the match.

In the first five minutes he offloaded a delicate pass over a defender's head to Geyer, who was playing his final home game. He scored. The whole team rushed in to celebrate. It was a worrying sight for the Rabbitohs. Storm was playing with passion. When Cronk gave a short ball to Hoffman on the left-hand side of the field before half-time the score was 20–4. Melbourne needed only to extend its lead by 10 in the second half. Slater made a 95-metre kick return in the 52nd minute for a try and then Folau broke the defence and ran for 40 metres. His inside pass bounced into the hands of Slater, who went over again.

Bellamy watched the clock. He *wanted* that Minor Premiership. Such was the desire of the home team – Storm's forwards even won a scrum against the feed. It was their night. The final score was 42–4. But there was worrying evidence that Melbourne was not in great shape for the play-offs. Dallas Johnson left the field with an injured knee in the 78th minute. The rest of the team appeared tired; striving for those late season wins had taken something out of them. Melbourne wasn't just saying goodbye to Geyer that night, although the crowd in the Tawera Nikau stand gave only him a standing ovation. Crocker was leaving for Super League in the United Kingdom at year's end. Israel Folau had been recruited to Brisbane on a rich deal. Keeping the young phenomenon was too hard even for Waldron and Bellamy. Anthony Kaufusi (North Queensland) and Jeremy Smith (St George Illawarra) were also leaving after the finals.

For once, Melbourne Storm was being worn down by emotion. This September, Bellamy's team was the rubber band being stretched. It would snap in a way no-one could have predicted.

CHAPTER 25

BELLYACHES

The weary champion from the southern capital lost its first final to New Zealand. It was the biggest upset in NRL finals history, the Warriors becoming the only team to finish eighth and beat the Minor Premiership holders. They did it with a winning try in the 78th minute to make the final score 18–15 after Storm led all night. A missed tackle from Folau had allowed New Zealand space to run. Five-eighth Michael Witt scored the special four points. Good night nurse.

Storm had one last magnificent performance in it for 2008. The problem was it needed to win three more matches to lift the trophy again.

In the second week of the play-offs Storm opposed the Broncos in Brisbane. Melbourne was losing by two points with one minute remaining. It had been a tough but fair contest of the highest standard. It seemed the season would soon be over for Smith and the rest of the players. Bellamy sat in the coach's box and made not a sound ... until the ball went to Inglis at the end of a splendid chain of passes. Inglis dived over the line with one arm out, like Superman flies, and touched the ball down. Storm won 16–14. Venerable Brisbane five-eighth Darren Lockyer screamed, 'NOOOOOOOOOOOO.' The other Broncos were left splayed on the turf like road kill.

Strapped around the head, blood staining his left eyebrow, Smith sat at the media conference after the game. Ask how he rated the win, he said,

> One of the best. It was a strange feeling when we went over at the end. Obviously very happy for our club and our team but I

> guess there's a feeling of disappointment for the Broncos, because I know how it felt last week. We got beat in the last minute and obviously I got a lot of good mates in the Broncos. They looked very disappointed. Last week a couple of our boys said it was tougher than losin' a Grand Final. Knowin' how much both teams threw at each other tonight, I think that game was up to Grand Final standard.

He hinted at the team straining under the weight of another campaign.

'I think players would prefer a week off,' Smith observed.

> It's pretty hard backin' up every week after you've played 24 rounds. But, I think Craig made a good point. If we'd have won last week it probably would've let a few things go that needed addressing in our game. That was brought up last Monday leading into this one and I think if we had won that game against the Warriors we probably would've struggled next week, thinkin' that everything's alright.

Then came the question that lit a bomb's fuse.

'What's your recollections of that tackle on Sam Thaiday?' a hack asked.

'Yeah, obviously there was a lot of us involved in that tackle and I see on the replay my arm was up around his head but ...'

That tackle happened in the 59th minute. It was a particularly physical period of the game. Shoulder charges were everywhere. A short fight had followed a high tackle from Crocker. Adrenaline was surging through the bigger blokes. Brisbane was in front 12–6. Inglis kicked the ball 50 metres. It went dead. Karmichael Hunt retrieved it. Then Sam Thaiday hit up ... Punches were thrown. Players ran in. What happened?

A whistle. Thaiday was furious – it was the tackle he didn't like. Cameron Smith was involved.

It had been building all season. Opposition coaches and players had been complaining about the way Storm wrestled in the tackle, attacked the head. In fact, there had been criticism for years. Storm had trained to debilitate the movement of a tackled player. Former Melbourne player Brett O'Farrell added spice to the allegations in April 2008 when he was quoted in the News Ltd newspapers, explaining the history of the Storm grapple.

'I know that Craig Bellamy has denied that they train to do it and all that sort of stuff,' O'Farrell said. 'They do. At the end of the day we were drilled over and over and over by John Donehue [wrestling coach] to do it and to hide it and to conceal it.'

Bellamy responded to grapple allegations at the time by declaring, 'I'm telling you that's a load of crap.'

Now Smith was being accused of grappling Thaiday against the rules. He had been put on report. The replays of the incident would not comfort the Storm skipper. In slow motion, it looked bad.

A commentator said, 'Is that the chicken, is that the chicken?' A chicken wing tackle is also treated with frowns.

Thaiday was on his knees, his feet pinned by another Storm man, being bent backward. His fantastic hair whipped like frayed rope. At the time, a touch judge came in, said to the ref, 'He [Cameron Smith] actually held the player by the neck, there's no need for it, just a caution.'

The referee lectured Smith about head-high tackles, and threatened to send the next errant tackler to the sin bin.

Smith said, 'Sweet.'

'Nervous about it?' the hack followed up in the media conference.

'Aw, not really,' said Smith. 'I don't think there was any intent involved ... I didn't try to twist or choke him or anything like that. But y'know that's not up to us.'

In the change room below the stadium Storm players were celebrating like they had won the competition. Then the news was passed around. Smith was in trouble. He was going to be charged.

In the following days, newspapers and radio talk-back programs filled columns and airtime with discussions about Smith's fate. Would he be suspended? The level of attention and flavour of the debate incensed Bellamy. He steamed about bias. The coach was right to be concerned but not by anything untoward. The tackle had been dangerous. Slowed down for television, it looked even worse. Storm's captain was subsequently suspended for two weeks – the rest of the season.

Storm beat Cronulla in the preliminary final 28–0, without its esteemed hooker, a rare feat. Cronk was at his best, organising the team as expertly as any West End director. The victory set up a Grand Final against Manly.

There was no joy, but instead enormous tension in the Melbourne camp after flogging the Sharks. Bellamy still wanted to make a public statement about his displeasure over the Smith suspension. He had been silent all week, biding his time. Storm's board representatives advised him to 'let it go'. Previously, they had planned to help him craft an address, but now what was the point? They had qualified for the season decider. Even Waldron thought it was a bad idea to rage against the NRL and judiciary at such an important time. But Bellamy no longer took counsel. He went ahead and ripped in. At the post-game media conference, when the journalists were expecting happy Bellamy they witnessed 'Bellyache' at his most aggressive.

'I don't think Cameron Smith got a fair go,' he began.

> Cameron Smith, ten minutes after the game last week, was hung out to dry. The press conference ... got hijacked by some of you guys in the media that had him hung out to dry straight away and then it continued for four or five days. There are some sections of the media that seem to have an agenda against Melbourne and certainly the grapple tackle. It's my player that misses out on a Grand Final opportunity and I think he's been hard done by here.

Bellamy went further, questioning the integrity of the judiciary process.

'Bookmakers and betting agencies, they don't guess, they've got good information – take that as you may.'

Waldron reluctantly sat with Bellamy in the conference and, as a show of solidarity, verbally attacked Cronulla coach Ricky Stuart, who had earlier given his opinion on the Smith tackle. 'Opposition coaches, opposition officials, other officials in positions of responsibility of the game should not be commenting before the judiciary,' the CEO stated. 'To allow Ricky Stuart to make those comments is an absolute disgrace and a blight on the game and we need to address it.'

Stuart later responded: 'Brian Waldron is a flip. Wally Waldron should go and learn the rules before he starts complaining about me making comment. I was the opposition coach, of course I was going to make comment. The more that flip goes on about it the stronger I will be about it.'

The game was forgotten. Bellamy's rant became the story. By questioning the integrity of the judiciary, Storm had erred, badly. A hurricane of contempt and a lawsuit blew back on the pair. An apology did not save them. The NRL fined the club a record $50,000 over the comments. The legal case against Bellamy and Waldron was concluded in October 2010, after members of the NRL judiciary accepted a $105,000 settlement. The judiciary chairman Judge Greg Woods said,

> The conclusion of these proceedings vindicates the reputation of the judiciary panel members, who have always said that the disciplinary procedures of the NRL are independent, fair and properly conducted. The payment of damages and the payment of all the legal costs makes it clear that Mr Bellamy and Mr Waldron accept that the reference to bookmakers in relation to the NRL judiciary case heard on 24 September 2008 had no basis, and should never have been made.

Only Bellamy's players could have been pleased with his performance. He was defending one of them. It was his ultimate 'us against them' speech.

Any hope of the title being won was gone. Storm played Manly a week later without Smith. Bellamy used different tactics to prepare his team for that Grand Final but it was no use. At half-time they were behind and the opportunity was lost. Manly was perfect. The game was a rout. The Sea Eagles scored 40 points. Storm nothing. It was the largest Grand Final winning margin in the history of the game. And it was the first time since 1978 a losing team did not go past zero on the scoreboard.

Ponissi recalls the hopelessness. 'I remember people telling me about emotional fatigue and I thought what's emotionally fatigued? You're either mentally fatigued or physically fatigued. I discovered what emotional fatigue was in that year, that month.'

It felt like the end of an era. With so many players moving on, Storm could have dipped and taken two or three years to regenerate. The salary cap was blown. Inglis needed more money to stay. Smith was being courted by Gold Coast. Slater needed a new deal. It was a dire situation.

But the football department and front office never grumbled. Instead, the club went to work securing its future. Its big hope was in TPAs. News Ltd could help with those ... Sponsors could help. At that time, money was never an issue. Neither was the will of agents or players.

In October 2008 Waldron called Gainey to discuss finalising Inglis's contract extension. Things had changed slightly. Waldron was still promising to give Inglis $550,000 a year (plus extras) but wanted to separate the playing fee from the TPAs.

Waldron said, 'I'm going to prepare an NRL playing contract just with a playing fee of $400,000 each season.'

Gainey recalls being skeptical. He felt certain the league would not register Inglis for that price because it would mean a pay cut from what he was already on. 'Schubert won't register it,' he told Waldron.

Waldron said, 'That's not your concern. I'll handle it with Gallop and Schubert. As I already told you, I have been in plenty of discussions with them about the third party agreements. Don't worry, I'll handle it at my end.'

Gainey told Waldron the league would know something was not right with the deal if he tried to register the player at $400,000.

Waldron was reassuring. 'Don't worry, I'll handle it,' he repeated.

The agent had good reason to worry about his client's TPAs not being involved in the official contract. Being promised money from a third party is one thing – actually receiving the money when it is owed is another. Often footballers were left short-changed by such arrangements.

St George Illawarra champion Mark Gasnier had reluctantly left the NRL for French rugby union a few months earlier for that reason.

Gasnier wrote a book with journalist Andrew Webster in 2012 (*Gaz*), detailing his financial turmoil during the 'the worst year of my life'. It is a startling insight into a world of deals and half deals and rules that prevent financial certainty.

The Dragon wrote, 'Later, in 2008 ... trouble was looming. The four external third-party agreements I had signed in 2006 – worth $650,000 over five years – were owing per season.'

The deals Gasnier had signed were not contracts but 'letters of intent'. One of the withholding 'third parties' explained to Gasnier's agent he had made the agreement with the 'best of intentions but nothing more'. Because of the salary cap rules, neither the Dragons nor the NRL could guarantee the deals.

Gasnier wrote:

> Well it wasn't 'best intentions' as far as I was concerned. I was told it was guaranteed money that would be paid by certain dates. I never

> saw a cent of it. I had loans to pay, investments. When you start missing your loan repayments – large repayments – you get yourself into massive dramas. The whole situation reopened up the debate about the salary cap and what players should be entitled to; whether they should be able to earn money outside of their clubs, like through sponsorships, and whether that activity should be restricted or not. We have all heard rumours about players being paid under the table, but I had never hidden anything from the NRL, who were across every aspect of the deal and the issues of parties not paying their commitments. It would've been easier to have worked outside the salary cap, done the dodgy thing, but we conducted our business with all transparently – and look what it cost me.

The player's experience made him ill.

> I was in a bad place. All the different scenarios were unfolding before me. Meanwhile, I still wasn't getting paid. I was shattered and struggling, and the only person who saw it more clearly than anyone was Claude [his wife]. I had shingles. I was losing weight. I didn't want to admit to any of this because I'm a proud person.

Soon after, Gasnier reluctantly left the country, to play rugby in France.

Ex-Bronco Gordon Tallis criticised Gasnier for his decision to opt out of the NRL. Tallis said prophetically, 'In the end the NRL and the Dragons have bent over backwards to keep him in Australia. And if the sport makes an exception for him [by allowing him to be paid more], then what happens next time a Greg Inglis or an Israel Folau comes off contract and starts making the same threats?'

Inglis was finding out the league was prepared to personally show an interest in his future. But without a guarantee of those extra payments, he would potentially be left with the same uncertainty Gasnier experienced.

Gainey continued negotiating with Waldron; by now he suspected the CEO had no intention of declaring the full deal to the league. If he was concerned, the agent did not raise it with the NRL. He wanted to secure his client the best deal. He also wanted to secure his client.

Gainey called Ponissi to say the deal was on shaky ground but did not get far. Ponissi said it was not his domain. He had not been privy to negotiations and did not want to weigh in now. It would only confuse things. It was Waldron's deal to make.

The agent then went back and asked Waldron to guarantee the TPAs and extras (boat, parents' rent etc.). 'I spoke again to Waldron on the telephone, and told him that Greg had to have some security, so that the $550,000 figure would be undeniable,' Gainey remembers.

Waldron tried to assure Gainey via email his client would be paid no matter what. It wasn't enough for Gainey, who requested a more formal confirmation. He wanted it signed off by a News Ltd entity.

The CEO and agent met once more. The following conversation took place, as recalled by Gainey.

> WALDRON: 'I am in continuing talks with the NRL ... about securing third party agreements for Inglis. The NRL, in conjunction with the Storm, should be able to source third party agreements with club and game sponsors for $150,000 per season. I will be making approaches to AAMI, Gatorade, Channel 9, News Limited, Telstra Bigpond and federal government Indigenous initiatives.'
>
> GAINEY: 'Brian, I still don't see how you will get that playing contract registered.'
>
> WALDRON: 'It's not your concern. I'm handling that with Gallop and Schubert.'
>
> GAINEY: 'I want written assurances that the $550,000 agreed by the Storm board is properly documented.'
>
> WALDRON: 'I'll see to it.'

The agent, on behalf of Inglis, subsequently received a guarantee (with all payments listed) signed by Waldron on behalf of the News Ltd company Valimanda Pty Limited, trading as Storm.

It stated: 'I make this offer in my capacity as CEO of Melbourne Storm and acknowledge that this agreement is binding on Valimanda Pty Ltd trading as the Melbourne Storm Rugby League Club.'

It was against NRL rules to make such a guarantee. The above was a clear breach of $600,000 over four years.

Inglis signed the document, which would later be referred to as a secret 'side letter'. He also signed a separate, different-looking NRL contract.

Having the TPAs guaranteed was a smart move by Gainey. Without the paragraph of promise on behalf of the holding company, Valimanda,

Inglis would have indeed been exposed to losses because the following season he would become embroiled in a criminal investigation for assault. That would deter sponsors and leave Waldron without avenues to pay the athlete.

Gainey says he initially took Waldron at his word when he said he had the authority of the NRL, News Ltd and the Storm board to do whatever it took to retain Inglis. 'I was fixated on the $550,000 figure and the items Greg sought,' he explains.

> In other words, the only issue was money, and it was never a real issue. Waldron readily agreed to our figure, which was sufficient to ensure Greg's loyalty long-term – and the salary cap implications were, as Waldron kept saying, a matter for him to handle with the NRL salary cap auditor. I had Greg sign both the NRL contract and the side letter, and witnessed his signatures. At the time, I believed what I had achieved was the best possible result for my client.

Gainey says he always thought Waldron was a 'person of significance in the NRL and with News Ltd'.

The agent still shakes his head at Inglis being registered by the NRL to play for $400,000.

'Schubert did register it,' he laughs. 'That's what happened. It got registered. Does it raise any alarm bells?'

The Inglis side letter is from Waldron to Gainey, on Storm letterhead. It reads:

> Dear Alan
> Re: Greg Inglis
> This letter is to [sic] written to establish agreement between Valimanda Pty Ltd trading as Melbourne Storm Pty Ltd and Greg Inglis is to confirm what Greg Inglis will be provided for the term of his contract with the Melbourne Storm for seasons 2009 to 2012 inclusive.
>
> His playing fee (inc. the value of Third Party Agreements) over the four (4) years will be $2.2 million. Any annual short fall of the agreed $550k per year will be paid no later than 31 October in each calendar year.
>
> Your client will receive provision of a fully serviced and maintained motor vehicle for the term of the contract. Your client

will be responsible for his own fuel costs. The vehicle will be supplied immediately upon acceptance and signing of the new contract. Your client will be subject to the accepted rules and regulations pertaining to maintenance of the vehicle in the event of an accident.

Medical insurance – The Club agrees to pay for the cost of full hospital and medical insurance at either the single of [sic] family rate for the contract period.

The $40,000 Deferred Playing Fee from the 2008 season to be paid as a lump sum by no later than 7 November 2008.

A one off Harvey Norman voucher to the retail value of $20,000 supplied upon request.

Rental Assistance – The Club to pay 50% of the assessed market rental for Greg's Altona property for his parents, up to a maximum of $200 per week. This agreement will commence upon Greg's parents [sic] relocation to Melbourne and will only be a [sic] maintained on the understanding and agreement they remain in Melbourne.

Dally M Player of the Year/Churchill Medal Winner – A $5,000 bonus for each award, payable in each year of the contract.

The Club agrees to provide to Greg's parents or family, four (4) return airfares to Melbourne in each year of the contract.

The Club agrees to supply your client with a boat of his choice to the value of $30,000.

The Club in conjunction with the NRL to provide suitable media training for Greg during the contract period, the cost of such to be paid by the Club or NRL.

I make this offer in my capacity as CEO of Melbourne Storm and acknowledge that this agreement is binding on Valimanda Pty Ltd trading as the Melbourne Storm Rugby League Club.

If you are in acceptance with the terms of the above offer made by Melbourne Storm please acknowledge by signing the section below which will have the force of making this agreement binding to all parties.

Kind regards
Brian Waldron
Melbourne Storm Rugby League Club

CHAPTER 26

THE REAL DEAL

Often player agents pretend they are misunderstood innocent parties to payments outside the NRL salary cap. Of course this is not always true. Generally, managers are clued in because they have to be. At different times they negotiate directly with chief executive officers, chief financial officers, heads of recruitment, directors, players, football managers, coaches and each other. In the battlefield of negotiations leverage is their ally and weapon.

Of the hundred-plus agents accredited to sign NRL contracts, no agent is the same. It is not fair to categorise them. Personalities spread from bookish to rockstar; their behaviour ranges from cavalier to scrupulous. It is wrong to label player agents the hounds of treachery, the cause of so much misery in professional sport, for they are more a symptom of a system with faults, burrows, back laneways and a code of 'look after your own'.

Waldron had his favourite player agents. The man who used to negotiate for Cameron Smith was not one of them. Jim Banaghan was the Queensland agent who signed Smith to a long-term deal as a teenager. The hooker broke away from him in 2008, during the play-offs.

The split made headlines because Smith was about to negotiate a new four-year deal. Being without a manager in contract negotiations with a football club is normally not wise. But Smith was in a privileged position. He was now regarded as the most complete player in the world, a stand-out performer for Queensland and Australia. His personal circumstances (his wife, Barbara, had given birth to their first baby,

Jada) made him think briefly about moving back to his home state to be closer to his broader family. Such a thought caused more than flutters in Melbourne's football department and front office. Storm felt it could not afford to let him leave.

Waldron would not let the team down. He'd get the deal done. The CEO told the press,

> We wouldn't be concerned if Cam wanted to negotiate on his own. Managers are a necessity and I do see a role for them outside of negotiating contracts. But maybe some players can manage their own affairs. If they know their market value and are confident in their own ability, they may not need a manager.

Smith stated,

> Yes, the Storm has made me an offer. We haven't really gone too far into talks at the moment but I'm quite happy with what they've come up with. Hopefully we can come to some sort of agreement with what I'm thinking and what they're thinking. The length of the contract is important, it's too short – I get to, say, 28 years old, am I risking not getting another good contract being too old? So obviously the length of the contract is a factor. I'm 25 years old now and it may be my last contract.

The captain was astute and displayed a deep understanding of his professional position. He knew well enough to not make his own bed. Soon Isaac Moses would represent him. The press asked Smith whether he would have to accept a diminished deal to stay with a team bursting at the salary cap seams. He replied,

> I'm aware of that. I think everyone's aware of that, with the squad that we've got, if we were to go somewhere else we'd probably get a fair bit more. At the end of the day I'm not going to be asking the club for overs. I don't think I'm a greedy bloke. I'd just like to be paid what I think I'm worth to the club. We've got a great squad and I really would hate to leave the club to be honest.

Smith didn't have to worry about taking a pay hit. Storm creator John Ribot had volunteered to find Smith a big TPA. He spoke to

Waldron behind the scenes. 'Why don't we see if we can get him some money through Fox?' Ribot said.

It was critical to the integrity of the NRL that the TPA did not look like a negotiating tool for Storm – a fat sweet. Gold Coast was offering Smith a large deal in competition to Melbourne. Ribot had to prove Fox Sports was going to pay Smith regardless of where he ended up playing. He says he gambled on Smith being loyal.

Ribot recalls setting up the TPA, 'I did everything transparently, even to the point of going to David [Gallop] and saying this is what I'm doing. I had letters drafted saying it doesn't matter which club he goes to [if he signs the deal with the broadcaster].'

News Ltd was involved in the deal too. Company COO Macourt was on the NRL board *and* the Fox Sports board. He explains, 'There was no problem with that Smith deal. It was perfectly legitimate. David Malone was head of Fox Sports. He negotiated that deal at an arm's-length basis.'

The TPA with Fox Sports was worth $100,000 a year. The only thing that would alter its legitimacy was if Waldron guaranteed it in another secret side letter. Negotiations between Waldron and Smith's new manager, Isaac Moses, dragged out until December.

Email conversations with agents were now Waldron's life.

The day after Waldron was quoted encouraging Smith to negotiate his contract, the player's *ex-agent*, Banaghan, sent the CEO an email.

Banaghan was still representing Storm forward Adam Blair. He demanded Waldron insert his management fee into Blair's NRL contract, as per league rules. He finished his email:

> If this is not done by 4pm today I will be requesting the nrl [sic] to sort out and advising of your previous attempt to pay me via an indirect path.

It sounded like a threat. Waldron coolly replied:

> Jim
> It is not surprising that you continue to hide behind you [sic] emails and text messages. You have a short memory of what assistance was given to you in your attempts to retain Cameron Smith. To blame us and then become vindictive is extremely disappointing. I have no issue discussing matters with you on

> the phone or face to face when you return. I will not however respond to your threats and bullying. I look forward to talking to you when get [sic] courage to call me. I will be happy to discuss all matters pertaining to your management of players when you do.
>
> Kind regards
>
> Brian

Of course, Waldron was being deliberately evasive. But he did not display any anxiety. In a subsequent email Banaghan appeared to make another attempt to unsettle the CEO:

> Do not worry about covering your bum now. Just do the correct thing on blair [sic] as requested by me one more time in this email ... Why you will not does show consistency in your considered and deliberate attempts to hide it off the cap.

The email was evidence of Waldron's potential vulnerability to agents. But it also showed his attitude when pressed. He was calm, almost always. On 4 December, Smith finally penned a deal with Storm to keep him at the club until the end of 2013. Waldron and Moses had come to an agreement.

True to form, Waldron signed a secret side letter for Smith. Isaac Moses wrote it. It contained several extras, including a car for his wife and an unusual system to pay for his house renovations. It also included clauses so he could potentially negotiate with UK Super League clubs and terminate his Storm agreement if Bellamy left Melbourne. The document was signed by Moses, Waldron and Smith. Critically, Waldron guaranteed the TPAs (there were other TPAs listed only as 'Publisher') – another large salary cap breach.

The CEO signed the side document because if he didn't guarantee TPAs the club might lose its hooker.

Cameron Smith's side letter was written *to* Waldron. It was entitled:

> HEADS OF AGREEMENT BETWEEN MELBOURNE STORM, CAMERON SMITH AND TITAN MANAGEMENT.

It read:

Dear Brian,
In consideration for Titan Managements Client Cameron Smith entering into a playing agreement with the Melbourne Storm for the 2009 – 2013 seasons dated the 4th December 2008, please agree to the following:

2009
$350,000.00
Family Medical
$100,000.00 Fox Sports – Melbourne to underwrite this incase [sic] circumstances change.
$100,000.00 Publisher – Melbourne to underwrite this incase [sic] circumstances change. This is to be paid no later then [sic] June 2009 or in monthly instalments.
$4,000.00 net worth of Flights
$22,500.00 plus gst if applicable payable to Three Pty Ltd as a scouting fee on the 1st July 2009

2010
$450,000.00
Family Medical
$100,000.00 Fox Sports – Melbourne to underwrite this incase [sic] circumstances change.
$50,000.00 Publisher – Melbourne to underwrite this incase [sic] circumstances change. This is to be paid no later then [sic] June 2010 or in monthly instalments.
$4,000.00 net worth of Flights.

2011
$450,000.00
Family Medical
$100,000.00 Fox Sports – Melbourne to underwrite this incase [sic] circumstances change.
$50,000.00 Publisher – Melbourne to underwrite this incase [sic] circumstances change. This is to be paid no later then [sic] June 2011 or in monthly instalments.
$4,000.00 net worth of Flights.

2012
$450,000.00
Family Medical
$100,000.00 Fox Sports – Melbourne to underwrite this incase [sic] circumstances change.
$50,000.00 Publisher – Melbourne to underwrite this incase [sic] circumstances change. This is to be paid no later then [sic] June 2012 or in monthly instalments.
$4,000.00 net worth of Flights.

2013
$450,000.00
Family Medical
$100,000.00 Fox Sports – Melbourne to underwrite this incase [sic] circumstances change.
$50,000.00 Publisher – Melbourne to underwrite this incase [sic] circumstances change. This is to be paid no later then [sic] June 2013 or in monthly instalments.
$4,000.00 net worth of Flights.

Option
Melbourne storm have an option on the players [sic] services for the 2013 season. The Club will advise the player and Titan Management of its intentions no later then [sic] 14th June 2011. If Melbourne does not take up this option then the player has an option in his favour for the 2012 season and beyond.

UK Super League Clause
Cameron has the right to negotiate with UK Super League Clubs for the 2012 and 2013 seasons. Notification on this needs to be no later then [sic] 31 August 2011 and 2012 season and no later then [sic] 21 August 2012 for the 2012 season.

Craig Bellamy Clause
If Craig Bellamy is no longer head coach at the club the player has the right to terminate his agreement.

Car
Barbare [sic] is to keep the current Suzuki Grand Vitara car which has 5,000km's [sic] on it. This is an asset for her.

Salary Cap Increase
If the Salary Cap has an increase of $100,000.00 or more in any given year the Storm agrees to review the playing fee for each year remaining on the player's contract.

House Renovations
The Melbourne storm will deduct $60,000.00 gross from the playing fee over the term of the agreement. From this Cameron will have $33,000.00 net to spend on house renovations. For this to be completed both the Storm and Cameron are to obtain separate quotes for the work and then both parties are to mutually agree on the price for each individual job which will come off the $33,000.00 net that has been put aside.

If this is agreeable could you please sign where indicated on each page.
Kind regards
Mr Isaac Moses
Titan Management

By Christmas 2008, Bellamy, Smith and Inglis had all agreed to long-term deals. Cronk had committed to Storm in July (he negotiated his contract with Ponissi and had no side letter). It wasn't only the cream being retained. Dallas Johnson, Jeff Lima, Adam Blair, Sika Manu, Anthony Quinn and Brett White had also signed long-term deals.

Ryan Hoffman was next. The back-rower had become a representative player and his agent, David Riolo, enjoyed significant bargaining power. Hoffman told the press he had offers to go elsewhere. Waldron did Hoffman's deal, after a series of emails throughout January 2009. Of course, the club was planning to pay Hoffman some of his money outside the cap. In one of the emails Waldron wrote: 'The grim reaper Schubert is visiting us next week.'

Slater was the only one left without a deal. Waldron was still trying to come to terms with the marvellous fullback and his agent, George Mimis.

Waldron made one more signing during that time that did make headlines. It was his retention of the reluctant Matt Hanson as a Storm executive. It did not come easily but it was nonetheless crucial for Waldron in the short term.

Hanson was popular from day one of his employment at Storm, despite his lack of interest in a permanent position. He slowly worked his way through the complexities of the salary cap. In 2008 the league had introduced an Under 20s competition called the Toyota Cup. The salary cap for the Toyota Cup was set at $250,000. That was another spreadsheet to master for the finance controllers. A few amendments had also been made to the NRL system. Club sponsors could now pay some extra money to players for advertising and promotion in marquee player agreements (MPAs). All of this Hanson was told, though he did not rush to learn it at once. He also became familiar with the club's overspending practices.

Hanson viewed his early employment at Storm as he might consider a holiday resort he didn't fancy all that much: this is not very appealing but I won't be staying, so it's alright – I'll just put up with it.

Several things struck him as strange regarding the salary cap breaching. He was surprised the club had pretended to vary contracts but promised to pay the players the amounts they were owed anyway through a third entity. He was staggered Waldron would involve so many people in the scam. It seemed fraught with exposure. He said in jest to Waldron, 'So you've only got about 300 people who know about this?'

He first became aware of smaller breaches through reading a file containing the letters of offer and formal NRL contracts. He noticed not all of them matched. The differences were not cavernous but they were obvious. He initially thought the extras might be tantamount to a salary cap concession, which he knew existed in the AFL. But knowing what he already knew about the other irregularities, he did not wonder whether the file contained breaches. His audit-trained eyes were drawn to the differences, back and forth – that's different, that's different, that's different. Not wanting the club to suffer sanctions so early on his watch, he separated the letters and contracts and filed each folder.

One day Schubert came to Melbourne. He regularly visited as part of his annual audits, inspecting and comparing contracts, invoices etc. Previously, Storm prepared for his presence by having papers ready.

This time was different. Schubert said to Hanson, 'Matt, where are all the letters of offer?'

Hanson said he didn't think they were relevant to an audit because they had been superseded by the NRL contracts.

Schubert pressed. 'Oh we need them.'

Waldron was not in the office. But his executive assistant was there. She overheard Schubert's request and offered, 'No, I've got them, remember.'

Hanson looked at the helpful assistant and said, 'Na I'm pretty sure they're gone.'

She said, 'No, no, I've got them, look here they are in the folder here.'

Hanson said, 'Oh, okay I thought you threw them out.'

Schubert was handed the folder. Now *he* could spot the difference in contracts between 2005–2007. It was an important piece of evidence against the franchise.

Despite the 2008 finals series debacle, the entire club was excelling in its pursuit of another premiership in 2009. Robbie Kearns was growing into his role as the club's intermediary between the training rooms and commercial offices. The former Australian captain was effective at urging players to help the business by complying with requests from the media and sponsors. Up until now, Kearns had been the face of the club. But now Smith, Slater, Cronk and Inglis were usurping him in profile.

One of Waldron's best appointments was Lizzy Joyce, a publicity manager with a background in theatre. She was asked to help players make the transition from appearing in the back pages of the newspapers to the social pages. This would give them a larger profile, which would then hopefully fill seats at matches, sell memberships.

Joyce was very popular among journalists and colleagues for her dry wit and warmth. She understood how newspapers worked; she was friendly with the staff photographers. She was one of the best in her line of work. She helped place the athletes and their partners in popular marquees at the Spring Racing Carnival, on the red carpet at opening nights, courtside at the Australian Open tennis tournament and on TV. Melbournians are so parochial; once they know their athletes they want to own them. 'Billy', 'Cam', 'Cooper', 'Hoffy' and 'G.I.' were players locals could like. At this time the players were not so guarded and untrusting of the public glare.

The down-to-earth publicity officer also helped Melbourne set up its ambassador program. This involved inviting famous Victorians – ex-swimmer and broadcaster Nicole Livingstone, comedian Dave Hughes, number-one ticketholder and future prime minister Julia Gillard, outspoken Catholic priest and radio personality Father Bob Maguire – to promote their support of Storm.

Joyce also befriended Molly Meldrum. Before one of the Grand Finals, Meldrum did more than 20 radio interviews. He was second only to Waldron in spruiking Storm's charm and excellence.

A publicity coup for Storm occurred when singer Dannii Minogue and her model boyfriend (a rugby league fan) came to quite a few games. The first outing Minogue went on with her first baby was a Storm game. She tweeted a picture of the bub from her grandstand seat, which Joyce had organised. That is how Storm grew its brand. Waldron was ultimately responsible for it. He employed skilled managers.

Gerry Ryan may have been the only director helping Waldron with third-party deals but he was not the only sponsor.

Honda's Tony Devers, who backed the club in the Ribot era, was now sponsoring the team through his position as a manager at Suzuki. The car company was using some players in its advertisements, paying them for 'image rights' contracts: approved by Schubert. Slater was (and still is) his number-one promotions player.

Devers's sleeve sponsorship is the most recognisable and therefore most valuable in Australian sport. 'The subliminal message of Suzuki in a tough game, a tough sport and winning team is very positive,' explains Devers, whose late dog was called Storm.

As part of Devers's sponsorship, he leases cars to the club. He says he did not know Storm was breaching the salary cap under Waldron's watch. But he was aware of the cap's reputation, through talking to Sydney dealers about against-the-rules services. They told him 'everyone is doin' it'. 'They [the people he talked to] were involved in other clubs,' Devers recalls. 'They were either lifetime members or supporters and being businesspeople at a reasonably high level they knew, heard rumours, about what was going on.'

It was not his job to report leased cars to the NRL.

'Nothing to do with us,' Devers says. 'If he [Waldron] says we want to give a car to somebody, they allocate the car, it's up to them to report to the league.'

Devers says he sold a car to Slater's mum, which the league allowed. 'If I was selling him a car perceivably below retail,' Devers says, 'they wanted to look at it under the salary cap. It was a 4WD up at Innisfail.' Devers added he did not deal with the NRL, rather Slater's manager. 'Once again, if Billy wants to buy a car, yeah, no worries. Love to have his mum, his brother, everybody driving 'em.'

Schubert contacted Devers to ask him about his leasing arrangements with Storm.

The car executive recalls, 'I actually did talk to Schubert and whether he misunderstood ... I said, "Look I want all the players driving Suzukis. I'm a sponsor and if the players are seen driving another product, you lose credibility." I think that was misconstrued.'

Waldron asked Devers to help him keep players happy. It was a loose agreement. Suzuki was pleased to help, as long as it went both ways.

'I'm quite disciplined about getting value for money,' Devers adds. 'I would never even give Storm, who I love, something that I didn't get value for my company from. The coach is probably perceived as the best coach in Australia. He drives one [a Suzuki]. The value of that is superb.'

Importantly, the players knew how to keep sponsors grinning. When interviewed by the media, they always name-dropped the companies.

Bit by bit, Hanson started to enjoy the company of Storm people. It was their passion that was winning him over. The players found him easy to talk to and treated him with respect, perhaps because he looked like one of them, handsome and fit. The CFO liked Waldron too. The pair would talk over lunch most days. The staff watched them become closer. Waldron was not threatened by Hanson's big-business experience.

News Ltd–appointed board director Craig Watt offers interesting analysis on the Waldron–Hanson partnership. On Waldron:

> When I think of Brian I see a very ambitious executive, someone who wanted to carve out a reputation as being the best football administrator in the land regardless of codes. He was a natural salesman that was sometimes short of detail. The board was well aware he was a fast talker and was forever bringing him back to the detail of many issues.

Watt says of Hanson: 'Matt came across as a very smooth operator and played the room almost as well as Brian did. He was a confident, athletic young man who was very popular with both the football and corporate departments. He was smart and always across the detail. Together Brian and Matt made a very persuasive team.'

In late 2008 Hanson quit, just as he said he would. He was only ever going to stay for a few months.

He handed in his typed resignation and gave a month's notice. He felt he could not continue working for his current wage (about $200,000 a year). Also, the work was not satisfying. A commercial pilot would not be stimulated taking Cessna joyrides around the city. Hanson was over being a CFO and his Storm position was taking away from his focus of finding a job back in the private equity sphere.

Waldron asked Hanson what it would take to keep him. Hanson said money alone was not important. It was the job description: he did not want to crunch numbers. He also did not want to handle any more player payments, as he was uncomfortable carrying out instructions that were leading to breaches of the salary cap. During this time Hanson had experienced the self-examination suffered by Vale. Should I blow the whistle and cause the club to suffer NRL punishment or should I quietly carry out Waldron's instructions, while looking for another job? He chose the latter.

But could he be talked into staying?

Waldron said, 'What about the new stadium?' The club was scheduled to shift into the new rectangular stadium from 2010. With Hanson's experience as part of the Docklands stadium executive in 2001, he was perfectly placed to manage Storm's relocation. Waldron added, 'Would you stay if I could get another chief financial officer in to look after finance and you concentrate on the move?'

'If there was a role purely getting you into the new stadium, I'm happy to do that,' replied Hanson. 'But once again it's a finite role, it's a 12-month thing, then I'd be out the door.'

The stadium relocation was no easy task. Storm was to be one of the major tenants. It planned to have a retail shop for merchandise. There was a cafe being built. All the offices had to be configured. The training facilities were to be shared with Melbourne Victory and Melbourne Football Club so lease agreements had to be drawn up. Negotiations would have to be held with Melbourne Olympic Park Trust on the user agreements, how match returns were divided up. That sort of work Hanson enjoyed.

Waldron went to the board touting Hanson for the role of chief operating officer, in charge of the stadium deal. The board weighed up whether to bring in external consultants or stay with Hanson, who could do it, for sure. Either way it would be costly. The directors resolved to pay Hanson a salary that was now comparable to some CEOs in the NRL.

Hanson had a nice Christmas. But he would long regret the two big decisions he had made that year: agreeing to help Waldron out for a few months and not following through with his resignation. This time next year he would be in charge of Melbourne Storm, drowning in Waldron's whitewater wake.

CHAPTER 27

A MILLION MEMORIES / A NEW NUMBERS MAN

Slater was now the world's best player. He had followed in the footsteps of Smith to become a winner of the international Golden Boot award. It was a good time for him to be negotiating a new contract. But not everything was peachy for Storm.

News Ltd journalist Peter Badel astutely wrote a story on 15 February 2009, raising the issue of Waldron's salary cap squeeze. Questions were being asked about Melbourne's extraordinary ability to sign superstars *and* outstanding role players.

The lede was, 'Melbourne chief executive Brian Waldron has hosed down rumours the Storm are in danger of breaching the salary cap as the club moves to sign Queensland sensation Slater to a new deal worth more than $1.2 million.'

Badel's story continued, 'The Storm have been buffeted by off-season speculation the club is under mounting pressure to offload key players to ensure the 2007 premier does not exceed the NRL's $4.1 million payment ceiling.'

The story ran a statement from Waldron that says more about the CEO and his well-developed hubris than it does about the truth of the payments to Storm athletes. It read,

> We're good as gold. It's nothing but scuttlebutt. Others can speculate but we know where we are at with the salary cap, we know what we have to do to keep players and make hard decisions

on other ones in due course. It's always a challenge. Nothing has changed since 2006. We're doing what we can to manage it. The best thing is we've got blokes here who are prepared to make sacrifices by taking less to stay to ensure we can keep our squad together.

Finally, the story quoted Slater's manager, George Mimis, saying Slater had options available to him but was eager to continue discussing a new deal with Storm.

Waldron added, 'We don't envisage any great stumbling blocks. The guys here realise that you can't have a million dollars – but you can have a million memories.'

Negotiations between Waldron and Mimis followed. By the beginning of March the boy from Innisfail, who was now 26 years old and in his prime, had come to an agreement with Melbourne. He would stay with his mates.

Like Inglis and Smith, the elusive number one had a side letter, which guaranteed TPAs. But Slater's was different. Firstly, Slater did not sign it and neither did his manager. Also, it contained paragraphs stating Melbourne was complying with the salary cap rules. It was penned by Waldron and read:

Dear George
The Melbourne Storm and its Board of Directors guarantees to undertake the following payments on behalf of the Melbourne Storm for Billy Slater and/or his nominee Slater Group Promotions P/L.

The following sums will form the guarantee:

- Payable 10 April 2009: Sponsor TPA $140,000.00
- Payable 10 April 2009: Sponsor TPA $50,000.00
- Payable 1 Nov 2009: Sponsor TPA $125,000.00
- Payable 1 Nov 2010: Sponsor TPA $100,000.00
- Payable 1 Nov 2011: Sponsor TPA $125,000.00
- Motor Vehicle Gross value $60,000 in 2009

The player agreed to refund $40,000 in bonuses received for the 2008 season once he has received the $140,000 TPA for 2009.

As discussed and agreed Billy is one of the most marketable players in the NRL. Should the Melbourne Storm not be successful in procuring the above sums via TPA sponsors, the Melbourne Storm guarantees the performance of these amounts on a lump sum basis on the dates outlined, and the Melbourne Storm guarantees that these amounts will be reflected in the Melbourne Storm Salary Cap.

The above sums form part of the player NRL contract salary package and the Club agrees to fulfil its usual compliance requirements, as required under the NRL rules.

Kind regards

Brian Waldron

Attracting TPAs for Slater would not be a hard task. Suzuki was already using him for promotions. Other companies would be pleased to have Slater as the face of their products. Had Waldron decided to adhere to the laws of the game, he would not have had any problems fulfilling his promise to pay the above amounts. But, as with the others, he felt compelled to *guarantee* the TPAs. In doing so, he had breached the cap by another whopping sum.

The three side letters of Inglis, Smith and Slater, signed by Waldron, were kept hidden.

Waldron figured if the league did not see them, it would be impossible to prove the breaches. The agents and players would not tell the league about the secret documents. There were no questions being asked by the football department, which was delighted to have retained the team's four stars. Now Bellamy, with all the footballing talent a coach could ever want, got on with marshalling from his super squad the effort required to create the dynasty he so desired.

While the footballers got back to work after a tumultuous six months, life in the front office was entering a phase of excitement and eccentricity.

The new entertainment service provider, McManus Presents, was creating a buzz.

Andrew McManus was a director of Andrew McManus Presents Pty Ltd, New Breed McManus Events Pty Ltd and Andrew McManus Presents (International) Ltd. His expertise was in rock 'n' roll, having started in the music trade as a manager for the ARIA Hall of Fame band Divinyls in the late 1980s. Since then he has organised Australian tours for some of the world's biggest acts. He was also famous in Melbourne for staging the best parties at Spring Racing Carnival.

Having a concert promoter as a contractor can bring all sorts of possibilities. Storm players often attended the Formula One Grand Prix at Albert Park. They were there when Waldron phoned through the news – wait for it boys! – Kiss was going to perform at the season opener. It would be the year's biggest entertainment coup. McManus was going to make it happen, so said Waldron. Some Storm workers were giddy with anticipation. A few of their colleagues said it would never happen. They were right.

Kiss never played before any Storm matches. But Noiseworks frontman Jon Stevens performed for the club and so did Kate Ceberano. Waldron was like that. He started at the top and worked his way down.

A Storm masquerade ball was held in a warehouse on the water's edge at Docklands one night. The function was fantastic. It is still talked about by those who attended. It was in late summer so the air was warm and drinks were cold. The band Rogue Traders rocked a short set before midnight that had everyone – staff and players – dancing and bobbing along. It felt delightful to be the NRL champion.

But a swell time didn't come cheaply. The entertainment costs at Melbourne began rising.

Front office staff noticed. The club's commercial workers had been told Rogue Traders was playing for free. Waldron boasted McManus (the band's live gigs handler) was 'looking after us'. But a hefty invoice came in. A Storm worker questioned the bill with Waldron, who assured his staff it was not a concern. Don't worry. He would take care of it.

Of course, while McManus was providing real entertainment, it was also helping Storm meet its commitments to players.

Later News Ltd's forensic investigation by independent accounting firm Deloitte confirmed that it worked like this: the McManus Group invoiced Storm on a monthly basis for 'consulting fees'. Hanson coded the invoices in the club's balance sheet under 'general accruals'. He then paid the money to McManus Presents, which paid Storm players.

Nine footballers – Cameron Smith, Ryan Hoffman, Cooper Cronk, Michael Crocker, Dallas Johnson, Anthony Quinn, Steve Turner, Antonio Kaufusi and Matt Geyer – had received payments using this method in 2008. This was during Hanson's first few months on the job. The CFO, on instructions from Waldron, had organised the payments to be made even while he was still trying to understand the complicated NRL salary cap system.

Early in 2009 the payments going through McManus Group companies became larger. Hoffman received $180,000 in three lots of $60,000. Inglis ($40,000) and Slater ($140,000 – as stated as first item in his side letter) also received larger amounts to satisfy the deals Waldron had done with the athlete's agents. This time invoices came to the McManus Group from managers or accountants representing the footballers.

In total, Storm paid its players about $800,000 through McManus Group businesses.

It was News Ltd's money. Why didn't the club's owner, through its internal audit and board representatives, notice that entertainment spending was rising? In short, it did. But it didn't mind. News Ltd's hierarchy had granted the franchise access to more funds. It let Waldron spend extra in an attempt to increase membership and sponsorship.

For a long time Waldron had argued passionately to increase Storm's marketing budget. Melbourne was competing against Australian rules clubs. He insisted the AFL was the best sporting competition in the country at client entertainment and corporate hospitality.

News Ltd COO Macourt explains,

> Having been to AFL functions from time to time, I totally agreed with Waldron. The AFL were incredibly professional at the way they ran their game-day entertainment and just the way they run their corporate boxes generally. So I actually supported Waldron increasing the marketing budgets and the game-day budgets to help him, particularly at Olympic Park, which was a dive, to help him build the brand of the Storm up.

'So the increase in entertainment and marketing costs wasn't remotely remarkable,' Macourt says.

Storm spent $18 million annually on its entire business.

The annual accounts for Storm were prepared by the club and inspected by News Ltd auditors. They were presented to the board at the end of each year. Once the board was pleased with the financial position, chairman Moodie and Craig Watt signed it off. Watt, the News Ltd–appointed director, was charged with monitoring the franchise's 'strategic direction and financial objectives'. He was the owner's point man on Storm spending.

Watt became an important figure at Storm, after replacing Jourdain. At the time (2008) it was discussed within News Ltd executive offices that long-time Storm supporter and Herald and Weekly Times Managing Director Blunden might be a suitable club director. News Ltd chief Hartigan says he stopped this because it would be a conflict of interest. So Watt was added, instead.

Watt grew up the son of the Footscray Football Club (now Western Bulldogs in the AFL) curator. A lanky ruckman, he played Aussie rules in Melbourne's western suburbs for 270 games. He is a life member of his team – Parkside Football Club.

He studied at Melbourne University, completing a Bachelor of Commerce degree in 1985 and began his career as a graduate accountant with HWT in 1986, going on to hold several senior finance roles at News Ltd, including general manager of finance and administration and company secretary from 2001. Watt enjoyed his involvement at Storm, perhaps because it reunited him with the feeling that comes from being part of a football team. He developed strong relationships with his colleagues, including the other News Ltd–appointed director, Stanton. He highly respected Moodie as chairman.

Here Watt describes his early time with Storm,

> Despite the fact the club was owned by News, the board took very seriously its obligations to help position the club in this AFL mad city. The board saw that it had a responsibility to promote, grow and develop the rugby league code in Victoria. It was active in lobbying the government to provide funding to support a Victorian junior program. Unlike the AFL, the NRL never really opened its purse strings to support the growth of the game in Victoria.

Storm relied on monthly money from News Ltd. Watt's role was to make sure the funding requests of the club were in line with the club's 'budgeted objectives'. The board also depended upon updates from the club's CFO. For half of 2008 it was Hanson. In 2009 a new numbers man joined the executive. His name was Paul Gregory.

Gregory grew up in the Melbourne suburb of Rosanna and worked at a large accounting firm, before eventually moving to a position at Kodak, where he worked happily for 13 years. A highlight of Gregory's Kodak career was when he was European finance director for the company's motion picture interests from 2001 to 2006. Gregory met a girl called Liz in London in 2005. She was Australian, working in banking and insurance. They would later marry. In 2006 Gregory was offered a job in Los Angeles. He declined. It was time to come home.

Back in Australia, towards the end of his employment at Kodak, Gregory was offered the role of chief financial officer for the company's Australian operations. He took it because he wanted to get back into a finance role. In early 2009 the CFO and managing director roles at Kodak were made redundant. He thought it a good time to do something else.

Through a friend of a friend Gregory heard about the vacancy at Storm (left by Hanson, who was being promoted to Chief Operating Officer). He was not initially interested because it meant a 50 per cent pay reduction from his last post at Kodak. The title was financial controller (with a view to being promoted to CFO later). Aside from money, he had nothing to lose. He agreed to meet Hanson for a chat.

The introduction went well. Gregory liked Hanson and respected his experience. The lure of being inside the professional sports industry was strong. He decided it might be an interesting move. A follow-up lunch was held and that was when Gregory met Waldron. He was hired soon after. It was definitely a love job, not a money job.

In March 2009, Gregory travelled to Europe for a mate's wedding. He took the opportunity to ski again. It was a delightful way to spend his time between jobs. When he arrived back in Australia he started at Melbourne Storm. He could not know at this time he was about to be involved in a professional train wreck that would ultimately drive him to consider the merits of suicide.

CHAPTER 28

STORM V EELS

The statistics in 2009 were un-Storm.

From round one the season was a flight through turbulence. First game: beat the Dragons by a point. Second game: lost to the Broncos by two points. Third Game: beat the Cowboys in Townsville. Fourth game: lost to the Gold Coast at home. Melbourne then pipped the Panthers, lost to the Tigers and drew with the Warriors. And on it went. The team hovered around fourth position on the ladder until August, when everything went haywire.

Inglis was arrested by Victoria Police and charged with assaulting his girlfriend Sally Robinson. It became one of the biggest sport stories of the year. The Melbourne media turned its attention to Storm like never before. The team went from having no-one at training to having cameras everywhere. The gates of Storm were locked. It was an uncomfortable time for the football department and front office.

But the leadership of Waldron, backed by his board, was superbly fair and forthright. The CEO stood Inglis down indefinitely. He told the press:

> People need to understand the decision we take on this type of issue is not a football decision. It's a club decision that will consider all stakeholders. We are very strong on our stance to safety to women. No matter what we do in relation to this matter, we are not going to please everyone. What that means for Greg, we are not too sure.

Inglis appeared in court and the case was adjourned for two weeks. Melbourne lost to Newcastle that weekend. The following round Storm opposed Manly at home on a Sunday afternoon. The Sea Eagles won 20–16 in front of about 10,000 people. The season looked terminal.

In the 24 hours after the match, another Storm leader found his best form: Bellamy. The coach had been urging his team to finish in the top four. It was critical to making the Grand Final. Now he spoke to the players in a deadly silent change room meeting: 'If we don't win the next two games, forget the top four, we won't even be in the top eight.' He was not just scaremongering. Many sides were bunched in the middle of the NRL ladder. It was going to be tight, indeed. Bellamy thought hard about how to save the season. That night he hatched his plan. He would scrap his team leadership model for the rest of the season.

Up until this point Bellamy had included his best players, namely Smith, Cronk and Slater, in all his big decisions. It is part of his successful method to allow players to have a say in selection and strategy and tactics and behavioural standards etc. Footballers who are engaged by the coach to help run the team take responsibility for their actions and teammates. Such a leadership model promotes 'ownership', a sporting buzzword of the 2000s. Bellamy trusted in this sharing of information and ideas but now he had decided it was coming at a cost. Ownership of Storm in such a tempestuous time was a heavy burden for the men in their mid-twenties, who were finding it hard enough to win games.

Bellamy told Ponissi of his plan to alleviate the pressures of leadership for the rest of the year. Ponissi thought it was an overreaction but he supported Bellamy's call. The coach was acting on intuition.

Next he told the players. 'I'll worry about everything else, you just play football.'

In the next few days, Inglis went back to court. The case was adjourned again until October. Inglis was allowed to resume playing. The NRL backed the decision by Storm's board.

With that, the Storm started winning easily. Round 25: beat the Roosters by 34 points. Round 26: beat the Warriors 30–0 at Mr Smart Stadium. Qualifying final: thrashed Manly 40–12.

In the preliminary final, Smith overtook Orford as the greatest all-time scorer for Storm as Melbourne, playing free and easy, beat Brisbane 40–10. That same night Bellamy's side became the first team since the Parramatta teams of 1981–84 to qualify for four consecutive Grand Finals.

The season decider was contested before 82,000 people. Storm would play the modern Eels, a fairytale team if ever there was one. Two-time premiership winning coach–commentator Phil Gould began the 2009 NRL Grand Final Channel Nine coverage with this monologue:

> The Melbourne Storm today play their fourth Grand Final in a row. During those years they have set the standard for rugby league in this part of the world. Meticulous, clinical, professional – they are constantly in search of rugby league excellence. Some even say they have been machine-like in their execution.

The television coverage was beamed live around he world, even into Melbourne. A Blackhawk helicopter was used to fly in and deliver the ball.

Storm team V Parramatta, Grand Final 2009

Billy Slater	Adam Blair
Steve Turner	Ryan Hoffman
Will Chambers	Dallas Johnson
Greg Inglis	Reserves
Dane Nielsen	Ryan Hinchcliffe
Brett Finch	Jeff Lima
Cooper Cronk	Ryan Tandy
Aiden Tolman	Scott Anderson
Cameron Smith (C)	
Brett White	Coach: Craig Bellamy

Fullback Jarryd Hayne was lugging the hopes of the blue-and-gold. His team had recovered from a poor start to the season to win nine of its last 12 home and away matches. It finished eighth. Finals victories against Minor Premier St George Illawarra, Gold Coast and Canterbury provided qualification to the biggest match of the club season.

Coach Daniel Anderson was riding his luck. His team had gelled. It was young and fearless. Storm held no terror for the Eels. Going back a decade Parramatta and Melbourne had a rivalry of close contests.

Wolfmother performed. Then Mark Vincent sang the anthem.

A peculiar sight on this evening was the Storm player wearing the number six jersey – Brett Finch, a former Eel, had come to Storm halfway through the year because he wasn't enjoying his football under Anderson. Parramatta was still paying him. Finch's manager, Steve Gillis, says allegations his client was being paid by Storm under the table were false. If the NRL had any evidence Finch was not complying with the rules he would've been exposed, Gillis says.

Parramatta's preparation included planning to nobble a pet Storm play, involving Smith passing Finch behind two decoy runners and a short ball to a barging Hoffman, as Inglis loomed large outside, as a distraction.

In the fifth minute, Melbourne ran that exact play and Parramatta could not defend it. Hoffman. Try. 6–0. For another 18 minutes both teams strained for a break. Dallas Johnson was hit hard and had wobbly legs. Cronk made the next big break, dummying to Slater and then bursting beyond a poor tackle attempt. He passed it to Adam Blair, who scored a try. Smith missed the conversion. 10–0. The pro-Eels crowd was frustrated. So was Anderson in the box. Bellamy sat beside assistant coach Stephen Kearney and sipped water.

Three minutes into the second half the young Eels found their legs. Broken play was their reward. Storm scrambled to protect its citadel but Eric Grothe Jr scored diving through defenders. 10–6.

Cronk kicked a high ball. It came down 5 metres from Parramatta's line. The defence waited ... waited ... Inglis angled his run from the wing and did not slow down or even jump. He kept sprinting and caught the Steeden as if it was a baby thrown from a balcony. It would not have broken if it were an egg, so softly did it meet his carriage. He was neither tackled nor bumped on the way through and scored under the posts and spiked the oval on the painted turf. It was the young man's 67th NRL try – his seventh in five matches.

The Eels went down the other end and again broke through Storm's defence. They were targeting a pocket on the right-hand side. Melbourne appeared vulnerable but it kept scoring. Cronk was again the maestro. He kept kicking for field position. Then he shot Blair through another gap. Slater was in support. Try. 22–6.

The final 15 minutes might have been another victory march ... but no. Parramatta didn't believe it should be beaten. Veteran Nathan Hindmarsh tackled like a bear trap. Hayne strained to make his mark. Storm was disciplined to hold its line. With ten minutes to go Eel

Joel Reddy sprang and caught a chip. Steamroller Fuifui Moimoi then crashed through defenders and carried Slater and Steve Turner as human cargo across the threshold for one of the best Grand Final tries of the decade. 22–16. The crowd spent the next seven minutes urging the men wearing blue-and-yellow to slay the interlopers.

Storm players in 2009 had an unusual theme.

Under the coach's direction, they had spent the season working out what it meant to play with a Purple Heart. The athletes wrote down how they felt about playing in Bellamy's team. One footballer per week stood in front of the squad the night before a match and read his thoughts. This was classic Bellamy. Not only was he finding out about his men, he was making them explore their own emotions. Such a thing can be powerful, for each young man comes from a different background. Each player has different motivations brought on by their upbringings. All are searching for meaning and somewhere to be loved and appreciated. Talking about comfort and loyalty and unity in front of friends is humbling beyond measure. Everyone listens. Tears are shed in such quiet moments. By now, Storm players believed they *were* members of a family

Defending a tryline is easier when you stand beside someone you perceive to be, at that very moment, your brother.

Hayne skied a bomb. Slater dropped it. Bellamy hung his head. The crowd clapped like thunder. But the tackles stuck. Slater shot up the middle and lost the ball. The Golden Boot winner – the world's best – had made two consecutive mistakes ... but luck was on his side. A referee's mistake gifted Storm a penalty that helped Melbourne set up for a field goal.

Three minutes and 22 seconds remained when Inglis, dropped the ball before his feet and booted it flatly. Goal. One point. 23–15. Premiers again.

Inglis's skill had landed the victory but courage in defence had saved them from defeat. Slater won the Clive Churchill Medal. He said, 'Cooper Cronk deserved it.' The statement was modest and true.

'There's always disappointment,' says defeated coach Daniel Anderson, remembering that day. 'I've learnt now it's never nice to lose but it's very hard to get there so you can't mope when you fail in a Grand Final. So cast off the disappointment and still enjoy the company of family and friends that night because it's a pretty big achievement.'

He does not feel his club was beaten by one of the great teams.

> I just felt they were a better team than us on the night. I thought we handled the game and situation well and fought hard. It's one of those things where you don't think about it but other people say, 'If they didn't have one of those big four [Smith, Cronk, Slater or Inglis] then, what would have happened?' And you go yeah, but it never happened. Personally I've always felt the privilege to be in my sport and especially in it professionally. A fair bit of stuff comes your way, negatively and positive. But no-one owes you anything.

Storm's staff and board – the rest of the family – joined the players on a slow victory lap. By now the Independent directors and News Ltd directors were great friends. Board member Craig Watt recalls it best:

> Being so close to a number of individuals I understood just how much work was put in – by a playing group, the office staff, the sales and marketing teams, the administration and the finance team – not to mention the numerous volunteers who gave up their time to give the club a hand. The memory I will forever savour is walking around the boundary of the Sydney Olympic stadium with my fellow directors after our great group hung on to beat Parramatta in a hard-fought game. What a fabulous moment.
>
> I also recall the great win we had in Leeds the following February, in almost Arctic conditions, to take out the World Club Challenge, surrounded by a group of passionate sponsors and club officials at the home of the Leeds Rhinos. At that particular moment Storm were effectively on top of the world. I had no idea what was about to unfold.

The in-house fire that had been sparked in 2006 had made its way past the foundations and into the walls. The blaze would soon be in the roof.

PART FOUR

CHAPTER 29

'THEY'VE GOT NOTHIN'.'

They were at a trendy pub celebrating being the NRL champion. Music and perfume and success were in the air. It was the Melbourne Storm Christmas party. Waldron, who had been at the club's helm for five years, said to Matt Hanson, 'If I left, you'd take over wouldn't you?'

Hanson said he didn't know. 'Why?'

'You'd like it, wouldn't you?' urged the CEO.

Hanson had long waited for an opportunity to become a CEO but enthusiasm wasn't his first response. 'Maybe.' He knew Waldron's job, if it ever went to him, would come with landmines. He had grown to admire and like most of his colleagues. He could see great potential for the club. Hanson looked around the room and wondered what people would say if they knew what he knew about the past six months. The only other person who understood his state of mind was the financial controller, Gregory.

Gregory's first few months at Storm were everything he had hoped. The staff – from the football department and front office – were warm and welcoming. He'd sat down with Ponissi every month to go through the football department spending. Bellamy was always polite and generous with his time. After-match drinks and functions were fun. There were so many young people on the staff; it was very different to the ageing workforce at Kodak.

Gregory took a while to twig that there were strange things happening with the salary cap. Although it was not initially obvious, he felt something was not right. Then the reality of Storm's overpayments became apparent and it made him feel uneasy, like Hanson before him and Vale before Hanson.

There was nothing he could do short of blowing the whistle. Each day he wrestled with his conscience. But at the end of those days he would walk out of the office and look around at all the people, his workmates, and see them applying themselves for the good of the franchise. He simply could not unburden himself. How do you bring down a place and shatter the people who love their jobs?

In July, Schubert had rung Gregory and asked him to provide all transaction records from the previous year between Storm and McManus entities. The McManus Presents payment of Storm money to footballers had ended but the paperwork was still there and Gregory knew it was not above board.

It was clear Schubert had received a tip-off. It could have been from anyone. A lot of people knew about the third-party payments.

With concern, Gregory told Hanson. Hanson rang Waldron, who was out of the office.

Hanson was aghast. 'He asked for all the McManus stuff.'

Waldron was typically optimistic. 'We'll get it sorted,' he replied. 'They've got nothin'.' For the next ten months Waldron repeated that phrase often.

After Schubert's request, Waldron scheduled a meeting on Tuesday, 14 July with an aim to make new invoices. The vaguely named 'consulting fees' invoices that were received from McManus companies were going to raise more questions than they answered. So Storm made a set of more detailed bills. One of the 'consulting fees' bills for $65,000 was renamed '*Promotional Fee for Masquerade Ball – event management, production staff, Rogue Traders appearance fee, MC, DJ, and other entertainment*'. Another 'consulting fee' invoice was transformed into: '*2008 Melbourne Grand Prix Hospitality Package – 29 March 2008 – Deposit*'. A $64,000 bill became '*Promotional Fee for 1300 Luncheon at Palladium Room Crown Casino ...*'

Two invoices were larger and more elaborately described than the others. An invoice for $143,000 – originally called 'consulting fees' was replaced by: '*Hire fee of Kearns Lounge marquee at Olympic Park as per Rental Agreement dated 1 March 07: 2007 – 13 game at $5.600 per game; 2008 – 12 games at $5,850 per game*'. The final one was similar. It was an invoice for $140,000. Originally it was called '*Digital Signage Rights – 2010 Rectangular Stadium*'. It was replaced by the description: '*Purchase of Kearns Lounge marquee by Melbourne Storm Rental Agreement dated 1 March 2007*'.

The Kearns Lounge Marquee was an entertainment section of Olympic Park.

As part of Storm's effort to cover its tracks, Gregory sent the new invoices to Schubert along with a purported rental agreement, signed by Waldron. The problem was: neither Storm nor McManus Group owned Kearns Lounge Marquee. Melbourne Olympic Park Trust managed the marquee. MOPT was established in 1995, after a merger of the National Tennis Centre Trust and the Olympic Park Committee of Management.

The money paid on receipt of these invoices had already gone from Storm through McManus Group businesses and was now with the players. Schubert was following a paper trail in search of evidence.

If Schubert was Waldron's grim reaper, the Storm CEO was now Schubert's white whale.

With Schubert investigating, Storm could no longer continue paying any players through McManus companies. The club was now searching for ways to meet its commitments to players for the third party agreements.

Sponsor Gerry Ryan arranged a third-party deal for Smith worth $100,000. Ryan says he believed it was a genuine deal. 'Not for me, for one of our subsidiary companies [Coast to Coast, which distributes and imports camping and leisure gear],' he explains. Ryan says Smith's role was to market the company. 'We were just about to,' he says. 'We had all the posters done and all the marketing ready to go. How do you reconcile saying yes it is [legitimate under NRL rules] and yes it's not, and how other clubs are allowed to have third party agreements similar to what happened to Cameron.'

The NRL was not informed about that TPA.

Ryan was still a Storm director, although he was considering standing down from the board due to increasing business commitments. In just over 12 months he would launch his first professional cycling team, to compete on the world tour and hopefully race in the Tour de France.

Trying to find money to pay players was starting to become a full-time job for Waldron. Inglis's assault charge had put a full stop on his potential to attract TPAs.

The deceptions were bringing Hanson and Gregory closer together. Both men were becoming sleepless and stressed. They only had each other to confide in. Whenever Hanson questioned Waldron's methods, the CEO explained that the whole league was cheating the cap. 'Everyone's doin' it,' he would say. '*Everyone*.'

To assuage his creeping discomfort, Hanson once asked a player manager whether it *was* happening at other clubs. The agent replied, 'I've got players with every single club and they've all got separate deals [to the NRL contract].'

That reinforced in Hanson's mind that Waldron was telling the truth – footballers across the breadth of the NRL were being paid secret third-party deals or cash on the side. Waldron used to tell anyone who would listen the Broncos were overpaying players. 'Look at the Thoroughbreds [a group of Queensland businessmen supporting the Broncos],' he said over and over.

In 2009 Brisbane fell under a brief but ultimately fruitless Schubert investigation, sparked by evidence given in the corruption trial of former Queensland government minister Gordon Nuttall.

Listening to Waldron say other clubs were cheating did not make Hanson feel comfortable about Storm's activities. But it did help ease the tension. And whenever the chief operating officer (COO) felt the weight of the situation, he reminded himself that Waldron's schemes to break league rules were in place before he arrived. Also, his job was to facilitate Storm's move into the new stadium. That was it. Then he would leave.

Gregory wanted to jump ship earlier. His position had become personally untenable. His insides were churning. The premiership had been hollow to him. Each day he felt lower and lower. The stress he felt was made more intense by his growing adoration for the football club and its staff. He felt like he was in the right place – but at the wrong time. Like Vale, he was not the type of person to confront Waldron and challenge him about what the club was doing. He started looking for another job.

In late 2009 he applied for a chief financial officer (CFO) role at an AFL club. Gregory spoke to Waldron about 'exploring other opportunities'. Waldron said he would support him if he wanted to leave but intimated he might also be leaving soon. 'There might be an opportunity for you to move up [to CFO] if I move on.' It was another hint that Waldron was considering a departure.

Gregory fantasised about what would happen if Waldron left. In his mind, Storm would possibly promote Hanson to CEO. Hanson and Gregory would be running the show. Then they could start afresh, operate the business properly. He decided to stay put for a while, see what happened in the new year.

On 12 November 2009, it was announced to the public that Victoria had finally won a bid to create a new Super Rugby franchise. 'This is a vote for commonsense,' said Australian Rugby Union CEO John O'Neill. It would soon emerge that wealthy media buyer Harold Mitchell was the new owner of a team called the Melbourne Rebels, which would play its home matches at the new rectangular stadium. Storm officials pondered whether a rugby side and rugby league club could both flourish in Melbourne, let alone at the same venue. But the Rebels' arrival had bigger implications for Storm than many thought. Harold Mitchell needed a start-up CEO. He asked Waldron to lead his club into the future.

Even with the Christmas party conversation echoing in his mind, Hanson just could not believe Waldron was ready to leave his beloved Storm. But things were about to start moving quickly.

Chairman Rob Moodie was sitting in a Sydney Airport lounge, awaiting a flight to Mozambique, when he received a call from Waldron, who said he was thinking about taking a job as CEO of the newly formed Super Rugby team. Moodie asked whether he had taken the job or was weighing it up. Waldron replied he was just contemplating it. But he was going, for sure. Moodie spent the next two weeks in Maputo wondering who would take charge of the NRL champion in 2010.

Waldron then spoke to News Ltd COO Macourt and said he had decided to resign. Macourt tried to persuade Waldron to stay. After all this time, Macourt still valued Waldron's contribution. He offered him more money. Even that didn't work.

Hanson was sitting at home watching the horseracing when he received a call from Storm director Peter Maher. Maher said, 'Can you meet me in 15 minutes?'

Hanson: 'Yeah.'

Hanson rang Waldron and explained the strange little conversation. Waldron said, 'Yeah, I've resigned. And they want you to sit in the role. If they think you're the right bloke to take it over, you should.'

Hanson met with Maher at South Wharf, near the old colonial ship *Polly Woodside*. Maher said, 'We're gunna conduct a search for a CEO. You'll have three months before the search is complete. Don't leave any stone unturned. Give it your absolute all.'

Hanson was appreciative of the offer and did not want to throw it back in Maher's face. If he rejected the position he would have to explain why. Not for the first time, Hanson baulked at telling Maher about the salary cap breaches. He considered that if Maher – or Moodie – knew about the breaches, then they would want to go straight to the NRL and the team would collapse before he could start mending it. At that moment, the interim CEO determined to accept the role and fix the mess. He rang Gregory and asked if he would be the new CFO. Gregory said yes but only if they started managing the franchise legitimately. They agreed to give it a go.

What made these two financial workers think they should try to undo what had been done? It was a huge risk without obvious reward. They would receive no bonuses, pats on the back or trophies. Certainly, they wanted to prevent the club from falling into a deep hole. It was a decision that would cause them to pay a heavy personal toll.

For the next three months Hanson was in charge of Storm, a role akin to driving a racecar without brakes or adequate steering.

Firstly, the interim CEO and CFO had to figure out how much was owing to players. The perfect scenario would be to pay outstanding amounts and then cut wages. Hanson and Gregory started talking about offloading one of the champion playmakers. Probably Inglis. They did not share their thoughts with Bellamy. It was the first time any Storm leaders even contemplated the reality of losing one of the big four to fit under the salary cap.

In the lead-up to Waldron leaving Storm headquarters for the final time, he gave Hanson the three side letters. Waldron told Hanson to keep them at home. Hanson read them and was stunned at the extras included.

There was no clear air for Hanson to breathe. Agents George Mimis and Allan Gainey, among others, began calling, chasing money owed to their clients. Hanson crunched some sums and figured out the club owed players $750,000 outside the salary cap for 2010.

For weeks Hanson stayed in contact with Waldron, still trying to understand what had been promised. Some things didn't make sense, like the item in Inglis's side letter that compelled the football club to pay Greg's parents' rent. Often Hanson would express despair. Waldron was calmer. He was no longer in the hot seat.

Schubert undertook a salary cap audit on Storm for season 2009 and found issues he wanted to explore further. One of them involved the TPA Smith had with Fox Sports. The other related to a termination payment to Dallas Johnson. The league was questioning whether it should have been included under the 2009 or 2010 salary cap. Hanson relayed Schubert's concerns to Storm directors at a board meeting in February. There was no panic. The Smith deal had been known by everyone for a long time. The Johnson payout didn't involve a lot of money and was not considered a big deal. Hanson did not declare that Waldron had guaranteed the Fox Sports TPA. He was waiting to see how things played out with Schubert. But the salary cap auditor was not about to show all his cards at once. He had more investigating to do.

Hanson was certain of one thing: he needed advice. So he went to a trusted friend – his ex-boss Ian Collins. The pair had stayed mates long after Hanson had worked for him at the Docklands stadium. They walked for exercise six days a week through Royal Park in Carlton, near Storm's offices. Collins was not only one of Melbourne's most influential businessmen, he had been president of Carlton Football Club in the AFL, stepping in after the Blues suffered salary-cap sanctions in 2002. He would know what to do.

Collins recalls,

> I would walk with him of a morning at 6am and we would discuss some of those issues and I just told him that because of the structure of the club and the rules and regulations, he ought to talk to the board about it and just disclose it all. I told him he should give no surprises to the board. He should tell the board and explain it all to them, what the issues were, that he's uncovered and I think he took that advice. The only thing he probably didn't do – he didn't call a formal meeting and tell the board all at once. He did it one by one. And I think that didn't go in his favour. Some of the board members said they weren't told or didn't know. It should've been a formal meeting with all present and properly documented, along with minutes.

Did Collins feel for Hanson?

'I did, because it wasn't of his making.'

The first director Hanson talked to was Ryan. He told the caravan king he needed to find $750,000 to pay the players. Ryan said he would try to help but instructed Hanson to tell News Ltd directors Watt and Stanton about the crisis.

Storm was about to head overseas for the World Club Challenge. Hanson agreed he should talk to Watt and Stanton. He felt better having a plan of disclosure and took off to Europe with the slightest hope he could save the club after all.

Meanwhile, Gregory got to work reforming some of Storm's management processes. He began a long-overdue overhaul of recruitment and contracting. The letters of offer were still ambiguous. So Gregory ensured General Manager of Football Operation Ponissi and scout Darren Bell started using more formal language. For instance, instead of an offer containing the vague promise of 'relocation costs - $5000' it would in future read: 'relocation allowance of up to $5000 on presentation of approved tax invoices from credible suppliers'. He wanted to make sure that he accounted for 'true costs' in the spirit of the salary cap. He wanted to be transparent to Schubert, who was no longer being referred to in Melbourne as the shadow of death.

The new CFO wrote a policy document. From 2010 he planned to submit letters of offers to the NRL for approval before transferring deals onto NRL contracts to be signed. That way there could be no confusion.

Gregory believed he was re-creating the accounting and reporting culture of Storm. He was determined to concentrate on what he could control, forget about the past as much as he could.

In Europe, Hanson decided to first speak about the salary cap pressures to Watt. The World Club Challenge was in Leeds but sponsors had been invited. A side-trip to Barcelona was included in the itinerary. Hanson was carrying his salary cap secret while still auditioning for the full-time CEO position. It was a balancing act. On one hand he was trying to be like Waldron, excel as a friendly and entertaining host to sponsors. On the other hand, he was attempting to be the anti-Waldron on salaries.

Watt was with his wife, Lisa-May, on this trip. Hanson spoke to him late one night about player payments, among other things. They were at a bar, drinking mojitos.

This is how Watt recalls it:

> Like any conversation that occurs late at night after several drinks we drifted from topic to topic. At one stage of the conversation I do recall him saying that he had a call from White's manager claiming that Waldron had promised an extra $60,000. It was very late at night and my comment went along the lines that I

> wasn't surprised that certain player managers would be trying this on, given Matt had only just replaced Brian.

Hanson did not tell Watt about the side letters. The men did not speak about the salary cap for another two months.

The trip ended successfully for Storm on the field and off it. The team beat Leeds. Cameron Smith was man of the match. The sponsors were giddy with excitement. Melbourne Storm Rugby League Club was on top of the world.

Some time after he returned from the UK, Hanson rang Stanton, the other News Ltd director, who lived in Queensland and had not attended the World Club Challenge.

Stanton was in his car on the Gold Coast when he answered. Hanson told him, 'There is a problem with the salary cap.' He outlined that Schubert had been investigating several issues, which Stanton knew about through the earlier board meeting. Hanson later claimed he told Stanton there was more to it. Stanton says Hanson did not give him any further details. Certainly, there was no mention of the side letters.

In the weeks approaching the season, Hanson was trying to promote his team, keeping up the façade of positivity. He was a guest for the first time on a national sports television program – ABC's *Offsiders*. The discussion was as much about News Ltd's future in the game as it was about Storm. Rugby league was moving very slowly to abolish the News Ltd–ARL partnership in favour of an independent commission, similar to the AFL model.

Host Gerard Whateley said, 'You've taken over at a fascinating time. This is potentially the fifth year of a dynasty or it will be the end of an era?'

'It's going to be a very exciting year this year,' Hanson replied, appearing a little nervous. 'Moving in the new stadium, there is a lot happening off the field as well. We'll probably see this as a watershed year for Melbourne Storm.'

Whateley: 'I have heard from time to time the phrase used of News Ltd that the Storm exists at the pleasure of News Ltd. When that pleasure dries up who's to say what the future will hold?'

Hanson:

> I think at a point in time, News probably will relinquish the ownership of the Storm. I think it's probably very important to

> note that the one thing I found in dealing with News is they very much want to see Melbourne Storm survive. I think that's very important and it's important to the future of the game. Victoria is the second-largest advertising market. I think all of the other clubs in the NRL have looked at Melbourne Storm and they acknowledge the commercial importance of the Storm to the game.

Offsiders' format revolves around a panel of commentators. On the program this day was Rebecca Wilson, a News Ltd columnist. Whateley asked Wilson: 'Rebecca, how many conditions will News put on its exit from rugby league?'

'News want to get out of the game, no doubt about that,' replied Wilson, who was also News Ltd boss John Hartigan's partner.

> They really feel they've set a benchmark, they've set the NRL up in a good way. But they won't get out unless it's absolutely fair, honest and transparent. They will not relinquish all of their control over the game that they have, the 50 per cent control they have, to the dinosaurs who used to run it.

Whateley to Hanson: 'What about the team? The recent history of football clubs will say four years, four grand finals is about as far as you can go. Can you extend a dynasty into a fifth year?'

Hanson: 'You shouldn't try telling Craig Bellamy that. We're very much of the view that there is no premiership window, especially I suppose with the free agency that we operate under.'

Storm's roster was brighter than it had been for years, and not because of any overspending. The club's Under 20s team had also won the Grand Final in 2009. The youth roster was flush with potential first-graders. A stand-out Englishman five-eighth, Gareth Widdop, was one player to watch. He looked like he might complement Cronk in the halves one day soon. Recruiter Darren Bell could take a lot of credit for the bumper crop, as well as Ponissi.

Hanson had performed well under the bright lights of the studio and warmth of the make-up. His pitch to become full-time CEO was going well. He had the backing of most of the board. If only he didn't have to handle Waldron's legacy.

Melbourne beat Cronulla in round one at Toyota Stadium. The next week it defeated the Knights in Newcastle.

During this time, Hanson scrambled to get back under the cap for 2010 on payments the NRL actually knew about. This was hard enough. He decided to honour commitments that had been made by his predecessor, so as not to create more problems with agents. One player's manager was in negotiations with Storm at that stage. He was pushing for a bit extra in his client's deal, outside the cap. Hanson resisted, determined to draw a line in the sand.

Among other things, the interim CEO successfully argued to vary Smith's contract by $120,000, shifting that sum to 2011. That was a small victory. But he was swimming against the stream's current, dodging driftwood every day.

Schubert did not yet have all the evidence he needed to prosecute the team. But he was readying to strike.

Agents continued contacting Hanson for money owed.

Ryan helped ease Hanson's load ever so slightly. Inglis's accountant was hounding Hanson to pay his client cash from the TPAs in the side letter. Ryan paid Inglis $50,000. At the time, he said it was a loan (as noted at a subsequent board meeting) but three years later says he was never paid back. Inglis's agent says the footballer paid tax on the lump sum.

By no means did Ryan understand how much Storm had overspent on players. He rang Waldron and said, 'Brian, you gotta tell us what the situation is.'

Waldron offered no concrete answers.

Ryan explains, 'It was a mess. I don't think probably Waldron realised the situation.'

Ryan was still holding the opinion that other clubs were breaking the salary cap rules.

'It's public knowledge that everyone does it,' he says.

> It's like Lance Armstrong saying I've never taken drugs. It is rife. The reason is because clubs don't get enough money from TV rights to pay the players what's rightfully theirs. You look at the NRL in terms of distribution and the salary cap compared to the AFL. Minimum wage ... we had senior players on $35,000, bustin' their arse.

Ryan also believed it was Storm's right to keep the players it developed. 'It just goes to show you how good a system they have down there [Storm football department],' he explains. 'You look at the number of players they've lost. And they've never gone out and said come to us and here's a car or an apartment. They're always trying to keep their best players and you look at the turnover, we couldn't afford to keep them all.'

During this time Ryan was an important figure for another reason. News Ltd COO Macourt arranged a meeting with him and club chairman Moodie to discuss the sale of the franchise. Macourt says the timing of the discussion had nothing to do with the salary cap crisis. 'It would've been a complete coincidence,' he says.

Ryan says he was keen on buying the club but was unsatisfied with what he was hearing from News Ltd. 'I couldn't come to terms with where the sport was heading,' he says.

Macourt also had discussions with Hanson early in 2010. They talked about the salary cap. 'We had a meal at Southbank and that's when he said they were being investigated for a salary cap thing,' Macourt recalls. 'And I would've said you've got to cooperate with them. From that conversation it wasn't apparent to me at the time that the breach was significant.'

CHAPTER 30

SCHUBERT MAKES HIS PLAY

The team was opposing Penrith in a twilight match.

Injured Slater had been in doubt right until the start of the match. But he played. In the 19th minute Cronk took a pass from Smith, and made a right foot step to disrupt the Panthers' defensive line. He almost broke through but was tackled. He offloaded. Slater ran onto another pass, had only the fullback to beat, and used Brett Finch, who scored the first try.

Penrith scored its first try in the 35th minute.

After half-time Cronk measured a 20-metre flat kick across field to Slater, who went over near the posts. It was perfect Storm. The half-filled stadium cheered when the Panthers got within six points with a few minutes to go. But Storm closed it out. The shot of the coach's box was not one of joy. Bellamy sat with his hand over his mouth. Ponissi was taking notes and Steve Kearney was staring straight ahead. Word was out that there was something wrong with the salary cap. Schubert was sniffing around.

That morning a bold headline appeared in the News Ltd press about an investigation into dealings between Gold Coast football club, a developer and five-eighth Scott Prince (Prince and his team were later exonerated). But there was a bigger rugby league story brewing.

Dave Donaghy was the Storm media manager. The former *Herald Sun* journalist had joined the club in 2008, after Bellamy's ill-conceived blow-up at the judiciary. The coach decided he wanted a close media advisor.

Donaghy and Bellamy had been cool on each other while Donaghy was writing for the paper, but now the young man was in the inner sanctum at Storm. He was intelligent, enthusiastic and extremely likeable. He would soon play an important part in saving Storm from extinction.

On the night of the Penrith game Donaghy's phone was ringing non stop. Fairfax was calling to ask about a deal involving Smith and Fox Sports. On the surface of it, the Smith deal was fine. John Ribot had brokered it with Fox Sports and made sure it was cleared by the NRL. News Ltd knew about it too, of course.

Donaghy sensed there was more to the story. He heard urgency and excitability in the journalistic voices at the other end of the line that told him this was no run-of-the-mill yarn. He went to Hanson and asked how bad it was. He plainly and intuitively probed, 'Are we fucked?'

Donaghy did not suspect Melbourne had been cheating. Even before he joined the franchise he was writing stories about how many ace players Storm had lost to free trade to stay under cap. Back in May 2008 he wrote for News Ltd:

> Jeff Lima will become the 16th player to leave Melbourne Storm since 2006 if he accepts a lucrative three-year offer from Canterbury. The extent of how much the salary cap squeeze has affected the defending premiers can be seen by the number – and quality – of players to have left the Storm since they made their first grand finals under Craig Bellamy.

Hanson saw Donaghy was worried.

'Well, we don't know, we don't quite know,' the interim CEO told the media man. 'They're looking into us and we don't quite know.'

Fairfax journalist Adrian Proszenko won a Walkley Award for his story, which hit the stands the next day, detailing the Smith deal. He wrote:

> The NRL is investigating Melbourne over alleged salary-cap breaches that occurred during its premiership triumph. Salary-cap auditor Ian Schubert has raised concerns over several issues around payments to Storm players, including a third-party deal between skipper Cameron Smith and Foxtel. But Smith last night said it was a 'non-issue' and was adamant it would not have any effect on him.

Smith told Proszenko, 'My job is to worry about my football. The things that are in my contract are obviously private but they are the things that our CEO works with the NRL to do. It's the first I've heard of this issue.'

Smith had signed the guarantee in his side letter. His agent had signed *and* authored the guarantee. But it was clear from Smith's comments he considered Waldron ultimately responsible for this type of contracting issue.

Ponissi had held talks with Gallop and Schubert about the Smith deal. Ponissi was quoted in Proszenko's story: 'There were negotiations with the NRL and the club in December 2008 and January 2009, whether it should be inclusive in the cap. There was debate and basically we have been waiting for 12 months for a decision.'

The real story was not yet clear. Gallop explains the Smith deal debate:

> We'd been arguing with the Storm about Smith's contractual arrangements with Fox Sports for months. Schubert's position was they're definitely guaranteeing this. Their position was we definitely haven't. It was a conversation I had with Waldron. I think I had it with [John] Ribot as well. And in the end it *was* guaranteed.

Donaghy didn't receive any more calls from journalists for a while. The media pressure went flat. He was hoping what he had witnessed was only a manic blip. Everything was calm.

On 2 April Melbourne hosted St George Illawarra at Docklands stadium. (The new rectangular stadium was not yet ready.) Storm won easily before a record regular-season home crowd of about 25,000. Some 13 years after it was born, it seemed Melbourne Storm was finally being appreciated by its local people.

Five days later Schubert went south on a fact-finding mission. He arranged though Hanson to meet McManus. Schubert recalled in a subsequent report of his investigations:

> While he was largely uncooperative, McManus agreed to provide me with a copy of group certificates for the small number of players that he said were employed by McManus Presents. He insisted that the employment (of players) had been genuine with payment being made for actual services provided.

Subsequently *The NRL Report of Salary Cap Auditor into Melbourne Storm Salary Cap Breaches* recorded that:

> No evidence was found that Mr McManus [or any staff of Andrew McManus Presents] knew about the payments or was aware that payments by entities associated with him could have contributed to the club breaching the cap.

Schubert stayed in Melbourne after his meeting with McManus. The NRL's chief detective had one more important matter to resolve. He met Brian Morris, representative of the Melbourne Olympic Park Trust. Schubert finally discovered that the Kearns Lounge Marquee was never the property of Storm or McManus Presents. No party other than the MOPT has any right to sell it, Morris explained. It was another breakthrough Schubert had been working toward.

Now to confront the club ... Schubert met with Hanson the same day. Armed with undeniable evidence the McManus Presents invoices were, in part, arranged to pay players, Schubert let Hanson try to explain. The interim CEO knew the ruse was no longer going to work. He conceded the marquee deal was a crock. In one last desperate play to buy himself time, Hanson explained the marquee deception was created by Waldron to somehow generate more money for match-day entertainment. Schubert didn't believe it. Worse, he knew it wasn't true. Not for the last time Hanson silently cursed Waldron for the mess he had left behind. But he still conceded no ground to Schubert on the secret payments to players.

The next day Schubert wrote to Hanson. He formally listed several discrepancies he had found in Storm's 2009 audit, including Smith's deal, Johnson's termination money etc. The total overspend he alleged was $183,345. Schubert also wrote that 'the matters pertaining to seasons 2006–9 will be addressed next week'.

Hanson decided enough was enough. He finally decided to tell all to the final three board members: Petra Fawcett, Rob Moodie and Peter Maher. He waited for the weekend to pass. Melbourne lost its first match of the season to the Gold Coast Titans. A round-five defeat meant nothing compared to the dark clouds over the club's future.

On Monday, 12 April, Hanson phoned Fawcett and asked if she would meet him. The pair sat at a bar in Melbourne and Hanson told her about the unpaid, undisclosed money. It was a short conversation, without great detail.

Fawcett urged Hanson to inform the chairman, Moodie, straight away. 'Or I will,' she said. 'The chairman's role is to govern the club.'

Recalling the moment she learned her club was a cheat, Fawcett says,

> I didn't ask any details and we didn't talk about it. I didn't really appreciate what he was talking about. I'm surprised anybody wasn't made aware of it earlier to be honest. I can't believe it can happen. I think when Matt took over ... I'm surprised it took a couple of months. I don't know what he was expecting would happen – if he could fix it when he was the CEO. I was devastated.

The next day at 1.35pm, Hanson sat down with Moodie at a busy cafe near Melbourne University, around the corner from the Nossal Institute, where Moodie worked as a professor of public health. There was a Storm board meeting coming up, so it was not unusual for the CEO and chairman to meet and discuss the upcoming agenda. Moodie read Hanson's countenance to understand this catch-up was different. Something was wrong.

Above the noise of students chattering and the grinding of coffee, Hanson said, 'I need to tell you about this stuff with the player payments.'

He then explained that Waldron had left him with a $750,000 payroll gap for 2010. Also, Waldron had been systematically cheating the cap. Hanson had known about it. So had others. Critically, Schubert now knew about it (some of it, at least).

Moodie's mood turned sour. He recoiled at the moment of disclosure. 'I felt physically ill,' Moodie recalls. 'This is like an unexploded time bomb full of crap. It's about to go off. And it has also completely destroyed my sense of what's right. I thought we were a legitimate, genuine, fair club based on a really strong work ethic.'

Moodie immediately phoned Maher and passed on what Hanson had said. Finally, everyone knew. But there was still uncertainty about the size of the problem.

Moodie rang Waldron and they arranged to see each other.

While Storm was staggered and fearful of what would happen next, the NRL was planning its next move. Schubert contacted a Brisbane barrister called Martin Burns S.C., who helped the league with cap queries. The cap auditor knew enough by now to realise that he did not know everything. He needed help in planning to extract more information. Gallop recalls bringing in expertise and legal resources: 'We don't go into this stuff shooting from the hip. We were using a very experienced senior counsel every step of the way.'

In the meantime the McManus Group emailed Schubert group certificates for three footballers. Hanson was copied in on the email. Strangely, so was the CEO of the Melbourne Rebels, though Waldron must barely have noticed. He was preparing to see Moodie at a cafe.

Moodie has an aura of fatherly decency. He is one of those people who can appear strong, dignified, confident, warm and generous in a single greeting. His head was spinning when he caught the first sight of Waldron the day they discussed the betrayal. The conversation was a short one, stripped of small talk and blokey banter. Moodie asked why Waldron did it. Why cheat? Why lie?

'Because everyone else does it,' Waldron explained. 'You have to do it to be competitive.' Waldron added he had felt the pressure from News Ltd to be successful, which was true.

News Ltd demands success from its managers. There was always a lot riding on Waldron's performance. The club's long-term survival depended on its improved finances, which related directly to the team's success or failure. Without the best players, you don't have a top team. Without a top team, attendances are diminished, membership falls, sponsors drop away, further losses are incurred – the team is not attractive to buyers. Waldron always had this on his mind.

But his actions weren't completely motivated by pressure from above – they were needled by something inside him. Waldron had always been driven by ambition. From his school-teaching days he burned to live a bigger life. Hard work as a volunteer at Oakleigh had catapulted him to Richmond. He became a young man in a new frontier and as the old Victorian Football League became the Australian Football League, Waldron could see opportunities opening up before him as gift to his imagination and fortitude. At Richmond he acquired a taste, perhaps an addiction, to professional football, a restless man's playground, where the working class can climb the invisible social ladder to vast respect.

Most men are in a hurry in their late twenties and early thirties. After that, life settles and flattens out a bit. Waldron always felt like he needed to do more, be more. At a time when married men with little children look for somewhere to put their feet up, Waldron found a new adventure. St Kilda gave him a lifeline. His brief successes and premature departure from that AFL club only fed his determination. Along came Storm, a club with young footballers and an obsessed coach, growing up together to become the best in the world. It was Waldron's perfect home. He could lead them anywhere. He could be anything, as long as everyone stayed together.

Waldron did not tell Moodie about the development money, the 2006 mistake that set him on his path to where he sat now. He did not explain why he did all the things he did after that. There was no time for explanations. And what was the point?

'I'm sorry,' said Waldron to Moodie, who was not as angry as he was dismayed. Moodie wondered whether Waldron was genuinely remorseful. He wondered about everything now. The colourless look of disappointment on the chairman's face told Waldron more than he could say. The men prepared to part ways.

'Don't worry,' Waldron added. 'They don't know enough.'

That was true too. The NRL did not know about the side letters. But they would soon find out.

Days after he met Waldron, Moodie was scheduled to make two addresses on the topic of leadership, for which he is renowned in Victoria and abroad. One speech was planned for a football club. His other audience was a crowd at Leadership Victoria, an esteemed development program. Moodie fulfilled his obligations but says now, 'I felt a fraud.' For the professor, the heaviness of knowing was becoming unbearable.

From that point, Waldron was reduced to a spectator in the fortunes of Melbourne Storm. Not that it stopped him from trying to influence the final score. He rang Gallop and said there had been no breaches. He offered to speak to Schubert. He made threats of legal action. Gallop recalls, 'I remember him threatening to sue if anybody suggested they'd breached the salary cap – he would sue them.' Gallop was not frightened. He was backing Schubert. Waldron's threat was without menace, but it shows he never gave up.

CHAPTER 31

THE BOMB HITS

Schubert's promised letter had still not arrived. Hanson was wondering what was taking so long.

Storm had a regular board meeting on 15 April. It was a Thursday. All directors attended, as did Hanson, Ponissi and four other department heads, including Gregory, who had just been married in a lovely ceremony on the Mornington Peninsula – the last joy he would know for a long time.

It must have seemed a peculiar meeting for those in the know. Some of the people in the room understood Storm was teetering on the edge of disaster. Others did not quite grasp the extraordinary circumstances.

Moodie tabled, as per the agenda, the minutes from the previous meeting. Next, Hanson provided his acting CEO's report. He worked through all elements of the club's function: membership ('It was suggested that the commercial operations team speak with MOPT to organise a membership marquee at the VB Test Match in order to increase member numbers.'); sponsorship ('It was noted that Sponsorship is currently $450,000 behind budget.'); staff ('Staff are generally happy but the long hours being worked are taking their toll.'); football department ('Injured senior players are beginning to return to the field ...'); World Club Challenge ('Robbie Kearns presence in terms of sponsor relations was noted as highly successful.') and so on.

Hanson then tabled a report on the 'salary cap audit.'

Notes from the meeting read:

> A letter received from Ian Schubert last week noted that Melbourne Storm is currently over the salary cap by $183k. The amount relates to fringe benefit tax (FBT) on management fees, Dallas Johnson's termination and grand final prize money being allocated to the player's [sic] fund.

Hanson outlined the club's defence. He said the club would refute the claims on the fringe benefits tax but 'will not refute the Dallas Johnson claim'.

Then he revealed Schubert's promised letter. The meeting notes reveal an understated tone: 'Ian Schubert has claimed that he has received a tip regarding salary cap issues between 2006 to 2009. Hanson has been advised a letter will be forwarded shortly detailing any claims.' The chairman noted that payments outside the salary cap are not to be made and it's not something the Melbourne Storm Board will do, or partake, in.

Another item on the agenda was Inglis's assault case. After seven months it had finally concluded. Ten days earlier the footballer had escaped a conviction and was ordered to attend a behavioural change program and pay $3000 to a women's health service.

The board notes read: 'The most important lesson learnt was the education, management and prevention of situations such as this.'

Gregory gave his finance report. Sponsorship was down. The World Club Challenge spend went $90,000 over budget. The meeting went on. Toward the end, Ponissi told the board the 2011 playing roster had been addressed and it was known that three players would have to be cut 'in order to fit into the salary cap'.

This highlighted the depth of the club's salary cap crisis. Waldron's secret payments aside, the franchise's wages were still bulging.

The board meeting was closed after two hours. The real situation of the salary cap was not actually discussed. Before and after the meeting, however, directors were scrambling to find out more about the breaches. Hanson was pulling together as much detail as he could from old and new contracts.

They painfully waited and waited for Schubert's letter. Another weekend went by. On Monday night, Storm hosted the Sea Eagles at Docklands. Melbourne lost its first match at that venue since 2001. Barely 14,000 people turned up.

Before the match a Storm player had received a strange phone call from one of his mates in Sydney. The friend told the footballer he had tried to place a wager at a betting outlet on Melbourne to win the premiership. But the agency would not take the bet. The athlete suggested there might have been something wrong with the system. Did he try again? Yes. The mate was adamant that something weird was going on. He simply could not back Storm for the title.

Hanson met with the board once more. This time he showed the directors on a spreadsheet what the players had been promised by Waldron in TPAs. He finally outlined the extent of the three secret side letters. They alone would cost the club at least $400,000 a year, on top of wages. The side letters were the cream of the deception. The details in those documents left jaws on the floor.

News Ltd director Craig Watt recalls from that meeting, 'The impression I got from Matt was that Brian had left him holding the can. With no third-party deals secured for these players and with Brian gone I don't think Matt knew how he was meant to find $400,000 to cover the guarantees.'

On Wednesday, 21 April, an emergency message went out to all Storm board members. Bellamy and Ponissi were also called in to the club's administrative headquarters at Princes Park, the shell of an old stadium, which Storm shared with AFL team Carlton.

Schubert's letter had arrived and it was frightening.

The leaders of the club arrived alone or in pairs, frowning. Hanson, Moodie, Maher, Watt, Bellamy and Ponissi. Not everyone could be there. Stanton, Ryan and Fawcett were absent. They were kept informed by phone.

All spoke in funereal tones.

The coach was aghast. He knew the club had been dealing with salary cap issues for weeks. But not like this.

Schubert's letter was labelled 'STRICTLY PRIVATE AND CONFIDENTIAL' and was addressed to Hanson. It read, in part:

> I have for some time been investigating the extent to which the Melbourne Storm has complied with its obligations under the NRL Playing Contract and Remuneration Rules.
>
> The investigation has discovered prima facie evidence of a number of serious and substantial discrepancies in the salary cap declarations that have been made on behalf of your Club. At this

> stage the investigation is focused on the declarations that have been made for the 2008 and 2009 seasons but it may also be necessary to investigate the declarations made for the 2006 and 2007 seasons.

Schubert revealed his investigation had 'entailed the sourcing of various documents and financial data'. He had also been provided information from 'parties external to the Club'.

It went on:

> Interviews of a number of persons have also been conducted – in Victoria, New South Wales and Queensland. The information gathered has been verified in [a] number of important respects and, more recently, I have taken legal advice from the NRL's solicitors as well as senior counsel regarding certain aspects of the matter.

In fact, the letter had been legally designed to emotionally rock the Storm hierarchy and compel a confession. Gallop explains, 'Schubert was doing a lot of work and I wasn't involved in it on a day-to-day basis. But he was getting information from people so we decided to send a letter drafted by our lawyers and flush some stuff out.'

Schubert wrote about his discoveries, including the letters of offer and the Kearns Lounge Marquee 'sham' agreement. He recalled the incident that led to the finding of the file in the office.

> I requested that I be provided with copies of the letters of offer for certain players. Your personal assistant overheard this and asked if I meant the folder in the cupboard, behind her desk ...

The league cap auditor used some figures as bait:

> Without wishing to compromise the integrity of the investigation, I am able to say that I am presently in possession of evidence that suggests that:
>
> In 2008 the Melbourne Storm failed to disclose payments made to players that totalled in excess of $220,000. These payments were in the form of undisclosed benefits, third party and ambassador agreements. There is also information from a third

party that I am investigating that suggests that further undisclosed payments of $80,000 were made;

In 2009 the Melbourne Storm failed to disclose payments made to players that totalled in excess of $200,000. These payments again were made in the form of undisclosed benefits, third party and ambassador agreements. These amounts are additional to the payments (that are) the subject of our present dispute in connection with the audit for the 2009 season.

The language was self-assured. Schubert then warned:

It follows that a comprehensive investigation must now be conducted to determine the full extent of the non-disclosure of remuneration, and the nature of the material unearthed to date necessarily leads me to suspect your Club may have failed to disclose remuneration with respect to not only the immediate past and current seasons but also with respect to earlier seasons. In broad scope, the next phase of the investigation will involve:

Conducting a full scale audit of the financial records of the Melbourne Storm;

Requiring all Melbourne Storm players during the 2006 and 2009 seasons to produce their taxation records for the period;

Conducting a full audit of the files for the relevant players held by their player managers ...

Schubert also flagged enquiries into 'any service provider and associated entities of Melbourne Storm who may reasonably be suspected of making player payments to the club', including McManus entities, 'New Breed and Andrew McManus Presents'.

It concluded with a stern invitation.

Given the seriousness of these allegations, I will require the full and immediate cooperation of not only the members of your Board and executive officers such as yourself, but also the full cooperation of your staff and the staff of all other Melbourne Storm related and associated entities, including sponsors.

Prior to embarking on the next phase, I wish to provide an opportunity for you, your financial controller and any other officer who wants to attend, to travel to Sydney to meet with me,

> the Chief Executive Officer and other relevant NRL officials. The purpose of such a meeting would be to provide your Club with an opportunity to make a full and frank disclosure of all payments made to players, particularly as they concern the 2008 and 2009 seasons, and all payments that you have contracted to make for the 2010 season that you have not disclosed. Such a course would obviously be preferable to what is now in contemplation but, of course, that is entirely a matter for your Board to consider.

Schubert proposed to meet the following Tuesday. That was six days away.

There was silence after the reading of the letter at Storm HQ. It was like a four-page death notice.

Bellamy was in shock.

He had made the club his life for seven and a half years. Though his name was not in that letter, his reputation was. He naturally turned his mind to possible sanctions. Maybe the league would strip the club of its points for 2010. That happened to the Warriors in 2006.

What now?

Moodie outlined his wishes. He wanted to be up-front and tell everything to the NRL, as soon as possible. The former Victorian Father of the Year didn't want to hide from his responsibility. He felt corrupted. Duped. Now that everything was clearer, he wanted to own up. It was the only way.

He recalls his reasoning: 'Ethics are important, honesty is important. I realise how hard being really ethical and being really honest in everything you do is.'

Moodie lectures about ethics at universities.

'I don't like people who are dishonest and I don't like that part of it,' he says.

> It's just the way I want to live my life. I want to be an honest person. I realise how hard in business and everything it is to be ... but there are degrees ... some people are just blatantly dishonest and two-faced and I just don't like that. Also, when you are dishonest it rebounds on you in the long run. I believe in karma.

With Moodie's intention clear, Bellamy started adding up the competition points ... They had won eight so far. No-one in that room mentioned Storm might lose its premierships. Losing credibility was their greatest fear.

Bellamy and Ponissi departed the offices to go home, thinking how hard it would be to prepare for the coming match against New Zealand on ANZAC Day knowing the club would send a delegation to throw itself at the mercy of the league two days after that. But after the football bosses left, the directors kept talking. Next Tuesday was too far away. Moodie wanted to go to NRL headquarters tomorrow. His conscience demanded it.

Moodie and Watt decided to call News Ltd management to discuss their next move. They went to another room in the building.

News Ltd already knew about Schubert's investigation. The NRL had been talking to its half-owner all week. COO Macourt, as a director on the NRL board, was dealing with it. He had passed it up the chain to CEO Hartigan.

Hartigan recalls, 'It was presented that the club had been involved in massive overspend on the salary cap.'

The phone call from Moodie and Watt went to Macourt. They told him they wanted to go to Sydney as soon as possible. Moodie said he wanted to give the league full disclosure. Critically, he informed Macourt about the side letters. Macourt was reassuring and said to come clean was a good idea. He was typically calm.

Many more phone calls were made that night. Storm called Gallop to say a delegation would be coming tomorrow morning. Gallop agreed to meet. He then called News Ltd. 'I spoke to Macourt that night and said they're coming up,' Gallop recalls, 'He said to me, "Just do what you've got to do."'

Moodie, Watt and Hanson would represent Storm in Sydney.

Meanwhile, Hanson had phoned Gregory to tell him about Schubert's letter. The CFO arrived at Storm HQ and stuck his head in Hanson's office to see what had been decided.

Gregory did not take part in the official discussions but hung around in the general offices for a while, in case he could be any help to anyone. He left Storm headquarters when it was getting late. He was walking down the stairs into the foyer when he noticed a father and his son lingering near the entrance. Gregory thought they must be aligned to a development squad with the Australian Rugby League, which also had an office at Princes Park.

The son was looking in awe at something behind the reception desk. It was the mock player lockers, adorned by the names of Melbourne Storm champions. Slater ... Cronk ... Hoffman ... Smith ... Inglis ...

'Whoa, look at those lockers Dad,' said the dreaming boy, strong and happy.

'Your name may be on those lockers one day son,' replied his father in a bright Polynesian inflection, proudly.

In witnessing this, the financial officer choked up. They don't even know, he thought. It's *their* club, and it won't be the same tomorrow. Nothing will be the same.

The boy's hopeful face stayed with Gregory for a long time. It was the look of innocence about to be lost. Gregory walked quickly to his car and sobbed over the steering wheel. After a while, he wiped his eyes and told himself at least from tomorrow he won't have to carry this burden any longer. But then what? It was the worst day of his life but only for a few more hours.

Before the sun shone on 22 April, word had passed around that Storm had been busted big time. In the earliest hours of the morning three gamblers placed $40 bets on Melbourne to finish last in the NRL season 2010. TAB Sportsbet took a bet for $200.

Sportingbet Australia spokesman Bill Richmond said later, 'You don't take a series of bets like that unless someone knows something.'

Within hours the odds of Melbourne winning the wooden spoon had dived from $250 to $1.01 – the sharpest and biggest betting move in Australian sporting history.

Storm director Gerry Ryan started his day in Sydney, before heading to New Zealand on business. His phone rang. It was a player agent who knew something. Ryan recalls, 'He told me Melbourne Storm were going to be fined a million dollars, they were going to lose a premiership and play for zero points for the rest of the year.' Hanson, Moodie and Watt had not yet arrived at the NRL offices.

The three Storm representatives flew in silence. On landing, they caught a cab to News Ltd headquarters. Moodie was thinking his club would suffer a hefty fine and lose the points from matches won in the first six rounds. Watt wasn't really thinking about sanctions. He was simply preparing himself to discuss the contents of Schubert's letter, plus the three side letters.

Both men noticed Hanson did not look at all well. It appeared he had not slept. In truth, Hanson had not slept soundly in the past year.

They went to News Ltd headquarters first, arriving at 10.15am. At that time Hanson's best estimate was that Storm had breached the cap by $900,000 over two years (2009 and 2010). There had been no admission of wrongdoing for 2007 and 2008. Hanson had only arrived at the club in mid–2008.

An inquisition began in the offices of the team owner. Macourt asked many questions of Hanson. News Ltd's chief general counsel Ian Philip (also a member of the NRL partnership board) was present. Hanson disclosed all he knew. Prior to this day he was more circumspect and guarded, fearful of what may happen to the football club. Now, with Moodie at his side, he was ready to reveal everything he understood of the Waldron era. By the time the questions and answers ceased, the best estimate of Storm's shame was $1.7 million in overpayments, including 2010.

The grimacing trio then headed to NRL headquarters at about 11.15am. News Ltd told them to 'go to the NRL and take them through it'. Philip went too. Macourt explains why the lawyer went along: 'To make sure what was told to the NRL was the same as what was told to us. To make sure that it's like a game of whispers, you hear exactly what they say and so News Ltd is not going to be hearing it second-hand.'

Storm had not sought legal assistance. Moodie considered Philip an ally. At that time he still believed News Ltd and the Storm board were on the same team and Philip was there for them. He looks back now and shakes his head. 'We did this openly and honestly, but what we didn't expect was to be set up, and in a modern-day public stoning,' he recalls. 'It would've been better off if Storm's board was chaired by a corporate heavyweight instead of someone from a university.'

Moodie, Watt, Hanson and Philip arrived at the NRL in a chauffeur-driven car.

Hanson spotted a news cameraman standing outside the building. 'What's the media doing here?' he asked. Watt was distracted by Hanson's phone, going off like a pinball machine. 'I can only assume that several player agents must have gotten word that he was about to sing and they were all trying to contact him, all at once, to persuade him otherwise,' Watt remembers.

One of the callers was indeed a player agent. He was chasing up monies owed.

Hanson said to Moodie, 'I'm just letting you know I'm resigning at the end of today, I'm done, I don't need this shit in my life anymore.'

Gallop's office was a small, thin room. Storm's men were ushered in. Watt sat in the corner. Hanson was on his left shoulder and Moodie was on his right. Gallop was in the centre of the room and Schubert beside him. Behind them were the NRL's lawyer and Schubert's staff assistant. There was also the NRL public relations manager.

Hanson answered rapid-fire questions from the league. He conceded McManus Presents had been paying players on Storm's behalf, the club was over the cap by at least $700,000 for 2010 and side letters existed for Cameron Smith, Greg Inglis and Billy Slater. The league's lawyer challenged Hanson to produce the three side letters. The interim CEO had left them back in Melbourne. A heated exchange followed. Hanson stood up to walk out. Gallop calmed the room. Talks resumed.

When pressed, Hanson estimated Storm had been over the cap in 2006 and 2007. That was before his time but he had seen the old letters of offer. He recalled his earliest memory at Storm was when he started in 2008 and Cameron Vale had warned him Waldron was 'doing stuff with the cap'. He summarised, 'Brian has left us with a situation that is now out of control. I suspect he knew that and that is why he left.'

Schubert talked about whistleblowers giving him information as evidence.

It was all moving so quickly. After about 45 minutes, the Storm delegation was asked to move into another room. Gallop mentioned likely sanctions: loss of premierships and playing for no points for the rest of 2010.

Hanson called Ryan and said, 'I'm getting machine-gunned here.' He was stunned by what was happening.

Half an hour later Gallop announced the full penalties. The club had been stripped of two premierships (2007 and 2009), three minor premierships (2006, 2007, 2008) and $1.1 million in old prize money. Also it would be fined $500,000 and forced to play for no points for the rest of the season.

The ticking time bomb had exploded.

Moodie's notes from that day read: 'We were absolutely stunned. Gallop told us we could think about it – and that there would be a press conference in the afternoon to announce the penalties.'

An impromptu full board meeting was held, with Hanson, Moodie and Watt phoning the other directors. Maher was back at Storm's training base with Petra Fawcett. He immediately raised the option of appealing or fighting or objecting the decision. 'Don't accept it,' he said.

News Ltd lawyer Ian Philip said Moodie should accept the ruling.

Hanson told Moodie to fight it. Moodie snapped, 'I don't think *you* can say anything right now.' It was a scolding he regretted later. The tension was overwhelming.

Watt recalls the moment:

> What sticks out in my mind with regard to this meeting was the fact that we dragged Frank Stanton out of a Townsville Cowboys (where he was also a director) board meeting and he was obviously having trouble hearing the full contents of the discussion between Melbourne and Sydney. Given Frank's long history as an NRL player, coach and administrator I'm sure that if he had been able to hear the conversation more clearly he would have ensured that the Storm demand that the NRL follow the full process of Rule 10 and he would have made a strong representation for the club to not accept the penalty on the day.

Rule 10 had not been mentioned in the meeting with the NRL. It would later be critical to court action arising from this day. Rule 10 of the NRL Rules states that:

> If the Chief Executive Officer forms the opinion, in his absolute discretion, that a breach of the Rules by a person bound by the Rules and/or a Club has occurred and the Chief Executive Officer proposed to impose a penalty in relation to that breach then Chief Executive Officer may issue a Breach Notice to that person and/or that Club setting out the alleged breach and the proposed penalty and specifying a period of not less than five Business Days during which the person and/or that Club may respond in writing to the Chief Executive Officer in relation to the alleged breach and the proposed penalty.

In short, the league's rules say Storm should have been served a breach notice and given time to formulate a response to the charges against it.

Gallop maintains he was very clear about the choice the club had on that day. 'Apart from giving them every chance to decide how they wanted to proceed that day, they knew what the process was,' he explains.

> They'd been fined every year. They'd been getting breach notices for everything from taking too long to take a goal kick to having the wrong person carry water on the field. They know the process. That wasn't what they wanted that day.

Moodie does not see it that way. He accepted the penalties on behalf of Melbourne Storm. But, he points out, 'I was certainly of the view that we had no right to any other course of action.'

There has since been much fascination about the discussions between the NRL and News Ltd before the penalties were dealt. Gallop says the sanctions were not preconceived. But News Ltd was not clueless. News Ltd CEO Hartigan says in the morning of 22 April he understood the penalty to be one premiership lost. Indeed, his corporate affairs manager, Greg Baxter, actually sent a draft media release to Storm HQ at 1.13pm stating the 2009 title would be taken back. It did not mention 2007.

Hartigan says, 'I'm pretty sure the Greg Baxter press releases reflected the actual events because I think there was initially one [premiership].'

Gallop concedes the original penalty *was* one premiership but became two during the meeting with Storm. In arriving at the penalties, Gallop relied heavily on Schubert's facts and figures. 'Schubert had the calculations, he knew,' Gallop says. 'Originally we discussed okay they're gunna have to lose that premiership [2009] and then as we found out more we discussed the position in 2007 and thought they're going to have to lose that one as well.'

It was the swiftest execution. The NRL pulled the trigger before even reading the side letters. It had come a long way in a short time since writing the flushing-out letter, which had only pondered that it might be 'necessary to investigate the declarations made for the 2006 and 2007 seasons'.

Within 24 hours, the league had stripped the 2006 Minor Premiership and 2007 Premiership. Gallop still bristles at any accusations of a set-up. 'This is the frustrating thing, they're trying to knit together some sort of conspiracy and there just wasn't one,' he says. 'We gave them a chance of telling us where they were at and they pretty much coughed up everything.'

Macourt says he never knew about sanctions. 'It's not a conversation I would've had,' he explains.

> When David [Gallop] rang me up and told me what the sanctions were I would've written them down but I was never going to be able to have an input into that. It's a conflict of interest. Hartigan was in a much better position to discuss them than I was. Me on the NRL board and me as News Ltd owning the Storm, I just can't possibly engage in a discussion around sanctions made by the NRL. Neither could Ian Philip.

Hartigan says he was fuming. 'I couldn't believe the gravity of the overspend and the sort of serial nature of it. I seriously couldn't believe that a club that we'd overseen could've engaged in this level of criminality.'

Embarrassment was chief among his emotions, for he was the man who had hired Waldron. Also, News Ltd had failed to pick up on Storm's crooked ways.

So began the media giant's relentless condemnation of Storm executives through its popular media outlets.

Moodie, Watt and Hanson had to drive back to News HQ.

They departed the NRL meeting via the back door. An excited gathering of news cameramen and journalists were waiting for them. The contingent had grown. Some of them were very informed about what was going on.

Watt says, 'We felt like criminals being ushered from a murder trial.'

Hanson elbowed a reporter who got too close. The News Ltd–driven car was pointing the wrong way, preventing a fast escape.

Once inside the car, Hanson informed his colleagues he wanted out, literally. He had decided to fly back to Melbourne. The other passengers did not want to drop him at the airport. So they let him step out onto a city footpath. Moodie and Watt were worried about him. He looked grief-stricken or worse. Hanson spent a while trying to hail a cab in Surrey Hills. Like a fullback, waiting under a bomb, he experienced a strange stillness.

When Hanson finally arrived at the airport he called Gregory and told him he had resigned. He warned him that everything was out in the open and the media would be coming.

Then Hanson phoned Waldron and told him what had happened. He explained how he had offered information about the three side letters. Waldron said, among other things, 'Oh you shouldn't have done that. They had nothin'.'

CHAPTER 32

LIGHTNING CRASHES

CFO Paul Gregory had turned up for work at Storm HQ early that morning. Though he did not know what the sanctions would be, he understood it was going to be a bad day. But he felt he needed to show his face.

Some staff knew Moodie, Hanson and Watt had gone to Sydney to offer a club confession. General Manager of Commercial Operations, Christine Finnegan, had been told. She, in turn, had informed her senior managers. 'They've gone up there and there is a real chance we could lose points,' she explained.

One finance worker asked Gregory whether he thought the club would lose its premierships. Gregory said he didn't think so.

For two hours the front office waited for more news and tried to behave as though nothing was wrong. The players' wives and girlfriends (nicknamed 'the girls' committee') held a conference at the club to discuss the seating arrangements for the new stadium. Waldron had always given five-star treatment to the partners and their children. One of the wives wanted to know how the kids would be catered for on match day. A Storm staffer was trying to answer their questions, knowing that the lives of these women would soon be altered dramatically. And they were worried about seating – if only they knew.

Gregory's phone rang. It was Hanson, who explained what had happened at NRL headquarters. Without a word, a sickened Gregory walked out of the office and cried his way home.

A short time later all Storm front office staff were asked to listen up. They rose to their feet. An announcement was made that the premierships were gone.

People were in shock.

At the same time, the players were on the training field. They were warming up. None of them could see Bellamy. He was inside, under the wooden grandstand, standing by director Maher, who was speaking on the phone to the other board members in Sydney. Maher was taking notes, writing down the penalties.

Bellamy was dumbstruck. Is this really happening?

It was becoming a game for the Storm footballers: trying to spot the coach. They looked all around the ground. Not there. Not there. They thought he was trying one of his innovations – hiding, watching to see how the squad trained without his presence.

Everyone was laughing, trying to figure it out.

Assistant coach Stephen Kearney came out of the change room and called for the players to go inside. 'Go straight into the meeting room,' he said with urgency. 'Don't take your boots off, head straight in there.'

The athletes thought maybe Bellamy had a video to show them.

The team jostled and prodded each other on the way into the room. The mood was light, jovial.

They sat and waited. The player whose friend had failed to get a bet on Storm to win the premiership a few days earlier worried first.

For some reason the conversation with his mate came flashing back. He had a presentiment of doom.

The anxiety started to spread. 'Why are we waitin'?' someone asked. 'Something's wrong,' another responded.

Then Bellamy entered the room, followed by Ponissi. The players looked at the coach's pallid face and fell deathly silent. There was a further pause. Bellamy and Ponissi, who often alternate speaking duties in team meetings, had not planned what they were going to say. All the football leaders knew was that they had to tell them. Ponissi waited for the coach to talk. Bellamy moved into the centre of the room, ready to deliver the news. But he did not speak. His face twisted, as it does when he is in deep thought, his mouth pointing off to one side.

The wait seemed to stagger for an hour. Eventually Bellamy tried to explain what had happened. There were so many penalties to list, so much to say but he couldn't do it. The coach, dripping a few sentences, began crying and could not finish his address. Ponissi stepped in and completed the task.

Some players broke down. Emotions bounded off the walls and collided. There was anger, bewilderment and shock. Perhaps the worst thing was seeing Bellamy so crushed. As painful as it was to learn the truth, it was just as confronting to see their father figure in distress.

Instructions were given. 'Just stay put,' Ponissi told the footballers. 'Don't go outside, don't answer your phone. Just stick together until we get our heads together.'

The Persian army was gathering at the gates.

That afternoon a news conference was called by the NRL. It was broadcast live across Australian on most channels. David Gallop, Rob Moodie and John Hartigan sat in front of many microphones, cameras and journalists.

Gallop began:

> Ah, ladies and gentlemen, eight years ago we announced a heavy penalty on the Bulldogs for breaches of the salary cap. At the time all clubs publicly supported the need for a salary cap system in our game. Our clubs continue to support the benefits that the cap brings to rugby league. Over the past few weeks it has come to light that the Storm has engaged in a long-term system of what might conveniently be called two sets of books. To their credit, this morning the Storm representatives have come in and confessed to a well-organised system of paying players outside the cap. On what we know this amounted to $1.7 million over the last five years, including approximately $700,000 in 2010. The elaborate lengths that they went to hide the payments was quite extraordinary ...

The league CEO read his statement, looking up to his audience after every sentence.

'These payments have allowed them to recruit and retain some of the best players in the game,' he added, before outlining the sanctions.

The language used by the NRL was colourful. Whether there were actually 'two sets of books' is arguable. And the club did not recruit 'some of the best players in the game'. It found them long before they were excellent.

Some questions were asked of Gallop. Hartigan seemed impatient. Then he interrupted. 'I'd like to say a couple of things,' he began.

> I believe today is a deeply regrettable day, certainly for sports fans generally, but certainly for rugby league fans. My knowledge of this has been only over the last few days and certainly the gravity of it only since last night. I certainly feel angry. I feel very, very disappointed and quite frankly I feel sick in my stomach. News [Ltd] doesn't tolerate behaviour like this.

He accepted the penalties.

'I think what you're going to see and hear of,' he went on, 'is collusion at such a level and such an orchestrated level of deceptive conduct that you may understand why over a period of years ... $1.7 million was able to be fraudulently misappropriated in smaller increments ... over that period.'

Hartigan announced he had appointed an accounting firm – Deloitte – to conduct a forensic examination of the club's finances and management, stood down two senior managers (Hanson and Gregory) and appointed Stanton to be CEO.

Moodie, dressed in a suit and purple shirt, then apologised to the Australian people, rugby league followers and Melbourne Storm fans. 'We do accept the referee's decision,' he said. 'The rules are clear, as David said. We've broken them. We offer no excuses whatsoever. It's obviously the lowest day for the club.'

A journalist asked Moodie, 'Is Brian Waldron the man to take responsibility for this?' The club chairman responded that an investigation would reveal who was behind the cheating.

Hartigan said, 'Our inquiries so far have indentified five people who knew about the effort to conceal these payments.' He did not name them all but he was referring to Waldron, Hanson, Gregory, Cameron Vale and Peter O'Sullivan. Spontaneously he uttered what would become his famous phrase: 'This club has had a couple of rats in its ranks and it's my intention to root them out.'

Of Waldron he said, 'He appears to be the architect of the whole shooting match.'

Storm's front office and football department watched the conference in distress.

Gregory saw it from home with his wife, Liz, who had rushed from work to be with him; the sacked CFO felt he was watching himself die.

Gregory and Hanson would suffer terribly in the days, weeks, months and years following 22/4. Their friends and families would see them deteriorate in the face of News Ltd's comments and coverage of the overpayments. The media company was as good as its word on trying to 'root' out the 'rats'. It ran an aggressive campaign and continually mentioned the likelihood of criminal charges against the club executives. If news coverage of sporting scandals were firestorms, this was Black Saturday.

Of course, News Ltd was not only driven by the flouting of NRL rules but by commercial and reputational damage control. There were high stakes for the owner. If the blame went further than Waldron and the other executives, what would happen to the club? What would happen to NRL advertising? What would become of the broadcasting contracts, present and future?

Most importantly for the company, what would Australians think of News Ltd?

Hanson flew straight home that night. His father was there to comfort him. Thereafter, he became very sick through stress. Director Fawcett says of Hanson, 'I was concerned for Matt. [He was a] mess, absolute mess. He went into hibernation. He was trying to help, was very open from the board's perspective but he was a mess mentally.' She was worried about him self-harming.

Gregory's mind became a black cave. Doctors prescribed him anti-depressants. He also used Valium and sleeping tablets.

'It's a pretty confronting time to go through,' he says, three years later.

Liz took time off her job to keep an eye on her husband. She found out she was pregnant not long after the scandal broke. Her husband could not be as happy as he should have been. The stress over being labelled a 'would-be convict' was all consuming. A miscarriage followed.

Gregory recalls, 'My health at the time was quite draining on her and for whatever reason she lost the baby.' On the three-month scan there was no heartbeat. 'She [Liz] was really, really low at that point,' he explains. 'We were both in a bad state. Whether it was stress-related, whether it was mother nature, I've got no idea but what I do know is it happened right at that time.'

Gregory saw a counsellor to deal with the trauma of being labelled a rat by the nation's bestselling tabloid newspaper. He experienced suicidal thoughts, wondering whether it would be better for him to take all the sleeping tablets at once.

'They were thoughts rather than real plans,' Gregory says. 'That's how I was at the time, purely emotional and trying to deal with a heavy topic.'

Fear of the unknown was his greatest tormentor.

> Just the fact it was so public and there was so much information in the papers, I just felt I was in a very lonely place. Seeing your name constantly mentioned, knowing I was at the club for a very short period of time, these things [the salary cap deceptions] were in place well before I was there and I felt that I was a bit unlucky.

Once, Waldron rang Gregory to see how he was. 'One of the last conversations I had with him he was apologetic,' Gregory says. It made the CFO feel better. 'I'd ask how he was going and he wasn't doing it easy either. He'd said a few things to make me think he wasn't in a simple situation as well.'

Hanson was no better off. His professional life was shattered. He had never even been in trouble at school. Now people would ask him if he was going to jail. He shared Gregory's hopelessness.

Other front office staff workers felt the sting of the scandal for a long time too. They had a really hard time with it because people they didn't know would say, 'Of course you all knew.' And they did not.

News Ltd was determined to punish its five co-accused.

Severe media scrutiny was dealt to O'Sullivan and Vale too, but they were employed by other football clubs and relatively protected. Journalists chased them, parked outside their homes. O'Sullivan told the press, 'I am shattered. I knew nothing about this. There's nothing else I can say.' He had left the club in 2007, well before the largest overspending, through McManus Presents and the three side letters, were created.

The AFL and North Melbourne stood by Vale, who released a statement: 'During my time at the Melbourne Storm,' Vale declared,

> I never engaged in any fraudulent behaviour. I welcome any ensuing investigations and will cooperate fully with the NRL and auditors as I have absolutely nothing to hide. I strongly object to being branded a whistleblower as the only contact I have had with the NRL has been at its instigation. I have not acted unlawfully and am willing to assist in any way necessary. I have sought legal

> advice and am deeply concerned about the nature of some reports currently being circulated about me.

The night the bomb went off, every media outlet in the country led their news bulletins with Storm's demise. Commentators sat on talk shows, dissecting the penalties. Some Melbourne fans discarded their merchandise at the entrance of the team's training base, as a symbolic gesture of disgust.

Moodie and Watt travelled back to Melbourne from Sydney. Watt says of Moodie's performance that day, 'Rob quickly became the face and voice of Storm during the media circus. I have nothing but admiration for this man. He is a very genuine human being who was deeply hurt by what happened at Storm during his time as chairman.' (Moodie was meant to go to Laos for a meeting on tobacco control. He cancelled it to stay in Melbourne and deal with the fallout.)

Channel Nine Melbourne called the scandal: 'Australian sport's darkest day'.

Respected leading sports journalist Tony Jones presented the news. At the end of his segment he editorialised:

> The blame game has already started and it promises to be brutal and bloody. Brian Waldron is very much the man in the gun at the moment. I did ask him via a text message earlier today is he available for comment. His reply: 'Clearly not mate, sorry.' Melbourne Storm plays the Warriors at Etihad Stadium on Sunday and it will be interesting to see just how many fans turn up there. It'll be just as interesting to see if Storm themselves turn up, because, quite frankly, why would they bother?

A half-hour later, after the news bulletin had finished, Jones started chasing what would be an exclusive interview with the man News Ltd started calling 'The Chief Rat'. The next day Jones caught up with Waldron in a suburban street. The Melbourne Rebels had stood down their new CEO. The interview was not wide-ranging. It was a play from Waldron to draw the media's attention away from his family: his elderly parents, ex-wife and children.

He subsequently released a statement.

My concern is for, certainly, the welfare of those around me. At the end of the day love is uncompromising for those that are family and friends and that's the way it should be and hopefully I can return that to the people who have been good to me. As time goes on and the facts become clear, people can make their own determination. It's best that I just say very little at this stage. Those that are with me are with me for the right reason and it becomes a difficult time for everyone involved. A long process will unfold no doubt and hopefully over time those that have been hurt by this can get over the pain.

CHAPTER 33

A LATE NIGHT CALL / A SECRET MEETING

Cronk didn't want to go home. He went to talk to Ponissi and asked, 'What do we do now?'

Ponissi had sat at the club for hours after the premierships were stripped. There were no plans for the team the next day (Friday). A special training session was scheduled for the new rectangular stadium on Saturday.

'I don't know,' Ponissi replied. 'Unless there is a manual that says, "In case you breach the salary cap and lose two premiership and this, this and this ..." I like to consider myself highly experienced, been involved in the game for 20 years but I haven't got a fuckin' clue what we do now.'

Cronk said, 'We gotta get together tomorrow.'

Ponissi and Cooper went to Bellamy and suggested the leadership group meet.

Finding a secret venue was difficult. Initially a text message was sent to all the leaders: 'Meeting tomorrow morning at 10am. Venue TBA.' The coaches started calling around. Assistant Stephen Kearney offered his house. That settled it.

Bellamy's phone rang late that night. It was Hartigan and he was steamed. The News Ltd boss confronted the coach over his position as football department boss at Storm. And he did not hold back.

Hartigan recalls, 'I needed to know that he wasn't involved.' The News Ltd boss said forcefully to the coach, 'You'll get a 100 per cent support from me if you're not involved but if you are then you'll get none but I need to know now, for you to tell me, to satisfy me you're not involved.'

Hartigan got the answer he wanted. Bellamy said he was innocent but the conversation unsettled him greatly. The next day it was clear News Ltd *would* support the coach. The *Daily Telegraph* ran a half-page tightly cropped picture of Bellamy beside a headline: 'I did not know one thing about this.' Bellamy was quoted saying: 'This is an absolute shock to myself, to our football staff, to our players. Personally, I am heartbroken.'

Some players had trouble avoiding news crews on the way to Kearney's house. Eventually all made it. No-one was tailed. The assistant coach's house felt like a sanctuary. Ten players and the coaches sat in a circle on the decking. There was no agenda. They just talked.

Bellamy told his charges about the late-night Hartigan phone call. He explained the News Ltd boss had ripped into him in an effort to ascertain his guilt or innocence. This incensed the players. For a brief time after that disclosure Storm did not want to play in the NRL. The players were fiercely protective of their coach. It was suggested the league should stick its competition. But that rage subsided.

The athletes' biggest worry was playing the rest of the season for no competition points. It was unprecedented in professional sport. If Gallop wouldn't allow them to compete for reward, why bother? That sentiment came and went throughout the meeting.

Kearney was the voice of reason. He spoke of News Ltd's power. He pointed out that if Storm didn't front up the media company had the money to wipe the team out and start compiling another roster from scratch.

Through the meeting, which was fast becoming a therapy session, more people arrived. An important visitor was News Ltd's human resources manager Keith Brodie. He came to pledge the owner's support to them. That helped repair the rift before it widened.

Hanson was invited and also showed up. He retold the events of the Sydney meeting. The players had no ill feeling for Hanson. (In fact, some of the players kept sending him supportive text messages throughout the season.) After a while, he left. He had one final duty to perform: handing over the three side letters to Watt, who would pass them on to News Ltd's highest officers.

Once it was determined the team would play on, the leadership group had to decide whether or not to press ahead with training. The members had been invited to view their seats. In three weeks the team was due to play its first home game in the stadium that Waldron and News Ltd had compelled the state government to build.

There was fear in the players' minds that their fans would not turn up. Worse, what if the members turned up en masse to hurl abuse at them? There was no way of telling what the reaction would be. After a short debate it was decided it wasn't the supporters' fault the club had cheated the rules. So the team would front up and cop whatever came its way. That created another challenge. The media would also be there. And reporters would want to interview the players and coach. Media manager Dave Donaghy was now playing an important role. He arrived to work through a crisis management strategy.

Donaghy said, 'We can't keep avoiding the media, someone's gunna speak to them.'

Moodie had so far shouldered the weight of questions, but the media was already growing tired of the chairman's voice.

Bellamy volunteered to speak. 'That's my job,' he said.

Captain Smith said, 'Well you're not gunna do it on your own, we're all there with you.'

The players eventually dispersed, promising to be united from that day forward.

White had provided a strong voice at the Kearney meeting. After being recruited by O'Sullivan as a self-conscious Dragons fringe player, White had grown into an impressive man. The prop went home that night, his mind still whirring.

At 4am the next morning he awoke. Unable to fall back to sleep, he fetched a pen and some paper and wrote Gallop a letter he would never send but always keep. It is a reminder of how he felt. It was a porthole into the Storm psyche a day after the team went down.

It read:

> Your suggestion was that we play for personal pride – obviously comes from someone that has never pulled on a pair of footy boots. That you'll offer us a counselling service to get over this shows your disconnection from the players of the game. At least have the decency to give us something to play for. Give us a reason to truly go out there and compete week to week. Give the fans a

reason to turn up each week. Give the members something to be proud of. Give us a chance to make our members proud again before our team is torn apart.

A few hours later White and the other players began the strangest weekend of their football lives.

A special guest was arranged to speak to the athletes before they went out onto the field for their debut training session at the new stadium. It was John Ribot, the club's creator. It had been more than 12 years since Ribot sat down with Chris Johns and mapped out the future of the team Lachlan Murdoch wanted to call the Monarchs. Fittingly, Ribot talked to the modern players about the club's history. In particular, he spoke about one event: the death of Mick Moore. It seemed so long ago that Mick had jumped into the harbour at Auckland and fatally hit his head, leaving a wife and three children behind. Ribot's message to Smith and co. was simple. 'This is serious but it's not death.' He talked about overcoming the grief of losing Moore, accomplished through unity.

After the humbling speech, the players prepared to face their questioners. Donaghy and board member Maher directed the next part of the morning so superbly it would be remembered as the catalyst for Storm's recovery.

The team was in the change room, out of view. A media pack was on the other side of the stadium, across the field. Reporters and camera operators were told not to stand on the grass because it was too new and precious.

Donaghy told journalists, 'Listen, Craig and the playing group will come out in about two minutes. Just to let you know, Craig will deliver an address on behalf of the entire playing group and the club. Y'know, there won't be any questions following it and that'll be it.'

Donaghy knew there would be questions. The story was too big to expect journalists would come from all over the country not to ask questions of the team's coach. And Bellamy could not be expected to shy away. Once the first question was answered, another would come. Then the players would be asked to say something.

The reporters nodded and smiled. Sure. No questions.

Maher was pulling the players together and preparing them for their performance. He told them to keep their heads up. 'Look straight ahead,' he barked. 'Don't you look anywhere except straight ahead.

Cam you need to be right behind Craig, all in tight, you need to be in tight. Walk across the field, all the microphones will be there, don't say anything, just stay behind Craig, and look straight ahead.'

A lot of what Bellamy had to say was based on notes from Cronk and White. They had cobbled together their thoughts on paper. Donaghy had polished it.

When it was time to go, Maher sent them out into the soft morning light. The first sounds that echoed in the new stadium were the shutters of cameras. Slowly the players walked across the field. Slater looked across nervously at his captain and tugged at his lip. Smith looked at his feet for an instant before remembering to look up. Once into stride, the team looked regimented and imposing.

Finally they made it to the microphone and lenses. The reporters were quiet. Bellamy delivered his finest speech. The Fairfax press would later describe it as being 'part-Churchillian, part-Braveheart'.

Bellamy read from his notes: 'This statement will be our only comment today. The ongoing investigation presently taking place at our club means we are unable to answer any further questions. We intend to show our absolute support to that process.'

He raised his eyes to make sure his audience was paying attention. The glance held just long enough. He rocked on both feet, took a deep breath and continued:

> This has been without doubt the toughest 48 hours of our sporting life. We have been gutted with what has transpired in recent days. Our greatest accomplishments and what we cherished most have been taken away from us by the harshest of penalties. These guys behind me, they work their butts off for 11 of the 12 months of the year to be the best that they can be on the field.

Smith and the other players looked increasingly comfortable, almost enjoying Bellamy's stand.

'The majority of them have been here since they've been kids,' the coach went on.

> They spill blood for each other, for this club, for our members and for our supporters, for the development of rugby league in Victoria. They do it to win premierships, something we have been stripped of having any chance to do this year. And they do it

> because they love to play for their teammates and the admiration they have for one another. We truly feel for our members and supporters. They are the most loyal and dedicated of fans.

The coach only stumbled over his words once. The imperfection did not detract from the impression he was making. Indeed it made him more impressive, for it gave listeners a sense his emotions were making his mouth dry.

> They have stood us, sorry, they have stood by us with tough times before, we ask that they stand by us now.
>
> And I want to thank all of the players' families, all of our staff's families for their unwavering support, for everybody here at our club.

Bellamy looked up at the lenses. Family was critical to him. And his would be hurting.

'We love you all.'

While the coach went on, Smith found a place in the distance to fix his stare. He was tight-lipped and squinting. His jaw was flexing.

'The two things that they can never take away is our dignity and our integrity,' Bellamy continued. 'That is why we welcome the full forensic investigation that is taking place at our club. We know we will be investigated. We welcome that.'

Journalists were silent. Donaghy tried to read their faces. He saw astonishment and awe. He wondered who would ask the first question.

'I love these players,' Bellamy concluded.

> These players love our club. This club is a great club, it's a strong club, it's a very proud club. It also has been a successful club. This is why we stand here today united. We are not going anywhere. We ain't gunna surrender. We, as people and as a rugby league club, have a huge role to play in Victoria, which we are most proud of. We will not walk away from this challenge. We will stand up for ourselves and we will fight our way back from here. That fight starts today. And tomorrow it starts on the field.

With that, Bellamy's message was almost finished.

> The ongoing investigation currently taking place at the club means we are unable to answer any further questions here today. This is an ongoing process and one that may take time and that process is one we welcome and then we can start rebuilding this great club. Thank you very much.

As Bellamy turned to walk away, Donaghy waited for the questions to fly. Astonishingly, there were none. The sheer power of Bellamy's words had caused a reaction of silence. Bellamy and his boys spun on their heels and went back into the sheds.

In the next half an hour Bellamy comforted himself by concentrating on the game of football. He talked to the players about the coming match against the Warriors. The players then went out to have a light session. There was still uncertainty about the fans' reaction to the team. No-one had turned up yet.

Bellamy, Ponissi and Ribot stayed under the stadium and were deep in conversation when a football department worker interrupted. 'Without being rude, I'd get your arses upstairs,' came the instruction.

The Storm members had been let into the stadium. And they were many. For the players it was a wonderful feeling. Far from being repelled by the scandal, the fans were inspired to show their support. The supporters that appeared that day were passionate and loud and caring.

It was at this moment the club was saved. There are many possible reasons for the public's immediate backing of Storm, despite its systematic breaching of the salary cap. Perhaps it was parochialism. Maybe there were anti-NRL or anti-News Ltd sentiments at play. More likely, the people just wanted to watch their footballers run around and pass the ball and lay tackles and compete. While the game behind the game goes on, and the media professionals look for scoops and dirt, some fans, even a majority of them, just want to watch the men they believe are heroes, regardless of who pays their wages, do what they do best.

When Bellamy went outside he saw a horde of purple and heard a chant: *Melbourne, Melbourne, Melbourne, Melbourne.* There were thousands of people wearing the team colours, waving flags and giving players high fives. The applause lasted five minutes. Players looked sheepish but soon engaged. Cronk started shaking hands with the members. Others followed his lead. The awestruck media rushed over. Cameramen and supporters mobbed the coach.

'It was like someone had given them this unbelievable medicine,' Ponissi says.

The tonic was still fizzing in the players' veins when they played the Warriors the next day.

Storm's first captain Glenn Lazarus was invited to say a few words before the team ran out. He had flown down from Queensland. Others came too. Chris Johns was there. Matt Geyer. Mick Moore's wife, Tracey, attended.

Melbourne won 40–6, playing for nothing. An unusually large crowd of 23,000 people turned up to watch. They cheered every try.

CHAPTER 34

THE REALITY OF NEWS

News Ltd's opposition newspaper group, Fairfax, began running stories about who knew what and when at Storm. It was clear *The Age* and *Sydney Morning Herald* had the club's owner in its sights.

So many questions were left unanswered regarding News Ltd's executive responsibility.

Waldron was a News Ltd appointee, given control of the club, despite misgivings about his style. 'He's sort of a bloke's bloke,' Hartigan had explained.

Hartigan did not even know that Waldron had been sacked from St Kilda.

Initially a clause had been placed in Waldron's contract by News Ltd to say he would be fined if Storm breached the salary cap. He was fined twice for breaches by the NRL, yet kept his job. Macourt had said, ' ... for a relatively small amount of money, sacking a guy who you perceived to be otherwise doing a good job was probably a bit harsh.'

Instead, Waldron received a contract extension and a bigger marketing budget. When he quit at the start of 2010, he was offered a pay rise to stay. This was News Ltd's man.

Was it reasonable to say there was no suspicion Waldron was breaching the cap, even after the club struck deals with Smith, Inglis, Slater, Cronk and several others within a single year? Someone at News Ltd had doubts. The media owner itself published a story in early 2009 to that effect. Peter Badel had written,

> The Storm have been buffeted by off-season speculation the club is under mounting pressure to offload key players to ensure the 2007 premier does not exceed the NRL's $4.1 million payment ceiling.

You don't need auditors to tell you superstars cause cap pressure.

At the time, Waldron responded, 'We're good as gold.' Was that all the News Ltd hierarchy needed to hear?

Did News Ltd ask why Waldron was exclusively handling the biggest contract negotiations after the club appointed a General Manager of Football Operations to oversee recruitment and retention of players?

Such questions would not be answered in the pages of a large percentage of Australia's newspapers after the scandal broke. Thereafter, Storm's owner was using its platoon of mastheads to cover the story without a hint of self-examination.

It was made easier to avoid accountability when News Ltd was granted permission by the NRL (which it still half-owned) to commission the only forensic investigation into Melbourne Storm's cheating.

And the biggest question remaining, regarding News Ltd's executive responsibility, boils down to that word: accountability.

After the breaches of the cap became public, there were fiery speeches and rallying calls from News Ltd executives. This included displays of shock, anger and hurt, amid the frantic finger-pointing.

But where was the onus on News Ltd to shoulder its share of blame for the salary cap breaches? The basic failings of systems and personnel – which News Ltd either put in place and/or had ultimate responsibility for – nourished an environment for such deception to take root, and ultimately flourish, right under the company's nose.

Organisations holding themselves to account is wishful thinking. In this case, by projecting a self-interested and simplistic narrative of events, through its range of media outlets, News Ltd – powerful and riddled with conflicts of interest – was unable (and probably unwilling) to objectively pose questions about accountability and responsibility in its role in the salary cap scandal.

Fairfax ran coverage of News Ltd's glaring conflicts of interest. The media companies and their star columnists attacked each other. It became personal and unseemly.

Amid the reportage and volleys of opinion pieces, Waldron engaged respected public relations expert Mike Smith to manage his public affairs. Waldron was approached many times to tell his side of the story but after some consideration he declined all offers, paid or otherwise.

Smith, a former editor of *The Age,* had a front row seat to the media brawling over the next few weeks and months. He explains News Ltd's strategy, as he saw it:

> Hartigan got involved directly in the story. It was really important from News Ltd's point of view that the damage be limited to Waldron and they went out of their way to portray him as the 100 per cent cause of the problem even down to that famous image of 'king rat' [front page of the *Herald Sun*], picking the most unflattering photograph with unruly hair like a marsupial. There couldn't be any clearer example of them trying to put all the blame on one man.

There is little doubt because of News Ltd's ownership position at Storm and chief role at the NRL at the time, the media company was better able to minimise the damage and fallout from the Melbourne Storm debacle than they otherwise would have. News Ltd's conflict of interest saw it not just as a combatant in the story but also a controller. That was good news for some but terrible for the five people Hartigan identified as responsible for the rule breaking.

All of this played out in public. Privately, Hartigan did lay some blame on the players of Storm. A day after the Warriors match, he turned up to Storm HQ. Deloitte's forensic team had arrived. There were a dozen auditors carrying boxes of files and they were all taken down into the boardroom, to be sorted and examined. Computers were being emptied of data.

A security guard was employed by News Ltd to watch the front office workers, fast becoming the forgotten victims of the scandal.

Up until now the footballers were not getting too much criticism for accepting payments outside the cap. But Hartigan was seething at their part in the breaches.

He confronted the team in a meeting at Princes Park. He recalls,

> Once you sort of rationalise the behaviour you've got to say the players were the greatest disappointment. Here were the people who were the pillars of the code. That the players could sit there among the rest of the players, who were paid considerably less

> and weren't tainted by this cheating, and could put up this veneer of anger that y'know, they've taken our premierships – hang on a minute. Turn around and look at your own behaviour and ... that boat in the garage [Inglis had been photographed with the boat the club arranged for him] and you know that was there. The fact that you were getting all this extra money, which wasn't catered for in the contract that was lodged with the NRL. That was just the fairy godmother plonking it in your bank account.

When Hartigan challenged the athletes, they did not hang their heads. He says they remained belligerent.

A week after the Storm scandal blew up, Hartigan had another scrap to attend to. The former *Herald Sun* editor-in-chief Bruce Guthrie (who had fought with HWT Managing Director Peter Blunden over sending a photographer to the World Club Challenge in 2008) was suing News Ltd for unfair dismissal. The case was due to go to trial on 27 April.

Guthrie expected his matter might be settled. 'Our first thought was Hartigan's got these two big balls in the air,' he recalls.

> And we thought it would probably be judicious of Hartigan to go well, we've got this very major issue playing out at the Melbourne Storm, can we at least get the Guthrie issue off our hands. But it says a lot about News Ltd's judgement or arrogance that they made no such attempt.

The case went ahead and Guthrie won. He has an interesting take on Storm's cheating. 'I know the culture of News Ltd at the time and it didn't surprise me that something like that could happen at a News Ltd company,' he says.

> And that's because working as a journalist and an editor of news, when you have the meetings with the senior managers, be it Rupert Murdoch or Hartigan or others, you don't talk about things like business principles or ethics, you only talk about outcomes. They're only interested in outcomes. For me it was audience and circulation and readership. And I presume at the Storm it was probably premiership points, profit and loss. And that's all you talk about. If the only message you're given is keep

> all those things going up, then it's not surprising to me that there might be a manager or group of managers who might just start to cut corners, just like there was in the phone hacking [in the United Kingdom]. Because if that's going to get the end result ... lesser managers might start to cut those corners.

Macourt says one of the reasons News Ltd didn't notice the overspend was because a lot of the money promised in the side letters was not yet paid. A large portion of it was for the Smith–Fox Sports deal. That had been okayed. So that wasn't going to ring bells of alarm. Hundreds of thousands in breach money were still owed. That is why Waldron fled the company, Macourt believes. He couldn't pay the players. So he bailed. Hartigan said at the time of the sanctions, the company conducted regular audits by Ernst & Young and presented to the board on an annual basis. Hartigan was always at arm's-length from Melbourne. He concedes, 'With the Storm, I always felt that rugby league, while it was part of the management of our company, I always kept it away from my desk.' He delegated to Macourt, who delegated to board representatives.

From 2008 the News Ltd manager in charge of Storm finances for Storm was Watt.

The former company secretary was as devastated as the other directors and Storm stakeholders when it was revealed the club had been grossly overpaying players.

'I felt that my professional reputation took a battering as a result of the whole ordeal,' says Watt.

> At the Herald And Weekly Times I always prided myself on knowing where ever cent was being spent. How could I not have detected these concealed payments? I have asked myself that question a million times.
>
> Perhaps I was too trusting of the people who were employed as senior executives within Storm. It is true that I got on well with Brian, Matt and Paul. We knew Brian was a natural salesman and a very talented football administrator, but I never took him for the liar that he turned out to be. I must say that I was always very wary of Brian's style, but the same can't be said for Matt and Paul, who I saw as smart, young professionals with their whole career ahead of them. I was completely blindsided by their involvement.

Watt was director in charge of charting and monitoring the strategic direction and financial objectives of the club. The club relied on funding from News Ltd every month for cash flow. Part of Watt's role was to make sure funding requests from the club were in line with its budgeted financial objectives.

There was also an annual NRL salary cap audit. Any issues that were raised by Schubert were relayed to the board by the Storm CEO and CFO. There were always minor issues floating around the franchise.

Watt has one significant criticism of the NRL process: poor communication. 'If Ian [Schubert] had concerns or suspicions around the remuneration numbers that Storm was signing off as part of the salary cap declarations process,' Watt asks,

> then why was this not raised with Frank Stanton or I, as the two News Ltd representatives on the board? It seems odd given the role that News Ltd had in the game that if there were concerns around the numbers declared ... that the NRL would not have contacted certain board members directly to voice these concerns. In all my time as a director at Storm neither Schubert nor Gallop raised any concerns of these issues with me; until we were notified by Hanson.

Watt, who is no longer with News Ltd, spent much time after 22/4 reading about corporate fraud.

> Most of the experts agree that when there is collusion at the highest levels in an organisation ... then it is very hard to detect fraud until someone blows the whistle.
>
> Yes, the board signed off the accounts, but we relied on the fact those accounts had been audited by Ernst & Young. We relied on the feedback from the NRL's salary cap auditor to identify any breaches. We relied on the finding of News Ltd's own internal audit process, which failed to detect any false payments in its own testing process. We relied on the executives appointed to the highest positions in the club to provide the board with an accurate and true representation of the dealings of the club.

It was later asserted by Schubert that the Storm board was asleep at the wheel on the salary cap breaches. Was it?

'No, I don't think we were,' Watt concludes.

> A well functioning board is not meant to manage the business. That is the responsibility of the CEO and COO. They are not employed to review every invoice that is processed. That is the job of the CFO. A board does have to take some responsibility for ensuring the organisation has appropriate controls and provides a strong corporate governance framework to ensure accountability to its shareholders. In our defence the board convened regularly, it asked the appropriate questions around compliance (on record in minutes) and relied on the expert advice from its regulators and auditors.

Here Watt is emphatic: 'Schubert and Gallop, to this day, have never spoken to me as a director about the whole affair. I find it extraordinary for them to pass comment as they did without first discussing my side of the story.'

CHAPTER 35

SUPREME ACTION

Gallop was asked recently on ABC television: 'What makes a good sports administrator?'

He replied,

> Someone with a good sense of process, a good sense of the importance of even-handedness, the importance of having structures in place that allow you to build your sport and obviously deal with the unexpected events as well. I think lawyers have good training in that regard. Lawyers are accustomed to rules and processes and also accustomed to looking at things carefully, making sure you have all the evidence before you make decisions.

After 22/4, it was Gallop's 'good sense of process' that was questioned.

When the shock of the sanctions became a dull ache, Moodie rang a lawyer, senior litigation counsel Robert Heathcote from the leading Collins Street firm Arnold Bloch Leibler. Moodie was now appalled by the way News Ltd was reporting the Storm story. The public health expert said, 'Coming up against News Ltd isn't easy. From my experience in health I'd compare their tactics to those of a tobacco company – they are just so powerful, they have so many resources and they can be very intimidating. I have been shocked by their approach to ethics.'

Also, he was having second thoughts about accepting the sanctions without a fight.

Without knowing Moodie had sought advice, fellow Storm director Ryan engaged another lawyer, Leon Zwier, one of Australia's top corporate lawyers. He too was from Arnold Bloch Leibler. Heathcote and Zwier discussed representing the Storm board of directors to challenge the NRL's decision and win the club and its fans back their premierships.

The legal team expanded further as the directors also sought the opinion of Allan J. Myers AO QC. Myers is one of the nation's top lawyers in administrative and procedural law.

On 10 May at 7pm the Melbourne Storm board held an extraordinary board meeting at Storm HQ. Present were Moodie, Stanton, Watt, Ryan and Fawcett. Maher, who had been using his media position and network to rail publicly against News Ltd, was an apology.

Notes from the meeting reveal the main discussion points:

> The preliminary legal advice given is that David Gallop and NRL have acted in contrary to their own rules and have not taken improper [sic] steps in imposing the penalties.
>
> Public figures have raised the question of whether the Board have done all they could in seeking fair and honest justice. Some Board members feel that it is their responsibility to seek this justice for the Club, players, staff, sponsors, members etc.

The board members resolved to make a subcommittee to seek a meeting with the NRL to have the 2007 and 2009 premierships reinstated. A vote was held. Those in favour of the proposal were Ryan, Fawcett and Maher (Moodie acting by proxy). Abstaining from the vote were Watt and Stanton. A meeting note read:

> Frank Stanton and Craig Watt felt due to their involvement with News Ltd they would be obliged to communicate the Board's proposed actions to News Ltd. The other attending Board members were understanding of their position and supported this.

The split was on.

The lawyers engaged by the board were staggered by the NRL's denial of justice and poor regard for due process. The lawyers issued in the Supreme Court a commercial list, which requires immediate attention. The directors wanted their claim heard in a hurry. At first, the NRL seemed dismissive of the court action, perhaps believing there was not enough time for a trial and a judgement before the 2010 season had been played out.

But the directors knew better. They anticipated a speedy remedy, particularly if the case was in front of Justice Tony Pagone, the judge in charge of the Commercial Court in Victoria.

Heathcote and Zwier served papers to the NRL and looked forward to a first directions hearing. Their plan was to have the court issue a directive to the NRL to surrender relevant documents. Another aim was to have David Gallop appear in the witness box to answer questions about his execution of the penalties. In such trials evidence can be submitted via affidavit or *viva voce*. The stung Storm directors preferred the latter.

Fairfax reported this lede on 24 May: 'The old High Court in Melbourne was packed on Friday morning as the latest instalment of rugby league's long history of litigation began before Justice Pagone.'

In short, Moodie, Maher, Fawcett and Ryan thought News Ltd and the NRL had stage managed the events of 22 April and in doing so denied the club the right to NRL rules of justice.

Gallop maintained Moodie forfeited rights to Rule 10 by accepting the sanctions on the spot. In fact, Gallop mentioned this in a letter to Moodie on 23 April. It stated: 'The above penalty was of course imposed pursuant to Rules 9 and 10 of the NRL Rules. In this respect, I record that your club accepted the penalty and therefore waived the requirement to proceed by way of a breach notice, etc.'

The NRL said it was confident of its position. Gallop maintains he was on firm ground.

'The only thing that I would add about the meeting on 22 April is that the context needs to be understood,' he explains. 'We sent the letter on 21 April setting out what we knew and advising in substance that there were whistle blowers who had shopped them.' He adds the letter also promised an investigation of the club and offered the Storm board an opportunity to make a full disclosure.

'The most telling fact is that the date proposed for the full disclosure meeting was 27 April,' Gallop adds.

> The club decided to come the next day – 22 April – but we didn't know until about 6.30 pm on the evening of 21 April that they were coming. How is that consistent with a set up?

> The other fact that is relevant is that when we sent the letter it was Macourt's intention to fly down to Melbourne on 22 April to get to the bottom of it. He didn't do this because the board knew it was all over once the letter arrived and gave up. What else could they do as Hanson had confessed to them what had gone on and the letter confirmed that the NRL could prove it?

The NRL was preparing to defend itself in court. However, the News Ltd hierarchy did not want this to happen.

Hartigan and Macourt tried to convince the directors to halt the legal challenge.

On 2 June, Macourt sent the independent board members a letter. It read:

> You continue to prosecute the court action you commenced against the NRL in the face of serious concerns we have raised with you about the damage that conduct will do to the ability of Melbourne Storm to field a team and carry on business in 2011.

Macourt pointed out Storm could only compete in the NRL the next season if it complied with the cap restrictions.

> We believe your conduct may result in Melbourne Storm being unable to field a team in 2011,' he added. 'That would spell disaster for the club, sponsors, and its fans, and for us as its backers. We challenge you to abandon your court action, and work with us to rebuild the club. We do need your response this week.

From day one Robert Heathcote told his clients there was a danger of the trial being avoided by News Ltd if the company decided to sack them. News Ltd ran the club through the holding company Valimanda (Ribot's former family-named company) and so directors of Storm served at the pleasure and mercy of News Ltd.

Aware that News Ltd and the NRL may indeed want the same thing – the court action killed – the legal team acting for Moodie, Ryan, Maher and Ryan informed News Ltd's parent company, News Corporation, at its highest levels of its plan.

The lawyers also made a chart of all the penalties handed down to sporting clubs globally for breaking rules of the leagues. Rugby.

American football. Tennis. Golf. Every sport. Everywhere. It was to be argued by the lawyers that the NRL penalty was objectionable, excessive, unfair and unprecedented.

Beyond that, the lawyers wanted to have the sanctions reconsidered. Storm, as represented by the independent directors, would then make certain admissions and certain denials. It would plead for the case to be re-examined by a tribunal. With witnesses giving evidence on oath – from both sides – the directors believed Storm was in a better position to win back its titles.

It was never going to happen.

When Justice Pagone set down a date and offered to bring it forward to July, Hartigan pulled the trigger and sacked Moodie, Maher, Ryan and Fawcett.

They no longer represented Storm.

In a two-minute hearing before Justice Pagone, Storm's lawyer, Leon Zwier, said the dispute was resolved. 'The parent-subsidiary and half-brother are now in agreement,' he told the court.

The judge asked if that meant the action had been ceased. Zwier said yes. Outside, Zwier said cheekily, 'While it's fair to say that our advice hadn't changed, certainly our instructions have. I remain confident that neither Mr Gallop nor the NRL will allow for repetition of the events that occurred on the 22nd of April.' In a final twist, Storm agreed to pay the legal costs of the NRL. News Ltd would reimburse its half-company. It would be glad to have the whole mess sorted. Why open Pandora's box, which had been riveted shut?

In July 2010, Deloitte released its findings of the Storm salary cap investigation to News Ltd, which then made public a summary only. Staggeringly, it declared Storm had not breached the cap by $1.7 million over five years but $3.17 million.

The *Herald Sun* ran a front page with the headline: *Rats Face Jail*. A strap ran across the top, which read: *THE GREATEST BETRAYAL*. In smaller text, under the names of Waldron, Hanson, O'Sullivan, Gregory and Vale, was written: 'The alleged architects of Storm's salary cap rort face four investigations – with penalties of up to 10 years' imprisonment if found guilty – after the independent probe revealed the full extent of the scandal that has rocked Australian sport.'

Hartigan held another media conference. This time News Ltd publicly named its five suspects.

Hanson and Gregory watched the conference on television together, having endured and barely survived the most difficult three months of their lives. Both men were fearful of the threat of jail but their criminal legal advice was that it was not very likely at all. It seemed strange the newspapers kept lumping the five Storm executives so carelessly together. They were in no way a group. Some of them had not even met. O'Sullivan had left Storm almost two years before Gregory arrived.

Three years later, Hartigan says he does not believe the coverage was unfair. He remains disappointed no-one served time. 'The severity of the wrongdoings was such that in my view they certainly deserved criminal charges against them,' he says.

Peter Blunden, still a managing director at News Ltd, was asked whether the company went too far in proposing jail terms for the executives News Ltd hired to run Storm. It was explained the Storm staffers had suffered greatly from the coverage. He replied simply,

> There's a lot of things that are covered in the media that are going to cause a lot of people a lot of stress. And our responsibility is to provide a fair and accurate coverage. I'm sure Oscar Pistorius doesn't enjoy the coverage of what's happening with him at the moment but it's reality.

(Oscar Pistorius has been charged with murdering his girlfriend.)

'I think the accusations against people who were running Storm were heavy,' Blunden adds.

Police investigated the actions of the Storm five but decided not to lay charges.

Victoria Police subsequently released a statement declaring that after a thorough assessment: 'We have decided not to pursue this line of enquiry as to do so would be extremely resource intensive and there is a high probability it would not result in any charges being laid.'

There would be no prison sentences. Not even a court appearance. The Storm managers were guilty only of breaking the rules of a football league.

Gregory was glad the report was being released. He wanted to know what was in it. He and Hanson had offered to cooperate with the Deloitte investigation but were turned away because they could not agree on terms. Three years later, Gregory says he still has not heard from Schubert.

> Deloitte, when they spoke to me – I wasn't in a good mental state at the time – I said that if I was going to talk to them I wanted Craig Watt to be there and Deloitte did not want that to happen. They said they'd consider it but they never contacted me again.

One of the interesting findings from Deloitte was that the players did not cooperate with its investigators. The club had set up appointments for certain players to be interviewed but the footballers failed to show.

The press asked captain Smith why the players didn't turn up. He replied, 'We'd like to think that we're given fairly good advice by the people that we trust. At the time we did what we thought was right for us.'

The NRL Report of Salary Cap Auditor into Melbourne Storm Salary Cap Breaches 2011 says of player involvement:

> All the players interviewed denied any knowledge of Salary Cap breaches by the Storm. In general terms, where they had arrangements where payments were made outside the Salary Cap, the players asserted that they thought they were either approved third party arrangements or arrangements which the Storm had said would be cleared with the NRL.
>
> ... While with one exception I have seen no evidence amongst the material that I have reviewed that conclusively establishes that an individual player knew that the Storm was not disclosing all his remuneration to the Salary Cap auditor, a number of players received payments and benefits negotiated with the Storm that were not contained in their registered NRL Playing Contracts.
>
> Given this, the alarm bells should have been ringing for these players ... I note that I have not seen the direct communications between the players and their agents, which may have shed some light on what was understood by alarm bells.
>
> ... The alarm bells were certainly heard and understood by a number of the player agents who represented the players but the idea that the player agents can be relied upon has similarly been demonstrated to be folly. The managers of a number of players have been shown to exist on a continuum somewhere between incompetent and essentially unscrupulous. The players rely on such persons at their peril.

... Rule 26(1) of the *NRL Playing Contract and Remuneration Rules* prohibits a player from engaging in any conduct that in any way assists a club to avoid compliance with the Rules. This does not mean intentional conduct; it could include conduct that constitutes reckless indifference or, even, negligence.

... I also wish to respond to the assertion that is often made that players do not know the total Salary Cap position for their club and therefore cannot be said to have known that their own irregular arrangements were being used by their club to cheat on the Salary Cap. This with respect misses the point.

The individual obligation that the player owes is to ensure that his NRL Playing Contract discloses all of the agreed remuneration and third party agreements. If he does not comply with this obligation and enters into arrangements that are in breach of the Salary Cap rules then he is enabling his club to breach its disclosure obligations and he really has no basis for thinking other than that this is the way the club operates across the board.

CHAPTER 36

BACK ON TOP

It was September 2012. A warm sun was shining on Storm's training field.

Players stretched and signed autographs. There was an old man visiting from America. His name was Rupert Murdoch.

It was more than two years since Storm was stripped of its premierships. At the time, the News Corporation chairman and chief executive said he was shocked by the scandal. 'It was very embarrassing,' he said. 'We're far from sure that we're the only club involved.'

Storm had made it back to the top of the league in a surprisingly short time and Murdoch was not embarrassed anymore. He wanted to congratulate coach Craig Bellamy and captain Cameron Smith for taking the shoulder charge and getting back up.

Ponissi was waiting with Rupert Murdoch in the boardroom. He phoned a trainer, who passed a mobile to Smith.

'Smithy, what are you doing?' Ponissi asked with some urgency.

Smith said he was just finishing up. 'I'll be there in ten minutes.'

Ponissi knew that meant he would be longer, for Smith is not a slave to time. 'Smithy,' Ponissi said, 'you're gunna think I'm jokin' but Rupert Murdoch's in the boardroom and he wants to meet ya.'

Smith walked from the field and into the boardroom with his boots still on.

Smith and Ponissi stood by while Murdoch and Bellamy chatted. New Storm CEO Ron Gauci was there too. The meeting did not last long. Murdoch simply wanted to say well done for winning back credibility. Then he wished the Storm leaders best of luck for the Grand Final.

'Thanks mate,' Bellamy said.

News Ltd saw Bellamy as critical to Storm's chances of surviving 22/4. No-one was sure he would stay. Luckily for the club and its owner, he saw rebuilding his shattered team as his greatest challenge. From that first match against the Warriors until the Grand Final two years later, the competitor from Portland produced his finest work.

Disgraced and playing for no points, Melbourne braced for hostile crowds in the northern states in 2010. First stop was Townsville. The coaches were pleasantly surprised by the reception there. Storm won again. Next week the team debuted at the new AAMI Park stadium. Director Watt had dedicated all his time to move the club into its new digs. It was a game against Brisbane. Sponsors were brought in to pledge their loyalty to the team before it ran out onto the virgin turf. Gerry Ryan and Tony Devers were among the backers who stayed with the team. Jayco took over the jersey sponsorship. The Broncos blew Storm away. It only got worse. The Canberra crowd gave Melbourne a horrible baking. Sydney matches were similar. Before long, the season started to grind. The unbelieveable medicine wore off. Bellamy used the rest of the year to blood rookies and rotate senior players. The season became a long, long preseason for 2011. Few teams get the chance to educate young footballers in first grade for such an extended period of time without counting wins and losses. Bellamy made the most of it. He started planning for next season, long before his nightmarish 2010 was over.

Stanton was brought in as interim CEO. The former coach of Australia watched from close quarters as Bellamy began coaching like it was 2003. 'His work ethic is what has made the club what it is,' Stanton says.

Inevitably, the playing list had to be trimmed to get under the cap. Stanton told Ponissi, 'You've gotta come up with a rescue plan.'

Ponissi locked himself in a room for two days and worked out the players contractually committed and what they were to be paid. He designed several possible squads that would comply with the NRL rules and presented them to Stanton and Bellamy at a cafe in Port Melbourne.

All up, he had four plans. Incredibly, one of them included Inglis, Smith, Cronk and Slater. 'Craig didn't like any of the plans,' Ponissi says. 'It was killing him. To lose players you've developed was the hardest.'

After all this time and trouble, it was still impossible to conceive one of the big four going to another NRL team.

But then the departures started happening.

Michael Maguire, a former assistant coach of the club, had gone to Wigan in the UK. He signed Brett Finch, then Jeff Lima and Ryan Hoffman. Then Brett White bowed out. The Raiders had offered him a deal.

'I knew within myself that the way my body was, and if the team was still going to be successful, it was the best thing for Storm for me to be one of those players who left,' White says from his home in Canberra. 'It comes back to what we were trained to do – put the team first.' It was a selfless decision, his thanks to Storm for the ride of his life.

On a bus trip to one of the matches, Greg Inglis went to Ponissi and said, 'I've got an opportunity to go to the Broncos and I think I'm gunna take it.' At his best, Inglis was more spectacular and damaging to opponents than any of his teammates. He could play any position on the field and be successful. It hurt knowing Inglis would spend perhaps his most productive years with another club. The silver lining on this stormcloud was that Slater, Smith and Cronk would stay. It seemed so long ago that Mark Murray and Anthony Griffin found those boys in Queensland. So much had happened to them. But their skills had improved every year. They were stronger than ever. They were in their prime. With such a spine, Storm could still achieve anything it wanted.

Stanton says of the triumvirate,

> In the modern game, it's a little bit different to a few years back. But I don't think I've seen better. Each of them in their own right ranks high in my estimation. Their contribution to that club is unsurpassed. Smith has proven himself as a fine leader of men. He leads his club, he leads his state and he leads the Kangaroos. And the other two are equally adept and I've no doubt the combination they have and the chemistry they have is a great asset at representative level too.

In 2011, despite losing key players and coaching staff, Melbourne Storm won the Minor Premiership, perhaps the club's greatest triumph.

Gallop was not very welcome in Melbourne after the salary cap scandal so stayed away. When he turned up to AAMI Park to present the J.J. Giltinan Shield he was booed by Storm supporters who resented his tough action the year before. Bellamy would never have to make an us-against-them speech ever again. Storm's existence was now a Spartan tale, at least to Melbournians.

The Warriors ended Storm's season in the preliminary final in 2011. Storm fell eight points shy of yet another Grand Final.

Schubert's report into Storm's salary cap affair was released in 2011. It stands as a testament to his tenacity and diligence.

Among those criticised in the report were four player agents: Isaac Moses, George Mimis, David Riolo and Allan Gainey. An independent committee, formed by the Rugby League Accredited Players Agents Scheme, held private hearings into the behaviour of the high-profile player managers. As a result, Moses, Mimis and Riolo were suspended for six months. Gainey was issued a caution.

The NRL released a statement, which read:

> The committee found that each of the agents had breached the rules of the scheme and the Code of Ethics for accredited agents. No further comment on this matter will be made by or on behalf of the committee.

According to the accreditation rules, the suspended agents (represented by Alan Sullivan QC in the hearings) could appeal their six-month suspensions through the arbitration courts. All three lodged appeal applications but Mimis withdrew before his hearing date had been allocated. Riolo and Moses continued with their cases and were given leave to operate as agents until it had been dealt with in the courts. The appeals of Riolo and Moses were dismissed on 26 October 2012 and they had to pay court costs. Their suspensions took effect until 28 March 2013.

After Schubert's report was made public new Storm chief executive, Ron Gauci, issued a video statement. He said,

> I'm addressing you today because I think it's important you hear direct from the club on the back of the NRL report that was released today on the events of 2010. We want to reiterate, as we've said all along, that this club is moving on and we choose not to dwell on the past. We have put in place processes and procedures and governance to ensure that we don't go through this again. The important message that came from the report is that our playing group and our coach have been cleared. And as

far as we're concerned, that's it. So we move on from here. And we want to focus on the future.

At the end of 2011, Craig Watt quit as a director of Storm. He explains,

> Surprisingly, despite the fact that News Ltd effectively saved Storm from extinction, many inside the club still saw News as part of the problem. A lot of people began to avoid me on game day ... it was like I was forever tainted in many people's eyes.

Storm's 2012 season was a perfect build up for finals. Wins early in the season made sure it was up near the top of the ladder. Its younger players, given time to mature in 2010 and 2011, were making their own decisions and complementing the stars.

The team then lost a handful of matches after State of Origin. Bellamy privately questioned whether his methods needed changing. Smith and Cronk reassured him he was coaching well. As defeats mounted, he couldn't work out what was wrong. But it was Billy Slater. His injured knee had caused him to miss matches. Slater rejoined the team before play-offs and the team rediscovered its mojo.

In the qualifying final against South Sydney, Melbourne faced Inglis, who never quite made it to Brisbane. He baulked at going to the Broncos at the last minute and went to the Rabbitohs. There was a drama with his contract and he did consider quitting the game and going to the AFL, like his former teammate Israel Folau (who had left the Broncos to play for AFL expansion club Greater Western Sydney), but Gallop intervened and made sure Inglis was registered at Souths.

Against his old club, Inglis looked a bit lonely or lost, if not passive. Storm found a slick pace early and cruised home 24–6. In the preliminary final two weeks later, Storm thrashed Manly 40–12. It set up a Grand Final against the Bulldogs, full of flair and self-belief.

Storm team V Bulldogs, Grand Final 2012

Billy Slater	Sika Manu
Sisa Waqa	Ryan Hoffman
Dane Nielsen	Todd Lowrie
Will Chambers	Interchange:
Justin O'Neill	Ryan Hinchcliffe

Gareth Widdop	Kevin Proctor
Cooper Cronk	Jaiman Lowe
Jesse Bromwich	Richie Fa'aoso
Cameron Smith	
Bryan Norrie	Coach: Craig Bellamy

Both teams looked calm and happy in the change rooms. The fear of such occasions was no longer with Storm's best men.

Cameron Smith led his team out for yet another season decider. There were more Melbourne Storm supporters in the crowd than anyone expected. About a fifth of the stadium was purple. More than a million Victorians were watching on television. The NRL was riding high all over Australia. News Ltd had let go of its half-ownership. A new commission had taken control of the sport. One of the commissioners' first acts was to appoint a new chief executive.

The headline act for this Grand Final was Bulldog Ben Barba, a dynamic fullback in the Slater mould. Barba looked tense. His face was tight.

Six minutes into the match Gareth Widdop, the best young Storm player, measured a short pass to Ryan Hoffman, who had returned from the UK in 2012, playing his fourth Grand Final. The defence edged towards Slater, who was running wider. Hoffman barged over for a try. Smith missed the conversion. In the celebration huddle Cronk was giving the instructions. A minute later Cronk kicked a high ball. Barba spilt it.

Several sets later, Smith kicked for penalty points but missed. The Canterbury defence was holding up well; its forwards were aggressive and sure. Melbourne tackled bravely, applying pressure out wide, where the Bulldogs were dangerous. Barba broke and passed wide. Storm winger Sisa Waqa, another youngster, finger-tipped it and saved a certain try.

In the 25th minute, Canterbury made a brilliant play down the right side, a grubber kick finding Sam Perrett, who scored a try. Slater was slightly out of position and his late dive annoyed Perrett, who reacted by sticking his tongue out at the champion fullback. A fight started and all players ran in. One of the Bulldogs, James Graham, bit the ear of Billy Slater, who was miffed.

In the next ten minutes Melbourne – or more specifically, Cooper Cronk – would win the match. About 10 metres from the Bulldogs' line, Cronk held the ball like a tease, Slater came from behind and the halfback, without turning his head, found the fullback with a sublime pass. It left Slater with one man to beat ... *left foot step* ... and he scored diving. Smith converted. 10–4.

With a minute to go before half-time, Cronk planned to better his passing feat. He set himself deep in attack. Smith passed it back. Cronk measured a kick to Justin O'Neill that travelled through the air like a wish. Commentator Phil Gould called it sheer perfection. He could not have walked up and placed the ball in O'Neill's hands with better precision. You can only have that type of performance without nerves.

No team scored in the second half. Storm was tremendous in defence. It also had some luck. Smith had his finest moment with a try-saving tackle in the 50th minute at the end of four consecutive sets in the line. Still Canterbury pressed.

Barba was frustrated he could not find space. Then, in the 62nd minute he produced the play of the game, weaving through broken play and kicking the ball in front of a close-to-flying Josh Morris, who toed ahead. All Morris had to do was pick the ball up. Slater gave chase. Morris waited for one more bounce. The ball hit its end and shot up into the air like a firecracker. It was enough to spoil the try. Slater, who was begging chance to save him, leapt and swatted the ball over the dead ball line.

For the rest of the game, Storm held the line as it always has.

Before the game Hoffman and Slater and virtually every other Melbourne player were asked whether winning in 2012 would banish the pain of the Waldron era forever. Every one of them said they were still proud of their 2007 and 2009 'premierships'. How do you take away a memory? And now, they were about to collect another special moment to take with them on the great tour of the rest of their lives.

Leading 14–4, Bellamy could not sit calmly. When full time came he lifted his arms. Cronk and Slater collapsed and embraced. Smith said, 'This team stuck strong mate.'

Cooper Cronk, the organiser, was the Clive Churchill Medallist.

After the victory lap, the change room was crammed with family, sponsors and directors – past and present. Moodie was the only former independent not present. He was working overseas. Ponissi quietened the crowd for Bellamy to speak. A cheer preceded the silence. The coach waited until everyone could see him. Here he was in the centre of the room again, with something to say. He kept it brief. 'We got what we fuckin' deserved.'

CHAPTER 37

WHERE ARE THEY NOW?

On 11 February 2013, Bellamy called a media conference to announce his future in coaching. He had been offered a rich deal to join St George Illawarra. Several club insiders turned up to the announcement, including club creator Ribot, sponsor Tony Devers and News Ltd's Victorian Managing Director Peter Blunden. They were smiling. Bellamy duly declared he was going nowhere. News Ltd reported the fresh agreement would hold Bellamy at Storm until the end of 2016, with a two-year extension option. 'I feel like a fan,' he explained. 'This is my club. The emotional attachment is very strong, particularly to the players. I found that too hard to break.'

A question floated down from a journalist at the back of the room.

> Craig, just one final one ... In deciding your future did you think much about the early days when Storm was different, when you moved down without your family and Slater was playing his first game in '03? Have you reflected on those early times, when Olympic Park was still standing?

'No, not really,' Bellamy replied. 'I haven't got much of a memory actually,' he smiled.

> I don't look back too far and I don't look forward too far; so try and live in the now and basically they're very nice memories, watchin' Billy play his first game but, as I said ... that's not really a consideration in what's happened last couple of months.

The press conference wound up. Bellamy, muscular and youthful even now, stood up and went outside to pose for some photos in the Melbourne sunshine before driving to the airport to board a plane for the United Kingdom. Later that month, Storm won the World Club Challenge. It was once again on top of the world of rugby league. This time, legitimately.

There have been many changes at the franchise since 22/4. Long-serving front office workers have departed. The club was devastated in late 2011 when recruiter Darren Bell died of a heart attack. His colleagues grieved the loss of a dedicated professional and Bell is still missed. His legacy lives on through the scouting of many young players, who are now providing Bellamy with a bright future. Frank Ponissi continues to stand by Bellamy's side. He is the reigning winner of the Mick Moore Club Person of the Year Award. The former board members are all still active supporters of Storm. Rob Moodie lectures on leadership. One of the lessons he teaches his students is: Beware the charismatic, overly confident leader. Gerry Ryan has just backed a new theatre spectacular: *King Kong*.

David Gallop is now the chief executive of Football Federation Australia. He has recently presided over a stellar year in the A-League. Ian Schubert remains at the NRL as salary cap auditor, the position he has held for almost 15 years. The new NRL boss, Dave Smith, has hinted at revamping aspects of the salary cap.

John Hartigan is no longer with News Ltd, which has gone through leadership and structural changes. Peter Macourt also moved on (now chairman of Sky Network Television Limited) and Craig Watt left too, after almost three decades with the company. News Ltd is no longer a half-owner of the NRL. It owns 100 per cent of Fox Sports, which broadcasts matches in a shared deal with Channel Nine.

John Ribot is still a big supporter of Storm, the club he built from scratch. He also holds a place on the board of the Victorian Major Events Company.

Peter O'Sullivan is still successfully running recruitment at the Roosters, a title contender in 2013. O'Sullivan's resume beams brighter every year, with Greg Inglis the best player in the game and Israel Folau enjoying rugby, his third code.

Cameron Vale prospered at North Melbourne Football Club. He was promoted from CFO to COO (winning a prestigious $20,000 Graeme Samuel Scholarship so he could further his professional study at an overseas university). In June 2013 he realised a professional dream when he became a chief executive. He is now the boss of Hockey Australia.

After suffering greatly from the Storm scandal, Paul Gregory has reclaimed his life, resuming his career working for an internationally renowned company. On his office desk sits a photograph of his first child.

Matt Hanson has moved back to Sydney to work in private equity. In 2012 he won the Australian Off Road Racing Championship and celebrated the achievement with his proud father.

All the former Melbourne Storm CFOs believe they are better executives now from having lived and learned through the Waldron era.

Brian Waldron has maintained a dignified silence since 22/4. He is now CEO of a sports apparel business. On Sundays Waldron coaches his son's Under 13s team. There he stands on the dewy sidelines, to the sounds of boys shouting excitedly for their teammates to kick it to them. After every game there are lollies and awards for the children who tried the hardest. There are neither scouts, nor agents at these contests and winning matters a lot, but only until the final siren sounds.

POSTSCRIPT

Following the Melbourne Storm scandal, News Ltd appointed respected Queensland-based newspaper executive Dennis Watt to the position of General Manager of Rugby League. Watt (a veteran Brisbane Broncos board member) joined the Storm board and oversaw the franchise's corporate revival. On 21 May 2013 News Ltd announced it had finally sold the Melbourne Storm to a private consortium gathered by a New Zealand entrepreneur. A month later it was revealed club sponsor Gerry Ryan was one of the new owners.

Incoming CEO, Mark Evans, told the press: 'Over a five-year period we would like to get this period to be self-funded and viable financially without seeing any deterioration in its playing performance. That's the aim. It's not easy, but we think it is doable.'

Storm is again heading to another finals series. With Smith, Cronk and Slater controlling the plays, the team might yet become the first team in NRL history to win consecutive premierships.

ACKNOWLEDGEMENTS

The people I interviewed made this book possible and I thank you all. Most are mentioned but some did not wish to be named for personal reasons.

Others have also played important roles in the telling of this story.

Ian Heads was unbelievably generous with his time and words, as were my ABC colleagues Tim Ayliffe and Simon Conway.

Hard-working members of the rugby league press have my respect and gratitude. I relied upon their stories to better research ageing events.

Mick, Joan and Jo Kennedy contributed off the bench.

Thanks to Hardie Grant for its outstanding support from day one. Pam Brewster's guidance was particularly valuable. Editor Alan Murphy was understanding and incisive.

To literary agent Clare Forster – thanks for making this book a reality.

On a personal note: a big thank you to Kim, Jack, Gus and Leo for your patience and encouragement.

SOURCES

Chris Anderson, Chris Appleby, Marcus Bai, Peter Blunden, Ian Collins, Gavin Darwin, Tony Devers, Petra Fawcett, Archie Fraser, Allan Gainey, David Gallop, Ron Gauci, Matt Geyer, Steve Gillis, Paul Gregory, Anthony Griffin, Bruce Guthrie, Bob Hagan, John Hartigan, Chris Johns, Peter Jourdain, Brett Kimmorley, Peter King, Dr John Lill, Peter Macourt, Peter Maher, Dally Messenger III, Dr Rob Moodie, Tracey Moore, Mark Murray, Brad Newton, Tim Pallas, Frank Ponissi, John Quayle, John Ribot, Gerry Ryan, Mike Smith, Frank Stanton, Richard Swain, Craig Watt, Michael Westlake, Brett White.

Additionally, many of my colleagues in the media have conducted interviews and written about this subject and their research has informed this book.

Lastly, I have drawn from a plethora of reports, announcements, statements, comments, board minutes, correspondence, affidavits, books and websites.